Heterogeneous Information Exchange and Organizational Hubs

T0122443

Heterogeneous Information Exchange and Organizational Hubs

edited by

H. Bestougeff

Professor,
University of Marne-la-Vallée, France

J.E. Dubois

Professor
University Paris VII, France

and

B. Thuraisingham

Chief Engineer,
Mitre Corporation, U.S.A.

KLUWER ACADEMIC PUBLISHERS
DORDRECHT / BOSTON / LONDON

A C.I.P. Catalogue record for this book is available from the Library of Congress.

ISBN 978-90-481-6030-3

Published by Kluwer Academic Publishers,
P.O. Box 17, 3300 AA Dordrecht, The Netherlands.

Sold and distributed in North, Central and South America
by Kluwer Academic Publishers,
101 Philip Drive, Norwell, MA 02061, U.S.A.

In all other countries, sold and distributed
by Kluwer Academic Publishers,
P.O. Box 322, 3300 AH Dordrecht, The Netherlands.

Printed on acid-free paper

Introduction

Hélène Bestougeff, *Université de Marne la Vallée, France*
Jacques-Emile Dubois, *Université Paris VII - Denis Diderot, France*
Bhavani Thuraisingham, *MITRE Corporation, USA*

The last fifty years promoted the conceptual trio: **Knowledge, Information and Data** (KID) to the center of our present scientific technological and human activities. The intrusion of the Internet drastically modified the historical cycles of communication between authors, providers and users. Today, information is often the result of the interaction between data and the knowledge based on their comprehension, interpretation and prediction.

Nowadays important goals involve the *exchange of heterogeneous information*, as many real life and even specific scientific and technological problems are all interdisciplinary by nature. For a specific project, this signifies extracting information, data and even knowledge from many different sources that must be addressed by interoperable programs.

Another important challenge is that of corporations collaborating with each other and forming coalitions and partnerships. One development towards achieving this challenge is *organizational hubs*. This concept is new and still evolving. Much like an airport hub serving air traffic needs, organizational hubs are central platforms that provide information and collaboration specific to a group of users' needs. Now companies are creating hubs particular to certain types of industries. The users of hubs are seen as communities for which all related information is directly available without further searching efforts and often with value-added services.

A critical component for organizational hubs is data, information and knowledge exchange and their management tools. Information has to be extracted from the data and exchanged across organizations.

Further developments in heterogeneous information processing lead to the *semantic web* which will enable systems to "understand" information. The key solutions to solve this problem are *ontology* definition and construction.

In pure science and technology, the heterogeneous knowledge management formal working facilities usually go through certain types of hubs. In some systems with human and/or social factors, this transiting through a hub can be blurred and require some expert tacit knowledge input, often with semantic tools to eliminate any fuzziness in the decision-making process. Moreover, the important aspects of security, confidentiality and privacy within networks are considered essential features of most sharing processes.

The present volume focuses on these aspects and should provide the reader with an insight primarily based on knowledge management presentation and its underlying concepts of explicit and tacit knowledge. Moreover, some knowledge management models or studies given here can be considered in the light of the Newtonian/Cartesian causality principles, still useful in most of our day-to-day circumstances.

Still others concern the complexity approach, implying multiple intercausal units. This makes it possible to consider human factors associated with formal and informal aspects dealing with Heterogeneous Knowledge Management Systems (HKMS).

The contributions in this book provide insights into building the heterogeneous information exchange. They present ongoing research or results of experimental work, which should help and inspire readers for new applications. Most of them are illustrated by extended examples, so the reader can understand how concepts are used in practical applications. They are divided into three major parts:

> *Part I   Heterogeneous Database Integration: Concepts and Strategies*
> *Part II   Data Warehousing: Models and Architectures*
> *Part III Sharing Information and Knowledge*

Heterogeneous database integration deals with developing architectures and frameworks as well as techniques for integrating schemas and data. The different proposed systems can be classified with respect to the degree of coupling between the original data sources and the resulting system. On the one hand *tightly coupled systems* where global schemas are merged from the original external schemas; on the other hand *loosely coupled systems* using various approaches to interrelate the source systems and user's queries. Some chapters also describe techniques for maintaining security for exchanging data.

However, integration is just a first essential step towards more sophisticated architectures which are developed towards management decisions support. These architectures, grouped under the term of *Data Warehouse*, are subject oriented and involve the integration of current and historical data. As the data warehouses are built to answer questions not focused on individual transactions but on the overall process the design must reflect the way users look at their application.

Dimensional modeling is used to represent the user's viewpoint of his data. Some attributes refer to measures and others link them within other relations. This leads to the well-known *star schema*, which represents the basic design structure for data warehousing. Not all dimensional models are implemented in relational databases. Some systems offer what are called *multidimensional databases*, which store information in structures called *cubes*. The advantage of these cubes is to allow users to change their perspective interactively by adding or removing attributes. On-line analytical processing (OLAP) tools can then provide data navigation, managerial analysis and knowledge discovery. Part II develops new and different data warehouse architectures and related management and querying tools.

The third aspect of heterogeneous information exchange concerns knowledge management, use of standards, information mining systems, and web information management. We cannot escape the web. It is now part of our lives and part of almost all organizations. Therefore, the databases and the warehouses have to operate on the web. Furthermore, we need to deal with unstructured and multimedia data such as text, images, audio and video. Part III describes some of these aspects.

Each part essentially builds on technologies provided by the previous one. That is, we first have heterogeneous database integration. We then use many of its strategies to build warehouses. Finally we have to ensure that these techniques work on the web. These are the essential components for building organizational hubs. Note that other aspects contribute to hub construction; they include networking, real-time processing and architectures. In order to build efficient hubs, all these components have to work together.

There are numerous papers on heterogeneous database integration, data warehousing and knowledge management. The chapters in this book synthesize and complement the existing literature and attempt to show how all of the data, information and knowledge technologies can lead towards collaboration among organizations.

Although oriented to specific problems, each chapter clearly situates its contribution, giving the general framework of the research presented, together with an extensive list of references, so readers can, if need be, obtain more detailed information for a particular domain.

Further developments will no doubt tend to build more sophisticated organizational hubs for specific domains, using some semantic web approaches. Moreover, rules and regulations that work across corporations, that may differ according to countries, must be defined. To achieve these objectives, there is a need for system managers, developers and researchers to work with each other. In addition, the support of sociologists, economists, psychologists and lawyers can help provide organizational hubs with semantically rich, safe and user friendly interfaces.

Numerous endeavours are opening up as we enter this millennium. It should entail new opportunities and challenges.

*   *   *   *   *

The Editors hope that this work will provide scientists, information specialists, engineers, managers and librarians with new insights in the field of heterogeneous knowledge management systems including critical aspects of databased decision making, backed by information sharing processes. It is also hoped that while readers will take advantage of the information provided here, managers will provide support for developing the tools and techniques mentioned in this book.

Acknowledgments

This book was realized with the support of CODATA* FRANCE and the Engineering Services Institute of the University of Marne-la-Vallée. We are grateful for their generous and constant support as well as for their scientific contributions. We acknowledge the valuable help of Ms. Tamar Blickstein in editing the English texts.

* Committee on Data for Science and Technology - Member of the International Council for Science

Contents

Chapter 1

Integration Methodology for Heterogeneous Databases

Gabriella Salzano
Université de Marne-la-Vallée, France
Email: gs@univ-mlv.fr

Abstract: During these last years, databases have been produced with respect to various user requirements and implemented by different technologies. The stored information is still valuable, but two important problems must be solved to create new target systems: these are database integration and legacy systems modernization. This paper presents a methodology that explicitly defines how the different integration steps must be inserted in the context of the evolution of legacy systems. The final section revisits the correspondence search problem in order to illustrate a particular important step of the integration methodology.

Key words: Software development methodology, information systems engineering, heterogeneous database integration, legacy systems modernization.

1.   INTRODUCTION

Quite a number of databases have been produced during these last years. The stored information is still valuable and users wish to globally access and share this information asset through some user friendly interfaces. However, the databases, produced over a relatively large time span, have been designed with respect to various user requirements and implemented by different technologies.

Hence, in order to build a new target system, two important problems must be solved: database integration and legacy systems modernization. Although not new, these two problems have previously been studied quite independently ([5,17,8,1,10], [11,7,16,3,13,12]); no global methodological process is currently available.

1

H. Bestougeff et al. (eds.), Heterogeneous Information Exchange and Organizational Hubs, 1–16.

This paper presents a methodology that explicitly defines the different integration steps in the context of the evolution of legacy systems. The advantage of this approach is that it enables us, through rebuilding, to get reusable parts and devise automation of some tasks for future modernization iterations. So, instead of solving heterogeneity problems a posteriori, our aim is to obtain a set of reference database components which reconciles heterogeneity between subsets of legacy databases that are related, and also takes into account target requirements. This implies that problems must be anticipated and solved in a pre-integration process and documented in such a way that evolution and maintenance of the resulting parts can be easily accomplished.

The idea is to build a conceptual model for a target integrated system starting from information known (or rediscovered) at different levels of the legacy systems: conceptual models, logical models or simply physical models, with data and programs. Decisions about how to design a target system must be driven by an understanding of what must be retained, what is redundant, and what can be reused. Documents and everything that can be called "project memory" form a fundamental source of information, although extracting relevant information may be costly and lengthy.

Figure 1 presents the integration process schema at different possible levels: conceptual, logical, and physical. However, for each level, system modernization steps must be considered.

More precisely, the four main steps needed for integration are the following [12,16]:

I1- Pre-integration

I2- Schema comparison

I3- Schema conforming

I4- Schema merging and restructuring

In our approach, these steps must be interwoven with the different steps of the system modernization process which are generally defined as [8]:

S1- Requirements

S2- Analysis

S3- Design

S4- Implementation

S5- Test

The remainder of this paper is organized as follows. First, we briefly establish a list of actions relevant to the different integration steps, and then show how these actions should be interleaved with the system development steps. This approach defines the tasks to be performed as well as the needed information, but does not explain how to produce that information. The last section further analyzes the correspondence search problem, for which some new ideas are presented.

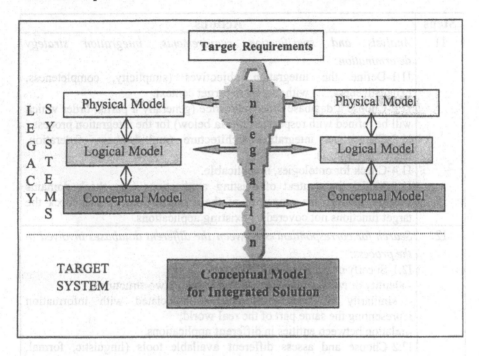

Figure 1. Integration Using Legacy Systems and Target Requirements

2. METHODOLOGICAL APPROACH TO HETEROGENEOUS DATABASE INTEGRATION

The semantic and structural heterogeneity of databases hinders an easy integration. To solve this problem several approaches have been studied based on:

- how well the local bases are structured,
- how well the local structure is known to the global system (for instance, the structures of WWW sources are not always accessible)
- how tightly the global system should be linked with the local databases.

Integration problems are stated explicitly in *multidatabases* with or without global schema or in *federated database* projects [7] or also in *data warehouse* projects [12] while in legacy system modernization approaches, integration problems are implicit. Considering the general integration steps, as defined above, we will now present the main actions in each step.

2.1   Actions in Integration Steps

Steps	Actions
I1	*Analysis and specification requirements, integration strategy determination:* I1.1-Define the integration objectives (simplicity, completeness, exhaustiveness,...) with respect to target context. I1.2-Choose a database order relevance (generally a partial order which will be refined with respect to criteria below) for the integration process. I1.3-Choose an integration architecture (multidatabase, federation, datawarehouse...). I1.4-Check for ontologies, if applicable. I1.5-Model the context of existing applications (i.e. check domains validity, analyze the properties of their intersection,...) and check the target functions not covered by existing applications.
I2	*Search for correspondences between the different databases involved in the process:* I2.1-Specify correspondence types to look for: - identity of two attributes or, more generally, two structures; - similarity of represented entities associated with information representing the same part of the real world; - relation between entities in different applications. I2.2-Choose and assess different available tools (linguistic, formal, cognitive, heuristic, re-engineering, data analysis,...) to help to detect correspondences; I2.3-Find correspondences: intentional analysis; I2.4-Find correspondences: extensional analysis; I2.5-Choose correspondence precedence for the integration.
I3	*Conflict resolution induced by the correspondences:* I3.1-Analyze conflicts induced by the correspondences; I3.2-Recommend solutions for classification and structure conflicts, following the integration objectives defined in the first step; I3.3-Recommend solutions for other types of conflicts (conflicts between data types, data and metadata, semantic constraints).
I4	*Integration of components satisfying all constraints:* I4.1-Design the conceptual model for new coherent common parts; I4.2-Design the conceptual model for supposed independent parts.

Figure 2. Integration Process

Figure 2 shows actions in integration steps. These actions must be refined with respect to some criteria, such as:

- Evolution policy of the information systems in a given company.
- Degree of knowledge about legacy systems (experts, available documentation).
- Cost and delay requirements.
- Number and volume of the considered databases.
- Effort needed for personnel training.
- Reliability and maintainability of legacy systems with respect to the new application requirements ....

2.2 Insertion of Integration Actions Into System Development Steps

As explained in the introduction, the proposed methodology tries to define how to design the organization of the different actions relevant to either integration or system re-development steps. System development steps and integration steps are defined with the same granularity. But several iterations of the same integration step(s) are possible and different tables of actions may be built.

Figure 3 gives a global approach. For instance, in the *requirements* step, all aspects of the integration should be considered while the *design* step is mainly concerned with I3 and I4 integration steps.

System Modernization Process	Integration Steps				Main levels		
	I1	I2	I3	I4	Conceptual	Logical	Physical
Requirements		√	√	√	√	√	
Analysis		√	√	√	√		√
Design			√	√			√	√
Implementation							
Test							

Figure 3. Integration Steps Inserted into System Modernization Process

The analysis may be refined by considering the different actions of each step as shown in Figure 4.

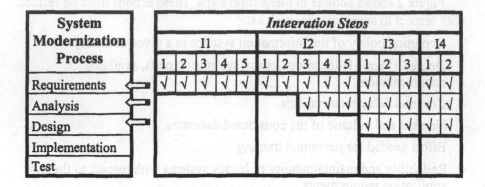

Figure 4. Integration Actions Inserted into System Modernization Process

From these last two figures, a list of needed actions can be established for the New Integrated System (NIS) process. Figure 5 gives a possible set of actions.

Steps	Actions
NIS1 Requirements	S1 + I1.1+ I1. 2+ I1.3+ I1.4 + I1.5 + I2.1+ I2. 2+ I2.3+ I2.4 + I2.5 +I3.1+ I3. 2+ I3.3 + I4.1+ I4. 2
NIS2 Analysis	S2 + I2.3+ I2.4 + I2.5 + I3.1+ I3. 2+ I3.3 + I4.1+ I4. 2
NIS3 Design	S3 + I3.1+ I3. 2+ I3.3 + I4.1+ I4. 2
NIS4 Implementation	S4 + ΔI
NIS5 Test	S5 + ΔI

Figure 5. New Integrated System Process: Steps and Action

It must be noted that NIS4 and NIS5 do not correspond exactly to steps S4 and S5, but are larger insofar as they take into account all the integration problems usually solved a posteriori. Hence the notation ΔI to indicate this fact.

2.3   Input / Output Documentation

The set of input information of the NIS process includes all knowledge on existing systems and elements which show their adequacy with respect to target requirements. This information can either be already structured inside available documents or could be partly rebuilt by some semi-automatic tools.

However, it is well known that, the expertise domain of each application and the correspondences between systems are, in general, barely recorded in any form. In brief, as illustrated in Figure 6, the input information for an NIS project is of two types: structured (i.e. documents, schemas, pre-defined process) and informal.

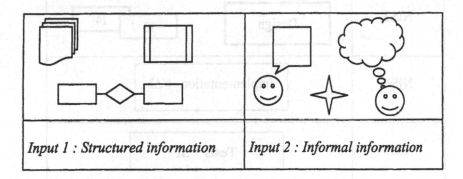

| *Input 1 : Structured information* | *Input 2 : Informal information* |

Figure 6. Input Information for NIS Process

In order to keep a "project memory " and follow each action, a set of documents must be either rebuilt or produced. The information contained in these documents could be functional or non-functional [6].

The output documentation of each NIS step can be synthesized as shown in Figure 7. It should be noted that integration documents and documents relative to modernization steps must keep the same granularity.

The whole set of documents is intended as input for the next system evolution (Figure 8).

At this stage, it may be useful to introduce some standards in order to facilitate the information reuse. In particular, a formalized structure of documents can make it easier to automate some integration steps. As noted further, XML formats are one of the possible choice considering in particular the available tools.

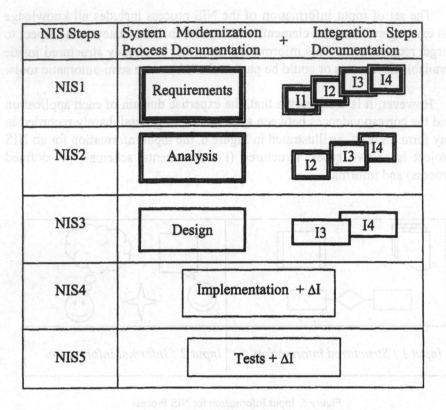

NIS Steps	System Modernization Process Documentation	+	Integration Steps Documentation
NIS1	Requirements		I1 I2 I3 I4
NIS2	Analysis		I2 I3 I4
NIS3	Design		I3 I4
NIS4	Implementation + ΔI		
NIS5	Tests + ΔI		

Figure 7. Output Documentation for NIS Process

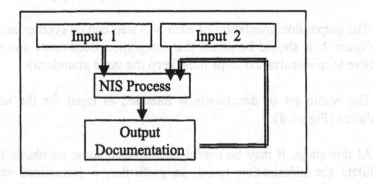

Figure 8. Iterative Reuse of Produced Information

2.4   How to Improve this Methodology Using Ontologies.

One of the difficulties encountered in database integration stems from the relational model, which does not support a unified language for schema definition, functional dependencies and integrity constraints. By considering a database as a kind of typed first order theory, it is possible to express schema, functional dependencies, integrity constraints, views and queries, in a uniform language [15, 2, 19]. By doing so, we define an explicit conceptualization of an application domain, which is exactly what Gruber calls an ontology [9]. Working in this more general framework, it becomes easier to detect and solve conflicts introduced by correspondences [4, 22,23].

In Artificial Intelligence, ontologies have been mainly introduced in the framework of knowledge base systems in order to support some common semantics or conceptualizations [23]. Different methods have been proposed to develop large ontologies applying top down or bottom up approaches. In relational database systems, the ontologies we are considering are not defined a priori but are built from all available information attached to the database system.

Our idea is to improve the integration process by using ontologies, and to work with two points of view (relational and ontological) and two levels (legacy systems and transversal). It is clear that the translation from the relational view to the logical view must be reversible in order to use either view when needed.

Steps 3 and 4 of the integration process could then be modified as follows:

NIS3.1 - Consider a weak universal relation [20] (i.e. a relation containing all data from relevant relations in legacy databases) and express the correspondences on this relation.

NIS3.2 - With each database, associate an "ontology" that is based on a typed logical theory describing the relational schema's, the constraints, the functional dependencies, etc.

NIS3.3 - Build a transformation ontology (TO) taking into account the universal relation, all previously found correspondences and constraints. This ontology reconciles some concepts from one context of application to another and is valid in a particular transversal context.

NIS3.4 - Extract useful rules from TO in order to build an Extension Ontology (EO) that reconciles concepts from different applications. This ontology is valid in the modified context with respect to the legacy systems, because it takes into account transversal notions and constraints. Keeping only coherent results may therefore reduce the contexts of initial applications.

NIS3.5 - Build an extended database from this Extension Ontology. This database satisfies all constraints (explicit and potential) generated from the integration process.

For the sake of simplicity, this process is illustrated for only a pair of databases but can be easily generalized. Figure 9 gives a global view, which is elaborated in Figure 10.

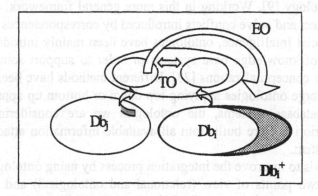

Figure 9. Transformation and Extension Ontologies

Notations : Db_i: i^{th} database; TO: Transformation Ontology; EO:Extension Ontology; Db_j^+: Extended j^{th} database

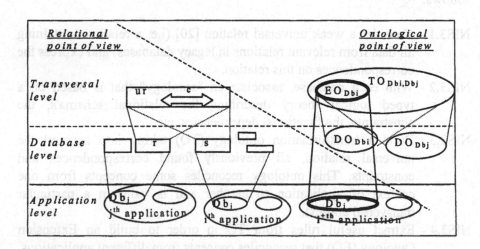

Figure 10. Different Levels and View Points of Transformation and Extension Ontologies.

In Figure 10, the ith and j^{th} applications are legacy systems; Db_i, Db_j are databases; r and s are relations; ur is a weak universal relation; c is a correspondence between r and s; DO_{Dbi}, DO_{Dbj} are ontologies associated to Db_i and Db_j; $TO_{Dbi, Dbj}$ is a transformation ontology between Db_i and Db_j; EO_{Dbi} is an extended ontology associated with Db_i and finally i^{+th} application is the system obtained by integration process, with its database Db_i^+.

Moreover we can note that:

- Ontological viewpoint ensure a coherent extension of a database. We do not have this guarantee with the relational point of view alone.
- Steps NIS1, NIS2 and NIS3.1 represent a starting point of integration. They do not take into account all possible conflicts and constraints, such as implicit constraints. All these elements are processed by logical rules and inference engines from NIS3.2 to NIS3.

NIS Steps	Level		Point of view	
	Database	Transversal	Relational	Ontological
NIS1	√		√	
NIS2		√	√	
NIS3.1		√	√	
NIS3.2	√			√
NIS3.3		√		√
NIS3.4		√		√
NIS3.5		√	√	

Fig. 11. NIS Process: Level and Viewpoint for Each Step

3. SEARCH FOR CORRESPONDENCES

The search for correspondences presents a difficult problem insofar as it implies semantic modeling and database design. This difficulty increases with the number of databases to be processed. Both human experience and adequate tools are used for this step.

Human experience concerns legacy database contexts, their specifications and constraints. In particular, they give different articulation points of view between several domains of application.

Tools are issued from different domains such as re-engineering, linguistics and data analysis [2, 21, 13].

Re-engineering approaches are very useful (especially when conceptual models of legacy systems are unknown), to analyze domains and allow to discover their business rules and undocumented logic. Linguistic tools allow us to discover some semantic links in the different databases (such as synonyms or related concepts) and to formalize the weight of the attributes in all databases. Data analysis allows us to discover some correspondences starting from the data, and to evaluate the nature of conflicts between correspondences.

In general, integration can be devised between databases belonging to one or several information systems. The two cases do not imply the same problems. In the first case, we can consider that applications are centered around different concepts and that the more frequent correspondences are therefore of the relation type, while in the latter case the same concepts can be described differently in various information systems. This generates more often correspondences of identity or similarity type.

By extending some notions presented in [14], we introduced two notions discussed in [18]: the *scope of a correspondence* and the *set of correspondent values*. These notions will be useful in the correspondence analysis. They are introduced in the relational context, but can be extended for the object oriented databases.

3.1   Scope of a Correspondence (SC)

Roughly speaking, the scope of an attribute A on a relation R is the set of all the values assumed by A on R. Moreover, if "c" is a correspondence between R on A and S on B, the scope of the correspondence is the intersection of the scope of A on R and the image (via the function f) of the scope of B on S.

We can characterize the correspondence c with respect to the scope of c: we will call it *equivalence* when the scopes are the same, or *disjunction* when the intersection is empty. Intermediate situations are *inclusion* and *overlapping* (see annex for complete definitions).

Insofar as we are working inside a single information system, we can estimate that data extensions of related entities or attributes are not too different, because they reflect the same point of view; so the data extensions will be generally equivalent, inclusive and more seldom overlapping. Thus, the probability of having correspondences of equivalence or inclusion type is high, while the probability of having correspondences of overlapping or disjunction type is low.

3.2   Set of Correspondent Values (SCV)

In order to find correspondences, it is also possible to start from data analysis on some subset of attribute values, even if these values do not seem semantically related a priori. If we find a "simple" function f, that relates one subset to the other, the attributes can be considered as candidates for a correspondence. (For instance, if the two sets have the same cardinality, we will find some injective, linear functions.)

The SCV notion is weaker than the SC notion. In order to detect some correspondences starting from data analysis, we shall only retain the SCV with a very large cardinality.

3.3   Choosing Precedence for Correspondences

From the previous analysis, we can deduce some rules for choosing the correspondences.

1. Among correspondences between two relations R and S, those implying database keys should be analyzed first.
    - If A_i is a key of R and B_j is a key of S then there is a high probability that the correspondence between A_i and B_j is :
        - an identity if type(c) is an equivalence,
        - a hierarchy if type(c) is an inclusion.
    - If A_i is a key of R and B_j is not a key of S and if there is a correspondence between attributes A_i and B_j, then A_i can be a reference for a foreign key for S.
2. The most interesting correspondences c are those for which the cardinality of SC(c) is the highest possible with respect to the cardinality of SA(R:A_i) and SA(S:B_j)

4.   CONCLUSION AND FUTURE DEVELOPMENTS

In this paper we have presented some general lines concerning an integration methodology for heterogeneous databases. This type of methodology enables the information system evolution process to be more easily handled, including, if needed, some new integration tasks, (i.e. mastering future iterations). To fulfill this objective, we may need to build a more formal « project memory » which would be processed and used by automatic tools. The first step we are looking at is the application of XML(S) format approach to specify input-output documents.

Our proposal is based on analyses of some rather limited cases. We therefore intend to subsequently extend our study to several large real-life cases, which would enable us to make certain steps more precise and to validate our proposed methodology.

ANNEX

Definition 1. Given two relations $R(A_1,...,A_n)$ and $S(B_1,...,B_m)$, if there exists i, j and a function f such that A_i and $f(B_j)$ can be interpreted as semantically equivalent, then a correspondence c between the attribute A_i of R and B_j of S, is denoted by

$c = c(R:A_i; S:B_j; f)$.

Definition 2. Given a relation R with attributes $A_1,...A_n$, defined on domains $D_1,...D_m$ the *scope of an attribute* A_i *on a relation R is defined as*
$SA(R:A_i) = \Pi_{Ai}(R)$

Definition 3. Given two relations $R(A_1,...,A_n)$ and $S(B_1,...,B_m)$, and a correspondence c=c(R:A, S:B,f) *then the scope of c, noted by SC(c) is* given by $SA(R:A_i) \cap f(SA(S:B_j))$.

Definition 4. Given two relations $R(A_1,...,A_n)$ and $S(B_1,...,B_m)$, and a correspondence c=c(R:A, S:B,f) *then the type of c, noted by type(c) is* defined by the following table :

for c $(R:A_i; S:B_j;f)$, type(c) is	if SC (c) =
équivalence	$= SA(R:A_i) = f(SA(S:B_j))$
inclusion	$= SA(R:A_i)$ and $SA(R:A_i) \subseteq f(SA(S:B_j))$ or $= f(SA(S:B_j))$ and $SA(R:A_i) \supseteq f(SA(S:B_j))$
overlapping	$= SA(R:A_i) \cap f(SA(S:B_j))$ and $(SA(R:A_i) \cap f(SA(S:B_j))) \neq \emptyset$ and $(SA(R:A_i) \neq f(SA(S:B_j)))$ and $(SA(R:A_i) \not\subset f(SA(S:B_j)))$ and $(f(SA(S:B_j)) \not\subset SA(R:A_i))$
disjunction	$=\emptyset$

Table 1. Correspondence Types

REFERENCES

1. Alhaji R., Documenting Legacy Relational Databases, in Advances in Conceptual Modeling, LNCS 1727, Springer, Nov. 1999.
2. Castano S., De Antonellis V., Fugini M.G., Pernici B., Conceptual Schema Analysis: Techniques and Applications, ACM Transactions on Database Systems, Vol. 23, n° 3, Sept. 1998.
3. Conrad S., Saake G., Integrating Heterogeneous Databases, EDBT'98, Valencia, March 23, 1998.
4. Conrad S., Schmitt I., Türker C., Considering Integrity Constraints During Federated Database Design, in "Advances in Databases, BNCOD 16, LNCS 1405, Springer-Verlag, 1998.
5. Cornella-Dorda S., Wallnau K., Seacord R.C., Robert J., A Survey of Legacy Modernization Approaches, CMU/SEI-2000-TN-003.
6. Dieng R., Corby O., Giboin A., Golebiowska J., Matta N., Ribière M., Méthodes et Outils pour la Gestion des Connaissances, Dunod, Paris 2000.
7. Elmagarmid A., Rusinkiewicz M., and Shet A. (Eds), Management of Heterogeneous and Autonomous Database Systemes, Morgan Kaufmann Publishers, Inc., San Francisco, California, 1999.
8. Gabay J., Berhanou Gébré, La Conduite des Projets d'Evolution des Systèmes d'Information, InterEditions, 1999, Dunod Paris 1999.
9. Gruber T.R., //www-ksl.stanford.edu/kst/what-is-an-ontology.html, 1997.
10. Haines G., Carney D., Foreman J., Component Based Software development / COTS Integration, SEI, Software Technology Review, 1998.
11. Hull R., Managing Semantic Heterogeneity in Databases : A Theoretical Perspective, 16th ACM Symposium on Principles of Database Systems, Tuscon, Arizona, USA, 1997.
12. Jarke M., Lenzerini M., Vassiliou Y., Vassiliadis P., Fundamentals of Data Warehouses, Springer, ISBN 3-540-65365-1, 2000.
13. Kingston J., The DARPA High Performance Knowledge Bases Programme, In Knowledge Acquisition, Modelling and Management, 10th European Workshop, EKA Workshop '97, Sant Felin de Crixols, Catalonia, Spain, Plaza E.,. Benjamins R., (Eds), LNAI 1319, Springer-Verlag, 1997.
14. Lee Chiang, Chen Chia-Jung, Query Optimization in Multidatabase Systems Considering Schema Conflicts, in IEEE Transactions on Knowledge and Data Engineering, vol. 9, n°6, November/December 1997.
15. Lenzerini M., Description Logics and Their Relationships with Databases, Beeri C., Buneman P., (Eds), ICDT'99, LNCS 1540, Springer-Verlag Berlin Heidelberg, 1998.
16. Parent C., Spaccapietra S., Intégration de Bases de Données - Panorama des Problèmes et des Approches, in Ingénierie des Systèmes d'Information, Vol. 4, n. 3, p. 333-358, 1996.
17. http://www.comp.lancs.ac.uk/projects/renaissance/project/Documents4.html

18. Salzano G., Bestougeff H., Finding Related Information in Distributed Heterogeneous Systems, in Proceedings of 16th International CODATA Conference – Data Management in the Evolving Information Society, New Delhi, November 1998.

19. Salzano G., Bestougeff H., Construction et Génération d'Ontologies pour Fédérer des Bases de Données Relationnelles, Université de Marne-la-Vallée, Rapport de Recherche ISIS, RR-99-19, 1999.

20. Ullman J.D., Principles of Databases and Knowledge-Base Systems, Computer Science Press, 1989.

21. Velasco M., Martinez V., Lloréns J., de Amescua A., Automatic Domain Analysis: Generation of Domain Representation, Proceedings IFIP Conference, Vienne, 1998.

22. Visser P.R.S., Jones D.M., Bench-Capon T.J.M., Shave M.J.R., An analysis of Ontology Mismatches; Heterogeneity versus Interoperability, in "AAAI 1997 Spring Symposium on Ontological Engineering, Stanford University, California, USA", Farquhar A., Grunninger M., (Eds), 1997.

23. Wiederhold G., Jannink J., Composing Diverse Ontologies, prepared for IFIP Working Group on Database 8th Working Conference on Database Semantics (DS-8), in Rotorua, New Zeland, Jan. 1999.

Chapter 2

On Transactional Issues in Federated Information Systems

Elena Rodríguez and Fèlix Saltor

Dept. de Llenguatges i Sistemes Informàtics, Universitat Politècnica de Catalunya Campus Nord- Mòdul C 6. Jordi Girona Salgado, 1-3. E-08034 Barcelona.
Email: {malena,saltor}@lsi.upc.es

Abstract: In this paper, we identify the main issues that must be taken into account in the design of a transaction model for a federated information system which accepts read-only transactions. These aspects include the definition of the federated transactions structure, the operations to be performed by federated transactions, the objects to be accessed by federated transactions, the federated transaction correctness properties, the federated transaction results and the correctness properties of the histories generated by the transaction model. We also present the execution architecture that is in place once the federated information system has already been built.

Key words: Federated information system, federated transaction management, semantic atomicity, nested transactions, compensating transactions.

1. INTRODUCTION

A *Federated Information System* (FIS) (see [15]) enables a collection of *preexisting*, *autonomous*, *distributed* and *heterogeneous* data sources to be accessed, through *integrated access*, as if they were a single one. Such integrated access implies that users of the FIS (also known as *federated users*) can formulate single queries and receive single, consolidated answers. Besides providing integrated access, an important requirement of a FIS is that local autonomy of the preexisting data sources should be preserved. In other words, the existence of the FIS must be transparent to the users and applications of the preexisting data sources.

In order to provide integrated access, we need to overcome *syntactical* and *semantic heterogeneity* and represent related concepts. This is

17

H. Bestougeff et al. (eds.), Heterogeneous Information Exchange and Organizational Hubs, 17–32.
© 2002 *Kluwer Academic Publishers.*

accomplished by means of an *integration process*. As a result of the integration process, in our project, a *7-level schema architecture* is obtained. This schema architecture extends the 5-level schema architecture of Sheth and Larson [15]. In [14] and [13] we discuss the reasons why the 5-level schema architecture of Sheth and Larson has been extended.

The different schemas obtained are: *native schema, component schema, export schema, federated schema, authorization schema, translated schema,* and *user schema*.

The native schema is the conceptual schema of the data sources that participate in the FIS and which is expressed in its native model. The component schema, export schema, federated schema, authorization schema and translated schema are expressed using the *Canonical Data Model* (CDM) of the FIS. Such CDM in our case is BLOOM (see [1] for a description of the revised version of the BLOOM model). In a FIS, the CDM plays a central role given that it is used to overcome heterogeneities. The component schema is the conversion of a native schema into CDM; the export schema represents the part of a component schema that is available to a class of federated users; the federated schema is the integration of multiple export schemas (it is important to note we assume that each federated schema supports one semantics); the authorization schema represents a subset of a federated schema which is classified at one federated security level; and the translated schema defines a schema for a user or a class of users.

Finally, the user schema is expressed in the user native data model which may differ from the CDM. In addition to the schema architecture, the integration process produces the corresponding mappings between the different schemas which are stored in the *directory* of the FIS [2].

Once the FIS has already been built, it should become operative. One of the most important issues to be addressed during the operation of a FIS, above all when data sources are databases (also known as *Component Databases*, or *CDB*), is the management of transactions that access data stored at different CDB that form the FIS; we refer to such transactions as *federated transactions*. In a FIS, the traditional transaction concept is very difficult to maintain due to the local autonomy of CDB, which makes it difficult to detect conflicts between federated transactions and local transactions executed at each CDB. Moreover, CDB can delay or reject the execution of federated transactions. All this implies that the *atomicity* and *isolation* properties of the traditional transaction model become compromised.

The aim of this a paper is to sketch transactional issues to be taken into account in the design of a transaction model for our project in the case that the FIS accepts read-only federated transactions. Section 2 explains the functional architecture, which includes different modules, involved in the operation of a FIS. Section 3 presents the transaction model that we want to support. Finally, Section 4 concludes the discussion and identifies directions for future work.

2.   OPERATION OF A FIS

This section presents the *execution architecture* that it is in place after the FIS has been successfully built giving rise to the 7-level schema architecture. As we stated before, the different schemas and their corresponding mappings are stored in the directory of the FIS. Furthermore, we partially demonstrate our schema architecture and our execution architecture through an example.

2.1   Execution Architecture

Figure 1 depicts our execution architecture at a functional level [13], showing all functional modules involved in the execution of federated queries. These functional modules are the *security manager*, the *query manager* and the *transaction manager*. Although in this paper we skip the security manager module, in [12] the reader can find a detailed discussion about security issues in FIS.

Federated users interact with the FIS through a *user interface module*. They pose federated queries expressed in terms of their user schema (FQ_{US}) and using a query language which will depend on the user native data model. The user interface module submits the federated query to the query manager where the *query transformer module* transforms the original query into an equivalent query expressed now in terms of the federated schema (FQ_{FS}).

After this, the *query decomposer module* transforms the FQ_{FS} into several subqueries formulated in terms of the component schema (FSQ_{CS}), and the *query translator module* translates every subquery FSQ_{CS} to equivalent subqueries expressed in the data model (FSQ_{NS}) and the language used at each CDB. Now, the query is ready to be executed under the control of the transaction manager giving rise to a *Federated Transaction* (FT).

We have shown the simplest case, i.e. the federated transaction includes just a federated query, but it could be the case that a federated transaction includes several federated queries. In any case, the federated transactions have a hierarchical structure which includes the FQ_{US}, the FQ_{FS} and the FSQ_{CS} and their equivalent FSQ_{NS} as Figure 2 shows.

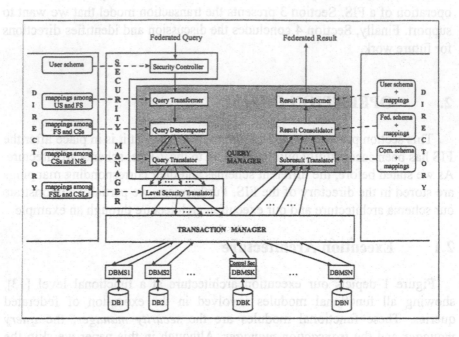

Figure 1. Execution Architecture

As we stated before, the transaction manager at the federated level is responsible for the coordination of the execution of federated transactions. This includes submitting the FSQ_{NS} (also known as *federated subtransactions*) to the CDB involved in the execution of the federated transactions, deciding which FSQ_{NS} can proceed in parallel and which others may have to wait for the result of other FSQ_{NS}, receiving subresults and making decisions about the final *commit* or *abort* of federated transactions.

If a federated transaction commits, its results are submitted to the query manager in order to invert the process to the one previously described. In other words, the *subresult translator module* will convert the subresults according to the FSQ_{CS} using the mappings between native and component schema stored in the directory, and its output will be processed by the *result consolidator module* which will produce a single and consolidated result to the FQ_{FS}. Finally, the *result transformer module* will produce the final result for the FQ_{US}, which will be sent to the federated user by means of the user interface module.

It is important to note that, in the previous discussion, some schema levels have been skipped such as the authorization schema and the translated schema levels, as well as the export schema level. In fact, the direct transformation between non successive levels is feasible if mappings between successive levels have been combined and stored in the directory during the construction phase. Moreover, the omitted schema levels deal with security aspects that are beyond the scope of this paper.

Finally, both the query manager and the transaction manager are distributed with a replica in every site where there are federated users since they are called (directly or indirectly) by the user interface module present at every user site. Furthermore, a replica of the transaction manager should also be present in every CDB of the FIS so that the different federated subtransactions (FSQ_{NS}) can be managed. Given the autonomy of CDB, it could be the case that some CDBs do not allow the placement of modules of the FIS. In the worst case, the transaction manager present at the site where the federated transaction was originated will be in charge of managing the execution of these federated subtransactions.

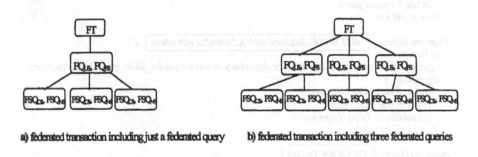

a) federated transaction including just a federated query   b) federated transaction including three federated queries

Figure 2. Structure of Federated Transactions

2.2 Running Example

The next example shows a FIS composed by two CDB. Each CDB belongs to an enterprise that transports industrial wastes (in the example called shipments) from the industry that produces them (hereafter called producers) to the company responsible for their final treatment (denoted in the example as receivers).

Figure 3 shows the (partial) conceptual schemas (i.e. the native schemas) and some data items of CDB_1 (a relational DB located at site 1) and CDB_2 (an object-oriented DB placed at site 2 which uses the revised syntax of the BLOOM model). Note that both CDB_1 and CDB_2 have shipments with shipment code 0111. In spite of this, they denote different real world objects and after the FIS has been built they must be distinguished as different.

Shipments	shCode	wasteCode	producerCode	receiverCode
	0111	060105	123	321

Wastes	wasteCode	wasteName	risk	precautions
	060105	Nitric acid	3	Explosive; keep cool

Customers	customerCode	customerType	companyName	address
	321	R	TRISA	Pl 2, Sant Boi
	123	P	CIQSA	Major 5, Reus

a) Relational CDB₁

class Shipments{
    aggregation_of
        waCode: waCodes *obligatory;*
        waName: String *obligatory;*
        risk: Int;
        precaution: String;
        producer: Producers *gral_aggr existence_dependency exclusive dependor_delete_effect block;*
        receiver: Receivers *gral_aggr existence_dependency exclusive dependor_delete_effect block;*
        shCode: String *obligatory;*
        class_key shCode;
}
***Shipments objects:** {* 0111, 060101, Sulphuric acid, 3, Neutralize with a base *}*
class Producers{
    aggregates_in Shipments *gral_aggr existence_dependency exclusive dependor_delete_effect block as* producer;
    aggregation_of
        companyName: String *obligatory;*
        producerCode: Int *obligatory;*
        industrialSector: String *obligatory;*
        class_key producerCode;
}
***Producers objects:** {* 123, CIQSA, Textile *}*

class Receivers{
    aggregates_in Shipments *gral_aggr existence_dependency exclusive dependor_delete_effect block as* receiver;
    aggregation_of
        companyName: String *obligatory;*
        receiverCode: Int *obligatory;*
        geographicalArea: String;
        class_key receiverCode;
}
***Receivers objects:** {* 321, TRISA, Baix Llobregat *}*

b) Object-oriented CDB₂

Figure 3. Running Example 1

As we said in the previous section, after the integration process a 7-level schema architecture is obtained. Below is given the federated schema that integrates the export schemas of both CDBs (not shown in this paper) and a user schema (Figure 4a); this user schema shows a portion of the federated schema used by federated users that work against the FIS using the relational data model.

```
class Fcustomers{
    alte_graliz_of    CustomersDb1,    CustomersDb2    by    dbDiscriminant
    delete_effect_propagate;
    alte_graliz_of Fproducers, Freceivers by CustomerType delete_effect_propagate;
    aggregation_of
        dbDiscr: dbDiscrs obligatory;
        fCompanyName: String obligatory;
        fAddress: String obligatory;
        fCustomerType: String;
        fCustomerCode: Int obligatory;
    class_key fCustomerCode, dbDiscr;
}
class Fproducers{
    alte_graliz_of        ProducersDb1,    ProducersDb2    by    dbDiscriminant
    delete_effect_propagate;
    alte_spaliz_of Fcustomers by CustomerType delete_effect_propagate;
    aggregates_in Fshipments gral_aggr existence_dependency exclusive
    dependor_delete_effect block as fProducer;
    aggregation_of
        dbDiscr: dbDiscrs obligatory;
        fCompanyName: String obligatory;
        fAdress: String obligatory;
        fProducerCode: Int obligatory;
        fIndustrialSector: String;
    class_key fProducerCode, dbDiscr;
}
class Freceivers{
    alte_graliz_of        ReceiversDb1,    ReceiversDb2    by    dbDiscriminant
    delete_effect_propagate;
    alte_spaliz_of Fcustomers by CustomerType delete_effect_propagate;
    aggregates_in    Fshipments    gral_aggr    existence_dependency    exclusive
    dependor_delete_effect block
    as fReceiver;
    aggregation_of
        dbDiscr: dbDiscrs obligatory;
        fCompanyName: String obligatory;
        fAdress: String obligatory;
        fReceiverCode: Int obligatory;
        fGeographicalArea: String;
    class_key fReceiverCode, dbDiscr;
}
```

class Fwastes{

alte_graliz_of WastesDb1, WastesDb2 *by* dbDiscriminant *delete_effect_propagate*;

aggregates_in　　Fshipments　　*gral_aggr*　　*existence_dependency*　　*exclusive*
dependor_delete_effect block

as fWaste;

aggregation_of

　dbDiscr: dbDiscrs *obligatory*;

　fWasteCode: String *obligatory*;

　fName: String *obligatory*;

　fRisk: Int;

　fPrecautions: String;

class_key fWasteCode, dbDiscr;

}

class Fshipments{

alte_graliz_of　　　　　ShipmentsDb1,　　　ShipmentsDb2　　*by*　　dbDiscriminant
delete_effect_propagate;

aggregation_of

　dbDiscr: dbDiscrs *obligatory*;

　fShipmentCode: String *obligatory*;

　fWaste: Fwastes *gral_aggr existence_dependency exclusive dependor_delete_effect*
　　　block;

　fProducer: Fproducers *gral_aggr existence_dependency exclusive*
　　　　　dependor_delete_effect block;

　fReceiver: Freceivers *gral_aggr existence_dependency exclusive*
　　　　　dependor_delete_effect block;

class key fShipmentCode, dbDiscr;

}

Shipments	shCode	wasteCode	Sourcedb

Wastes	wasteCode	wasteName	risk	precautions	Sourcedb

Figure 4a User schema

Assume now a user at site 1 asks the following SQL query in terms of the user schema presented in Figure 4a:

```
select *
from Shipments, Wastes
where Shipments.wasteCode=Wastes.wasteCode;
```

This relational query will be transformed by the query manager giving rise to a federated transaction FT^1 having the structure shown in Figure 4b.

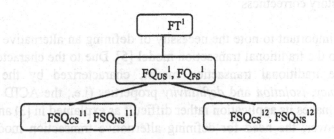

Figure 4b. FT^1 Structure

Now the transaction manager is in charge of controlling its execution; this implies the submission of federated subtransactions to the implied CDBs, the reception of subresults and making a final decision about the commit or abort of the federated transaction. The FT^1 includes two federated subtransactions FSQ_{NS}^{11} and FSQ_{NS}^{12} that will be executed respectively in parallel, at CDB_1 and CDB_2. In case FT^1 succeeds, the subresults will be sent to the query manager which will obtain a final, consolidated result. Assuming both FSQ_{NS}^{11} and FSQ_{NS}^{12} commit, the final result would be:

shCode	wasteCode	wasteName	risk	precautions	Sourcedb
0111	060101	Sulphuric acid	3	Neutralize with a base	db2
0111	060105	Nitric acid	3	Explosive; keep cool	db1

Table 1. FT^1 Result

3. TRANSACTIONAL ISSUES IN A FIS

The aspects to be considered in the design of a transactional model for a FIS are mainly related to the characteristics of the environment under consideration, i.e. the autonomy, heterogeneity and distribution of CDBs. In this section we want to sketch the issues that must be taken into account in case the FIS accepts read-only federated transactions. Basically, the transaction model must specify:

- The structure of federated transactions
- Operations to be executed by federated transactions
- Objects to be accessed by federated transactions
- Federated transactions correctness
- Federated transactions results
- History correctness

It is important to note the necessity of defining an alternative transaction model to the traditional transaction model [5]. Due to the characteristics of a FIS, the traditional transaction model, characterized by the *atomicity*, *consistency*, *isolation* and *definitivity* properties (i.e., the ACID transaction model), makes its application rather difficult as explained in [3] and [4].

Moreover, the need for defining alternative transaction models is also suggested not only in a FIS but also in other application domains where cooperation is required, as it is the case in engineering environments (CAD/CAM, software development), office automation, publication environments and so on. For these reasons, different transaction models have been proposed, not exclusively for FIS. Further, all these models have been developed taking into account the characteristics of the environment in which they have been applied (in [9], [11], [8], [6] the reader can find some of these proposals).

3.1   Structure of Federated Transactions

Federated transactions have a hierarchical structure (also referred to as a *nested structure* in the literature) which is represented by a tree of height 3, as Figure 2 shows. At the leaf level we have the different FSQ_{NS} that need to be executed. Each FSQ_{NS} will be executed exclusively in one CBD although we do not exclude the possibility that the same federated transaction needs to execute different FSQ_{NS} at the same CDB.

Given the autonomy of CDBs, we assume that the transaction manager at the federated level can not perform additional control over FSQ_{NS} once they have been submitted to the CDBs. Therefore, the only decisions that the transaction manager at the federated level could make with regard to FSQ_{NS} would be whether to send them for their execution, decide if they can proceed in parallel, retry their execution or disregard their results in case of abort of the federated transaction. Consequently, the properties of atomicity and isolation of ACID transactions become compromised for federated transactions; for this reason the federated transactions have an *open nested structure* (one of the first transaction models having an open nested structure was Sagas [10]). Since federated transactions are read-only transactions, one possibility to ensure atomicity is to disregard the results of the committed FSQ$_{NS}$. Concerning the isolation property, it could be the case that local transactions being executed by local users at CDB can interfere with federated transactions. From the point of view of local transactions, and given that federated transactions are read-only transactions, interferences will not appear.

3.2   Operations and Objects Accessed by Federated Transactions

We consider that federated transactions can perform two types of operations which include either transaction primitives or operations on DB objects. These two kinds of operations are known in terms of ACTA ([7]) as *significant events* and *object events*. In turn, ACTA classifies significant events in *initiation events* and *termination events*. As initiation events, we have the begin transaction management primitive whereas commit and abort are termination events. Both FT and FSQ$_{NS}$ perform these operations, but the precise semantics of such primitives can differ in the case of termination events. While the semantics of the commit and abort primitives applied to FSQ$_{NS}$ is fixed by the local transaction managers present at every CDB, the semantics of such primitives applied to FT can be defined at the federated level, as we will see later on.

With regard to object events, at this stage we only consider read operations. These read operations will take different forms depending on the specific node of the open nested structure associated with federated transactions (see again Figure 2).

With respect to objects accessed by federated transactions, it is important to note that, in general, federated transactions do not directly access objects since the objects are distributed and stored in the different CDB that form the FIS. So, the access is accomplished through the FSQ$_{NS}$ and the only objects accessible are those represented in the export schemas of CDB, and therefore in the federated schema of the FIS.

3.3   Federated Transactions Correctness

Federated transactions can complete their execution in two different states: *aborted* and *committed*. In the case of aborted state, the results produced by FSQ$_{NS}$ if any, must be disregarded. On the other hand, when a federated transaction ends its execution in a committed state, the results retrieved by its FSQ_{NS} must be passed to the query manager in order to produce a consolidated answer. So, the main point is to define in a precise manner the conditions that will cause a federated transaction to be in one of the two previous states. Such conditions could be specified by different user profiles, depending on the type of federated transaction we consider and the number of FQ_{US} (or alternatively FQ_{FS}) included in the federated transaction. In Figure 5 we show the different possibilities that must be considered.

According to the kind of *federated transaction* dimension two possibilities are distinguished: *predefined federated transactions* and *ad-hoc federated transactions*. Predefined federated transactions are defined in advance by the federated administrator and the federated designer and are available to federated users.

On the other hand, ad-hoc federated transactions are unknown and are directly posed by federated users. Depending on the *number of FQ_{US}* dimension, federated transactions may include more than one FQ_{US} petition or just one FQ_{US} (both cases are depicted in Figure 2).

If we combine these two dimensions we have different possibilities. When ad-hoc federated transactions include more than 1 FQ_{US} (upper right corner of Figure), the federated user can via the user interface module specify which FQ_{US} have to be successfully committed in order for the federated transaction to also commit.

These FQ_{US} are referred to as *vital* for the commitment of the federated transaction. Furthermore, if an FQ_{US} aborts, the federated user can specify how many times it must be retried if at all. In the case of ad-hoc federated transactions including just 1 FQ_{US} (lower right corner of Figure), the federated user is not allowed to specify additional conditions because s/he does not know the open nested structure associated to her/his federated transaction.

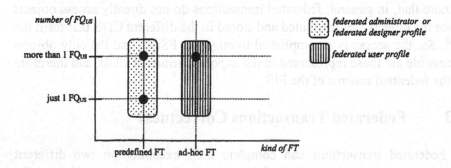

Figure 5. User Profiles

Finally, in the case of predefined federated transactions, the federated administrator and the federated designer are aware of the open nested structure associated to the federated transaction. Therefore, they are allowed to specify the previous conditions both for FQ_{US} (or alternatively to FQ_{FS}) and for FSQ_{NS}.

Assuming that the query presented in the running example (see subsection 2.2) is a predefined query, the federated transaction designer/administrator could have specified the following predicates that indicate the conditions for the commitment of federated transaction FT^1:

$$aborted(FQ_{FS}^1) \leftarrow aborted(FSQ_{NS}^{11})$$
$$committed(FQ_{FS}^1) \leftarrow ((committed(FSQ_{NS}^{11}) \wedge committed(FSQ_{NS}^{12})) \vee (committed(FSQ_{NS}^{11}) \wedge aborted(FSQ_{NS}^{12})))$$
$$aborted(FT^1) \leftarrow aborted(FQ_{FS}^1)$$
$$committed(FT^1) \leftarrow committed(FQ_{FS}^1)$$

In summary, the previous predicates state that FSQ_{NS}^{11} is vital for the commit of FQ_{FS}^1 and FQ_{FS}^1 is vital for the commit of FT^1 (this is a trivial case given that FT^1 is composed by just one FQ_{FS}).

3.4 Federated Transactions Results

With respect to the results produced by a federated transaction, it is necessary to specify what they are. We consider that these results can include:
- Retrieved data from CDBs involved in the execution of federated transactions
- Information related to the data origin (i.e. CDBs involved in the execution of federated transactions), when such information was represented in the user schema
- Additional messages informing where federated subtransactions have failed

3.5 History Correctness

A *history* (see [5]) represents the concurrent execution of a set of transactions adhered to a particular transaction model. In terms of ACTA [7], a history includes all the events (both significant and object) invoked by the transactions and indicates the partial order in which these events occur. In DBs that follow the ACID transaction model, the correctness criterion used is the *conflict serializability criterion*. This criterion guarantees that a history is correct if it produces the same results as some *serial history*, i.e. a history without interleaving of transaction operations, in which all or none of the transaction operations are performed. Correct histories (also known as *serializable histories*) do not have interferences and guarantee that DB integrity is maintained.

Again, in case of FIS, the *conflict serializability* criterion is too strict and the autonomy of CDB makes its applicability difficult. Since we consider read-only transactions, the histories produced at the federated level which only include read operations, are serializable histories (remember that operations executed by local transactions at each CDB are not considered at the federated level because they are unknown).

Moreover, the local transaction managers will also guarantee serializable histories at each CDB. But if the global history (i.e. the history including both local and federated transaction operations) could be reproduced, it could be the case that local transactions caused indirect conflicts between federated transactions, in turn giving rise to the possibility that such a global history was a non serializable history ([3] and [4] show examples that illustrate this situation). Again, this results in side-effects on isolation property at the federated transactions level.

At this stage we accept this possibility, and we just consider serializable histories at the federated level. In addition, it is also required that the transaction manager at the federated level enforces the federated transaction correctness properties specified either by the federated users or the federated designer/administrator (see subsection 3.3).

4.   CONCLUSIONS AND FUTURE WORK

Throughout this paper, we have sketched the transactional characteristics that must be taken into account for an FIS that deals with read-only federated transactions. In summary, we believe that a realistic assumption in FIS is the relaxation of the isolation property for federated transactions and the possibility for the user to specify the correctness properties for federated transactions. The transaction manager at the federated level must guarantee that those properties are enforced.

Future work includes research on the additional problems that appear when read-write federated transactions are considered and how these problems can be tackled. Concerning read-write federated transactions, we plan to apply semantic compensation techniques. Such techniques ensure that the effects produced by a partially committed federated transaction are undone by means of a compensating federated transaction which incorporates compensating federated subtransactions that execute the inverse operations of those that were previously committed.

It is important to note that, when federated transactions to be compensated have executed partially committed update operations, additional problems will appear. Committed local transactions that could have used these partially committed federated results must be also considered, compensated and executed again.

In order to make feasible the application of compensation techniques, we will focus on the following:

- the development of mechanisms for tracing the operations performed by local transactions that are susceptible to being compensated;
- the detection of all those local operations to be compensated and their compensating order;
- the generation of the federated subtransactions that must include either the inverse operations performed by local and federated subtransactions,
- the local operations that must be executed again.

ACKNOWLEDGMENTS

This work has been partially supported by the Spanish Research Program PRONTIC under project TIC99-1078-C02-01.

REFERENCES

1. Abelló A.,. Oliva M., Rodríguez E., and Saltor F., The Syntax of BLOOM99 Schemas. Technical Report LSI-99-34-R, Dept. Llenguatges i Sistemes Informàtics, Universitat Politècnica de Catalunya, 1999.

2. Abelló A.,. Oliva M., Rodríguez E., and Saltor F., The BLOOM Model Revised: An Evolution Proposal, in ECOOP'99 Workshop Reader (Poster Session), pages 376-378, Lisbon (Portugal), June 1999. Springer.

3. Breitbart Y., García-Molina H., and Silberschatz A., Overview of Multidatabase Transaction Management, The VLDB Journal, 1(2):181-240, October 1992.

4. Breitbart Y., García-Molina H., and Silberschatz A., Transaction Management in Multidatabase Systems, in Kim W., (Editor), Modern Database Systems: the Object Model, Interoperability and Beyond, pages 573-591, Addison-Wesley, 1995.

5. Bernstein P.A., Hadzilacos V., and Goodman N., Concurrency Control and Recovery, in Database Systems, Addison-Wesley, Reading, MA, 1987.

6. de By R. A., Klas W., and Veijalainen J., (Eds), Transaction Management Support for Cooperative Applications. Kluwer Academic Publishers, 1998.

7. Chrysanthis P.K., and Ramamritham K., Synthesis of Extended Transaction Models using ACTA, ACM Trans. on Database Systems, 19(3):450-491, September 1994.

8. Dogac A., Kalinichenko L., Özsu M.T, and Sheth A., Workflow Management Systems and Interoperability, NATO ASI Series, Series F: Computer and System Sciences, Volume 164, Springer, 1998.
9. Elmagarmid A.K., (Editor), Database Transaction Models for Advanced Applications. Morgan Kaufmann Publishers, San Mateo, CA, 1992.
10. García-Molina H., Salem K., SAGAS, in U. Dayal, I. Traiger, (Eds), Proceedings of the 1987 ACM SIGMOD Int. Conference on Management of Data, San Francisco, CA, pages 249-259, ACM SIGMOD Record, 16(3), ACM Press, May 1987.
11. Jajodia S., and Kerschberg L., (Eds), Advanced Transaction Models and Architectures. Kluwer Academic Publishers, 1997.
12. Oliva M., and Saltor F., Integrating Multilevel Security Policies in Multilevel Federated Database Systems, in Proceedings of the 14th IFIP 11.3 Working Conference in Database Security, Schoorl, The Netherlands, August 2000.
13. Rodríguez E., Oliva M., Saltor F., and Campderrich B., On Schema and Functional Architectures for Multilevel Secure and Multiuser Model Federated DB Systems, in Conrad S., Hasselbring W., Heuer A., Saake G., (Eds), Proceedings of the Int. CAiSE'97 Workshop, Barcelona, pages 93-104, Otto-von-Guericke-Universität Magdeburg, June 1997.
14. Saltor F., Campderrich B., Rodríguez E., and Rodríguez L.C., On Schema Levels for Federated Database Systems, in Yetongnon, Hairiri, (Eds), Proceedings of the ISCA International Conference on Parallel and Distributed Computing Systems, Dijon, France, pages 766-771, September 1996.
15. Sheth A.P., and Larson J.A., Federated Database Systems for Managing Distributed, Heterogeneous and Autonomous Databases, ACM Computing Surveys, 22(3):183-236, September 1990.

Chapter 3

Semantic Integration in MADS Conceptual Model

Anastasiya Sotnykova, Sophie Monties, and Stefano Spaccapietra
*Swiss Federal Institute of Technology in Lausanne, Database Laboratory, 1015 Lausanne,
Switzerland. Email: {Anastasiya.Sotnykova,Sophie.Monties,Stefano.Spaccapietra}@ epfl.ch*

Abstract: Our vision of a viable way for transparent and meaningful processing of
heterogeneous spatio-temporal data is to put data semantics in the foundation
of an integration process. We present and correlate means of integration as
components of the mediation level of an interoperable system. For our domain
of interest we present MADS domain ontologies and MADS conceptual data
model dedicated to modeling of spatio-temporal data. Using the example of
two MADS schemas we outline an integration methodology based on semantic
interschema correspondence assertions and integration goals.

Key words: Heterogeneous spatio-temporal data, semantic integration, ontology, MADS
conceptual model, canonical data model

1. INTRODUCTION

The interoperability problem arises in heterogeneous systems where
different data resources coexist and there is a need for meaningful
information sharing in the system. The heterogeneity of the data can be
originated by semantic, syntactic, and structural differences of the data
sources. One of the demonstrative realms of diversity of data representation
is the spatio-temporal domain. In the spatio-temporal domain the same
objects can be, and usually are, represented from multiple and greatly
diverse points of view. For example, a building can be represented from four
different points of view as shown in Table 1.

In contrast to thematic data representation, spatio-temporal data
heterogeneity largely lies in the semantics of the data. Thus, it is definitely
insufficient to establish a correspondence between attribute value domains,
for example. An adequate amount of integration work has to be done before
we can establish a correspondence on the attribute domain level. The core of

H. Bestougeff et al. (eds.), Heterogeneous Information Exchange and Organizational Hubs, 33–58.

an interoperable system that operates spatio-temporal data should be based, first and foremost, on the semantic information.

Purpose of representation	User
Architectural style and fitting in the neighborhood environment	Architect department of a city administration
Robustness of the construction of the building and the materials it is built of	Rescue crew of the city
Condition of the building and suitability for living in it	Renovation construction company
Location and dimensions of the building	Cadastral department of the city administration

Table 1. How a 'Building' Object Can Be Represented

As illustrated in Table 1, it is a challenge to propose rules from which it can be inferred that two or more different data representations portray the same object from the real world. Such rules or correspondence assertions are a viable way to express the fact of common population, spatial, and/or temporal features of objects from different applications. The derivation of semantically driven assertions is feasible if this process is founded on an equally semantically expressive data model for the application domain.

This implies that the application data should be remodeled or pre-integrated at the conceptual level[1] in a semantically rich model. Such a model is called Canonical Data Model (CDM). A CDM should have a minimal number of concepts while at the same time being sufficient to capture the semantics of the application domain and tasks to which it is dedicated. In this paper we present our view of the appropriate architecture for an interoperable system, CDM, correspondence assertions expressions, and an integration methodology for spatio-temporal domain.

We begin our paper by presenting a generic view of the interoperable systems and proceeding by refining the scope of possible architectures to agent-based and mediator-based systems as most widely approved by the research community. In Section 2 we discuss the main features that can be accomplished within each architecture and point to the one which is more suitable for our domain. Within this architecture in Section 3.1 we define the system component for which we contribute some proposals of our own. Section 3.2 presents the conceptual data model, which we use as the CDM for pre-integration of the spatio-temporal data. A provisional integration methodology is presented in Section 4 and illustrated by an example introduced in Section 3.3. Section 5 concludes our paper.

---

[1] as the implementation independent level

2.   INTEROPERABLE SYSTEM COMPONENTS.

Generally, an interoperable system consists of three main components as shown in Figure 1. At the foundation level there are heterogeneous legacy data sources. The mediation level supports exchange of queries and results between legacy data sources and applications. At the application level the interaction with the users is carried out [13].

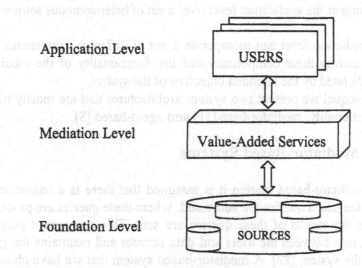

Application Level

Mediation Level

Foundation Level

Figure 1. Generic Structure of an Interoperable System

Without the 'Value-Added Services', the structure presented would be an ordinary information system architecture, designed for a particular group of users operating a specific set of data sources. Nowadays, when modern information systems increasingly address information and knowledge acquisition issues over heterogeneous data sources [9, 19], this is no longer an answer for an information system architecture.

An information system with an intermediate level between 'USERS' and 'SOURCES' levels is called *mediated*. The mediation level that provides users with services based on the data collected and operated previously with other purposes, and within other information systems, would allow for defining such a system as *interoperable*.

In the literature many different implementations of the mediation level can be found [18, 1, 3, 5, 2]. Among these, the components distilled by the practice are the following:

– *application ontology* - a dictionary containing all the concepts and their hierarchy for the application domain;

- *agents* - intelligent components that can serve different purposes in the system, for instance, location of the data sources in a distributed system, matching user requests with the services available;
- *translators* - translate user queries to a CDM;
- *wrappers* - translate the heterogeneous source data to a CDM;
- *integrators* - perform integration of heterogeneous data sources based, for example, on an ontology or a CDM;
- *mediator* - a complex component which provides transparent access and processing at the application level over a set of heterogeneous source data.

The mediation level can incorporate a set of different components. The choosing among these components and the functionality of the mediation level are dictated by the intended objective of the system.

In the sequel we present two system architectures that are mostly distant in the functionality: mediator-based [1] and agent-based [8].

2.1   Mediator-Based Systems

In a mediator-based system it is assumed that there is a component to which all the user's queries are addressed, where these queries are processed, and where the results of these queries are sent. This component plays the mediation role between the users and data sources and maintains the global vision of the system [22]. A mediator-based system that we have chosen as the illustrative example is presented in [1].

Figure 2 shows a simplified architecture of the system. As the basis for data integration, a CDM was used. The authors have chosen the object-oriented data model whose capabilities in modeling semantics and relationships were suitable for the application area. The local schemas of component databases are translated into the CDM and are enriched semantically if necessary. The federated schema is a schema constructed in CDM based on the user specifications on the data subset of their interest.

Thus, the users view the system as a single database containing the data they requested. User queries are directed to the mediator component of the system where the queries are decomposed and then translated into the local schema query languages.

Although the technique described in this paper suits the application requirements, the authors do not address issues such as semantic conflict resolution or integrity constraints management. In addition the disadvantage of the system is that the component databases are not operable locally and that the data sources updates are done globally.

Presenting the system capabilities, the authors mention that:

> ... *the schema integrator provides facilities for integrating the schema exported from the component databases into the federated schema. It needs to generate mapping between the exported and federated schemas and must have a reasonable capability for detecting conflicts between data...*

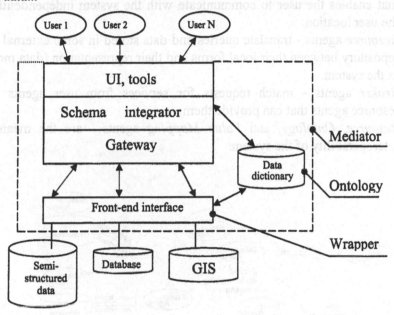

Figure 2. Mediator Based Approach.

However, no real example of the schema integrator functionality is given in the paper. The authors propose the use of a mapping table[2] for object representations matching.

2.2 Agent-Based systems

As an example of an agent-based architecture we consider the InfoSleuth system presented in [8]. InfoSleuth is a distributed system where the data sources and the users reside on different sites and are connected by sets of different agents. System agents communicate on the basis of a system ontology which is the only global component of an agent based system. An *ontology* is a specification of how to represent the objects, concepts and other entities that are assumed to exist in some domain of interest and how to

---

[2] which can be seen as a simplified ontology

represent the relationships that hold among all these entities [6]. An ontology does not represent a global structural vision of the system data sources but only the set of terms the system is aware of.

In an agent system three main agent types can be pointed out [8]:

– *User* agent - maintains the user state and provides the system interface that enables the user to communicate with the system independently of the user location.
– *Resource* agents - translate queries and data stored in some external data repository between their local forms and their representation (data model) in the system.
– *Broker* agents - match requests for services from user agents with resource agents that can provide them.
– *Resource*, *Ontology*, and *Value Mapping* agents - are the means of interoperability of the system.

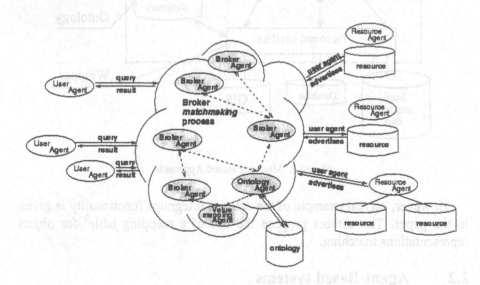

Figure 3. Agent-based Approach.

All the types of heterogeneity - structural, syntactic and semantic - are solved by resource agents and value mapping agents in InfoSleuth, based on the developed ontology. The value mapping agents map query terms to and from the canonical value domain, which is defined by the system ontology. The canonical value domain reduces heterogeneity only in terms of allowed attribute values but not in terms of data representation. Users query and view data in whichever value domain they prefer, and their user agents perform the value mapping necessary to communicate with other agents in the canonical value domain. To perform a value mapping a user agent contacts a value mapping agent. Thus, all the operations related to data interoperability are done through consultation with the ontology of the system. Referring to Figure 3, it can be seen, that the functionality of the *user* and *value mapping* agents is similar to that of the *query translator*. On the other hand, a resemblance can be found for the *wrapper*'s (in Figure 2) and the *resource* agent functionalities.

The partial knowledge of the available data and its location is maintained by broker agents. The information stored by broker agents is partitioned in such a way that the whole set of broker agents 'knows' about all the data available in the system[3]. The system ontology stores the data hierarchy that the system is aware of. When the user queries the system, it is the broker agent(s) functionality to determine whether the data requested can be found in the system data sources. The user does not have a global view of the system data and does not know whether his/her request can be met. The partition of the knowledge and communication between the broker agents ensures that the user agents and the resource agents are fully connected, i.e., any user can potentially reach any resource.

As it follows from the system description the users are assumed to pose SELECT-type queries. This system does not allow UPDATE-type queries. The broker agents are oriented towards locating requested data, matching the semantic and syntactic information of the user agent and a data source. Done automatically, the matchmaking process restricts the amount of semantic information that agents can operate. The last observation together with absence of a global vision of the system limits the application area of the agent-based systems.

2.3 Comparison

Comparing the approaches presented above, we bear in mind the following characteristics of an intended interoperable system:
– at the foundation level there are heterogeneous spatio-temporal data sources;
– at the application level there are users with their vision of the universe of discourse;
– users expect transparent operations on geodata stored in different formats, with different resolutions, and for different purposes.
Let us first briefly summarize the pivotal characteristics of the two approaches to make our reasoning about their applicability to spatio-temporal domain more clear.

---

[3] Depending on the system design redundancy may be allowed or even required.

Agent-based
- system ontology is the only global component in the system,
- the users do not have a global view of the system,
- updates are allowed on the local level and may not reflect the system ontology.

Mediator-based
- a mediator stores either the schemas of component databases and the relationships between them or a federated schema of the system, depending on the implementation,
- users have a schematic partial or global view of the system,
- updates are theoretically allowed from both the global and local levels, but with no clear methodology for updates propagation. The global consistency of the system is an open question.

The desired interoperable system characteristics can then be stated as follows:
- a global schema is constructed based on semantic and syntactic information. Conflicts are resolved at the global level;
- consistency of the data is ensured during the integration process;
- updates are allowed from the global level as well as from the local. Consistency of the component databases is ensured by an updates propagation mechanism.

The agent-based system is hardly a viable way to accomplish such a task. Agents are more oriented towards determining the location of data sources in a distributed system: the data sources available are heterogeneous in the sense that different objects are stored in different locations. Whereas, if dealing with the spatio-temporal data it is also likely that the same phenomena would be presented in different ways. Consequently, to establish a relation between different objects, a semantically based methodology should be employed which requires a semantically rich integration platform. Semantic information carried by agents in the InfoSleuth system is not sufficient for integrating spatio-temporal objects.

Moreover, in the spatio-temporal domain, the global vision of the data and data structure is an indispensable property of the system. An attempt to enrich the broker agents with more semantic information would lead to an increase in the system response time and therefore to a decline in system performance.

Another potentially incompatible feature of the agent-based system architecture with respect to the spatio-temporal integration process, is that the matching process is automatic. This advantageous feature of the agent-based architecture is not yet applicable to the spatio-temporal domain. To the best of our knowledge, there is no methodology which would support an automatic matching process for spatio-temporal objects modeled within different applications.

More features that can be adopted in the spatio-temporal domain are borne by the mediator-based approach. The example given in Table 1 suggests that for integration purposes the data sources should be implemented or translated (on the conceptual or physical level) into a model in which diverse semantic aspects of the data objects can be expressed. In addition there should be an expressive language which enables the user to define interrelations of spatio-temporal object types. In [16] the authors provide a picture of the integration approaches leading to system interoperability. In Section 4 we present our integration methodology in more detail.

One common system component in Figure 2 and Figure 3 is the system ontology. The notion of ontology is ambiguously perceived by the database community, whereas ontology plays a key role and for some implementations is the only means of integrating the system data sources. In the following section we present a notion of ontology and conceptual models as the next level of abstraction of an application area.

3. INTEROPERABILITY : ONTOLOGIES AND CONCEPTUAL MODELS

Guarino in [10] distinguishes several ontology levels, as shown in Figure 4. Top-level ontology is a representation of the 'truth', i.e., the representation of the real world without any inference services in mind. The top-level ontology is the most generic type of ontology where concepts like space, time, matter, object are presented. The taxonomy of top-level ontologies is simplest from the structural point of view. The only relation that is used for top-level ontologies is subsumption. Thus, a top-level ontology has a non-cyclic tree structure without multi inheritance. An example of such an ontology can be found in [12].

The reasoning behind constructing a top-level ontology lies in the four meta-properties borne by the things of the real world. These meta-properties are: *rigidity, identity, unity* and *dependence* described in detail in [10] and [11]. In brief, identity is related to the problem of distinguishing a specific instance of a certain class from other instances, by means of a characteristic property, that is unique to it.

A rigid property is a property that holds for all the instances of a class. For example, imagine two classes PERSON and STUDENT. From the point of view of rigidity, PERSON is rigid - all the instances of this class are of PERSON type. On the other hand, STUDENT is not rigid - the same individual can be STUDENT in one context, and non-STUDENT in another. From the previous example, we can conclude that rigid classes supply the identity, and non-rigid ones just carry an identity.

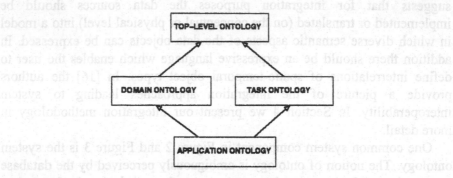

Figure 4. Kinds of Ontology from [10].

Unity is related to the problem of distinguishing the parts of an instance from the rest of the world by means of a *unifying relation* that binds them together. An example of an identity query would be 'What is this country?' and of a unity query would be 'Does this canton belong to this country?'. If existence of an instance of a class implies a necessary existence of an instance in another class, then the former possesses the dependence meta-property. One example would be a CANTON class that implies the existence of a COUNTRY class.

Ascription of those properties to classes imposes certain constraints on the positional relationship of these classes in the top-level ontology. For example, one of the imposed structural constraints is that a dependent class cannot subsume the class it depends on.

The role of the top-level ontology is to formalize the real world in a widely sharable, multidisciplinary way to be used further as the pattern for different domain and task ontologies.

For the spatio-temporal domain, the top-level ontology is one of the subjects of research and agreement of the OpenGis consortium [15].

When an ontology contains some domain specific concepts or concepts related to general features of an application we step down the ontology hierarchy. Such an ontology is a subjective, refined representation of the same concepts as in the top-level ontology, but domain and task ontologies already can be used in the integration process.

3.1   Ontology and Conceptual Schemas

Domain and task ontologies contain the classes that are further used in the conceptual schemas. When we start to model the roles of the domain ontology classes while performing a certain activity we are at the level of application ontology, the most specific and application dependent type of ontology. The main thread passing through the structure shown in Figure 3, is that domain, task, and application ontologies are structurally compliant with the top-level ontology. In the light of the above presentation, we believe that an ontology notion in each particular utilization should be differentiated and clearly distinguished from the next level of knowledge presentation, namely conceptual modeling.

The objective of conceptual modeling is to represent application data together with the rules of the application domain. In other words, conceptual models enables the user to represent his understanding of the universe of discourse. The task of designing a modern information system becomes more complex with the progress of information technology and with users becoming more demanding for the functionality of the information systems. In such circumstances conceptual modeling gains importance, as it is the starting point for understanding the users' needs.

The most important properties that a conceptual model should have are: abstraction, non-ambiguity, ease of understanding and verification, and implementation independence [14]. The last property implies that a conceptual model should be expressive enough for the same conceptual schema to be valid, even when software paradigms are upgraded or replaced.

Conceptual schemas are the representation of the user perception of the application domain, therefore they would constitute the basis for integration of heterogeneous domain sources in an interoperable system. In the integration approach presented in Section 4, we chose a conceptual representation as the starting point for corresponding heterogeneous data sources. The choice of an appropriate conceptual model depends on the completeness of the representation it allows, formal semantics, and simplicity of use and interpretation.

In this section we described two levels of metadata representation that are components of the mediation level of an interoperable system. An ontology constitutes the representation of the real world without bearing in mind any application of this representation. Conceptual schemas are implementation independent representations of the application area, containing the users' vision of the application domain.

The link between an ontology and a conceptual schema is that the conceptual schema of an application domain should be structurally compliant with the ontology of the same domain. Nevertheless, in our research we base our approach only on domain ontologies and conceptual schemas without making any reference to a top-level ontology since we are not aware of the existence of an approved top-level spatio-temporal ontology.

In the following section we reason about our choice of the spatio-temporal canonical data model.

3.2 MADS Conceptual Model as a Canonical Data Model

Applications manipulating geodata are difficult to model due to the particularity and complexity of the spatial and temporal components. More facets of real-world entities have to be considered, e.g., location, form, size, time validity; more links are relevant, e.g., spatial, temporal links; several spatial abstraction levels often need to be represented. Thus, modeling spatio-temporal databases requires advanced facilities [20], such as the following.

- Objects with complex structure (e.g., composition/aggregation links, generalization links), at least equivalent to those supported by current object-oriented models. This should achieve full representational power in terms of data structures;
- Alternative geometry features to support both discrete and continuous views of space, representations at different scale/precision, multiple viewpoints from different users;
- Spatial objects with one or several geometries associated to different resolutions or user points of views;
- Temporal objects with complex life-cycles that allow users to create, suspend, reactivate, and eventually delete objects;
- Timestamped attributes that record their past, present, and future values;
- Spatio-temporal concepts for describing moving and deforming objects;
- Explicit relationships to describe structural links as well as spatial (such as adjacency, inclusion, spatial aggregation) and synchronization links (such as before, during). The knowledge of the topological links between real-world entities is an essential requirement for applications;
- Causal relationships describing the causes and effects of changes that happen in the real world.

The model must also allow defining schemas that are readable and easy to understand. A key element for achieving this double objective is the orthogonality of the structural, temporal, and spatial dimensions of the model (and more generally of the concepts of the model). Thus, whatever the concept of the model, e.g., object, relationship, attribute, aggregation, the spatial and temporal dimensions may be associated to it.

In our research we employ MADS conceptual data model [17] as the CDM. MADS stands for Modeling of Application Data with Spatio-temporal features. The MADS model was specially designed to fill the niche of conceptual data models for spatio-temporal applications. In [17] the authors analyze different spatio-temporal data models along the axes of expressiveness, simplicity and comprehensiveness, formalism, and user friendliness, making the conclusion that none of the existing models satisfied all the demanding criteria.

MADS includes a set of predefined spatial and temporal Abstract Data Types (ADTs) that are used for describing the spatial and temporal extents of the spatio-temporal elements of schemas. Spatiality and temporality may be associated to object and relationship types, aggregation links, and attributes. The MADS structural, spatial, and temporal domains are orthogonal, meaning that spatial and temporal features can be freely added to any schema designed in MADS.

3.2.1   MADS Structural Dimension

Structurally MADS is an object + relationship data model. Thus, it allows us to represent basic concepts from entity-relationship model, e.g., entity type, relationship type, IsA link, as well as more complex structural components, e.g., aggregation links, multi-inheritance, complex attributes. The MADS data structure notation is shown in Figure 5.

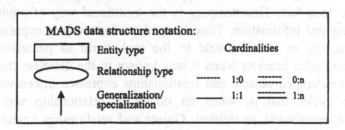

Figure 5. MADS Data Structure Notation.

3.2.2   MADS Spatial Dimension

MADS predefined Spatial ADTs (SADTs) are: point, line, oriented line, simple area, simple geo, point set, line set, oriented line set, complex area, complex geo, geo. The spatial domain ontology is presented in Figure 6, that also shows the icons denoting each SADT.

The most generic SADT is geo, which generalizes the simple-geo and complex-geo SADTs, and whose semantics is *'this element has a spatial extent'* without any commitment to a specific SADT. These three SADT are abstract and are never instantiated. The spatiality of an element can either be defined precisely (e.g., point, oriented line), or left undetermined, (e.g., geo).

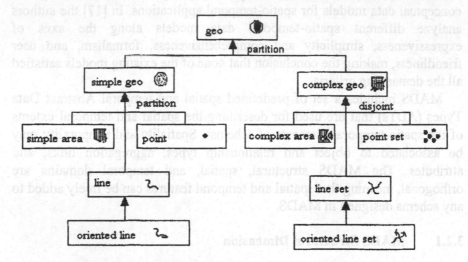

Figure 6. MADS Basic Hierarchy of Spatial Abstract Data Types

3.2.3 MADS Temporal Dimension

Temporal ADTs (TADTs) support timestamping, i.e., associating a timeframe to a fact. Timestamping is the traditional way of modeling so-called temporal information. Timestamped attribute values express when a value was, (is, or will be) held in the real world as perceived by the application (valid time) or when it was known in the database (transaction time). Timestamped objects and relationships expresses information about their life cycle: that is, when an object or relationship was created, suspended, reactivated, or deleted. Object and relationship timestamps are also based on either valid time or transaction time. Currently MADS supports valid time. Figure 7 shows the MADS hierarchy of temporal data types.

The spatiality/temporality of an application is reflected by the existence of spatial/temporal entities, but also by the existence of space- and time-related relationships between these entities. Is important to be able to explicitly describe space-related relationships in conceptual schemas. This enriches the schema, allowing these relationships to be named and described with attributes and methods.

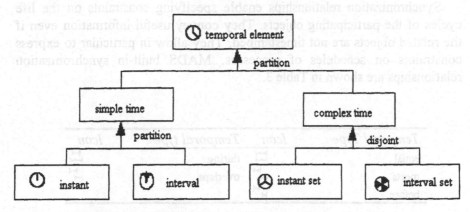

Figure 7. MADS Basic Hierarchy of Temporal Abstract Data Types.

3.2.4 MADS Constrained Relationships

MADS constrained relationship types are relationship types that convey spatial and temporal constraints on the objects they link. MADS includes topological and synchronization relationships as built-in constrained relationship types. For example, a topological relationship type inside may be defined to link object types Canton and Country, expressing that the geometry of a canton is within the geometry of the related country. The list of MADS predefined topological relationship types and their associated icons is shown in Table 2. Every MADS topological relationship type is characterized by its spatial type, which is visually represented by an icon. Although these icons represent surface objects, these symbols are valid for every spatial object type.

Spatial type	Icon	Definition
disjunction		the linked objects have spatially disjoint geometries
adjacency		geometry sharing without common interior
crossing		sharing of some part of interior such that, the dimension of the shared part is strictly inferior to the higher dimension of the linked objects
overlapping		sharing of some part of interior such that, the dimension of the shared part is equal to the dimension of the linked objects
inclusion		the whole interior of one object is part of the interior of other object
equality		sharing of the whole interior and of the whole envelope (for spatial objects of the same dimension)

Table 2. MADS Topological Relationships

Synchronization relationships enable specifying constraints on the life cycles of the participating objects. They convey useful information even if the related objects are not timestamped. They allow in particular to express constraints on schedules of processes. MADS built-in synchronization relationships are shown in Table 3.

Temporal Type	Icon	Temporal type	Icon
equal	⊔⊔	during	⊔⊔
meets	⊔	overlaps	⊔⊔
before	⊔		

Table 3. MADS Temporal Relationships.

3.3   Motivating Example

Figures 8 and 9 show two examples of schemas that will be used throughout the rest of the paper to illustrate the integration methodology we present in Section 4.

Schema S_1 is a part of a hypothetical schema for a park administration of a city. The objects this park administration is interested in are the green plantations within the city area, their geometries and types, (e.g., flower bed, park, field). In addition there are bordering objects included in the schema, such as crossroads or build-up areas. For these objects, the park administration merely needs to know their name, (e.g., crossroad), or their geometry, (e.g., road, water body, build-up area).

Schema S_2 is a part of a hypothetical road network schema for road management department of the same city. The focus of this schema is the detailed representation of road network elements, their classification and the relationships among them. Both schemas model real world elements geographically located in the same area - a city. As such, the populations of these schemas have some common instances providing an integration ground.

There are some concepts used in these schemas which are peculiar to MADS data model. For example, the Park entity type being non-temporal can have temporal attributes, illustrating the concept of orthogonality of the structural, temporal, and spatial dimensions of MADS data model. FlowerBed entity type has multivalued attribute FlowerType with *1:n* cardinality.

From the point of view of MADS spatial domain ontology, the IsA hierarchy of spatial entity types is coherent with it.

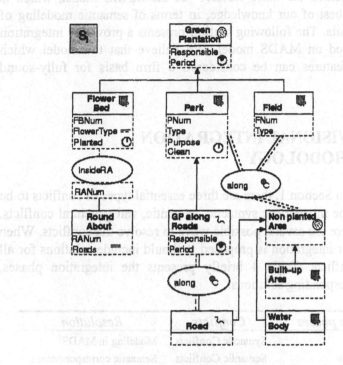

Figure 8. Park Administration

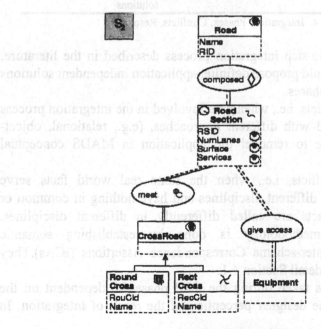

Figure 9. Road Administration

We have presented the basic features[4] of the MADS model, which is complete, to the best of our knowledge, in terms of semantic modeling of spatio-temporal data. The following section presents a provisory integration methodology based on MADS model. We believe that the model which possesses such features can be considered a firm basis for fully-sound integration.

4.   PROVISIONAL INTEGRATION METHODOLOGY

As described in Section 1, there are three essential types of conflicts to be resolved during the integration: syntactic, semantic, and structural conflicts. For each type, there are several possible ways to resolve the conflicts. When a methodology for integration is proposed it should include solutions for all the types of conflicts. Table 4 briefly presents the integration phases, conflicts and corresponding solutions.

Integration phases	*Conflicts*	*Resolution*
Pre-integration	Syntactic Conflicts	Modeling in MADS
ICAs formulation	Semantic Conflicts	Semantic correspondences
Integrated schema generation	Structural Conflicts	Set of possible structural solutions

Table 4. Integration: Phases, Conflicts, Resolution.

Following the three-step integration process described in the literature, we realized that we could propose definite, application independent solutions only for the first two phases.

For syntactic conflicts, i.e., when data involved in the integration process are logically designed with different approaches, (e.g., relational, object-oriented), we propose to remodel the application in MADS conceptual model.

For semantic conflicts, i.e., when the same real world facts serve different purposes for different disciplines and have nothing in common or when the same objects are called differently in different disciplines, resolution in our methodology is done by establishing semantic correspondences or Inter-schema Correspondence Assertions (ICAs).They are presented in more detail Section 4.1.

Structural solutions taken during the third phase are dependent on the application, and on the designer perception of the result of integration. In

[4] A more detailed specification of the MADS model can be found in [17].

addition, different structural solutions have their merits and shortcomings that might not be clear to the designer. Therefore, there is a need for an intermediate step in which the designer is guided through different possible structural solutions.

Generally, having independently two entity types *A* and *B* on the semantic correspondences existing between them, the resulting structural solutions can be different, thus, adding another dimension to the set of the decisions to be made during the integration process. In Section. 4.2 we present in more detail the intermediate phase called *'Choosing an integration goal'*. The results of this phase allows to solve structural conflicts of the next integration phase.

4.1 Interschema Correspondence Assertions

For semantic conflicts resolution we propose an integration language similar but more comprehensive and expressive than those presented in [21] and [4]. This language allows to formulate correspondences between different database schemas. The correspondences are called Interschema Correspondence Assertions, and are defined in four levels. Semantic Correspondences (SC) state the fact that there is a correspondence between two object populations.

At the next level there are Property Semantic Correspondences (PSC) where the domain mismatches are resolved. The Matching Rules (MR) uniquely identify the same object instances represented diversely in several schemas. The Integrity Constraints (IC) inherited from the component schemas complete the set of correspondences and allow to deduce those that are not inferable from the component conceptual schemas.

SCs are the most general notions stating that there is something in common between the real-world objects modeled in the databases.

The syntax of the SC is the following:

```
EntityPath Operator EntityPath;,
```

where `EntityPath` is composed of the name of a schema and the name of an entity type,

`Operator` is one of the following set operator: $\{\cap, \subset$ or $\sigma, \equiv\}$.

Set operators associate the populations of the entity types involved in the assertion. The choice of $\subset$ or σ operators depends on whether it is possible to state a condition for selecting a subset of an entity population. If it is the case, then the inclusion operator can be replaced with the more precise unary operator σ. Refining inclusion in such a way allows to establish a clearer correspondence between integrating entities' populations.

Example. Population links between the schemas shown in Fig. 8 and 9 exist between crossroads, e.g., RoundAbout and RoundCross entity types, and roads modeled as Roads entity types. The SCs are the following:

S₁.RoundAbout ⊂ S₂.RoundCross;

S₁.Road ⊂ S₂.Road;

Here we use the ⊂ operator, because the population of S₁.RoundAbout consists only of those round crossroads that contain a flowerbed, whereas the population of S₂.RoundCross includes all the round crossroads in the city. The same is true for road sections modeled by the schemas.

Property Semantic Correspondences make more precise the semantic correspondences defined by SC assertions. The syntax of a PSC is the following:

[Function]AttributePath Operator
[Function]AttributePath;,

where Function is a pre-defined or user-defined function over an attribute domain, AttributePath is composed of the name of a schema, the name of an entity type, and the attribute or attributes' name(s)[5], and Operator is one of the following:

– equality of the domain values – {=},
– user-defined correspondence of the domain values – {↔},
– topological relationship - ◑°, ◓, ◔, ◕, ●, ◉,
– temporal relationship - ⊨, ⊏, ⊢, ⊣, ⊦.

PSCs assertions state general correspondences between two value domains. They establish a *translation function* between the two value domains and are employed for example in the case of reversible integration to restore the attribute values for component schemas. The existence of a PSC via the = or ↔ operator implies that there is a population intersection within the entities involved in this PSC. If the entity types corresponded by a PSC possess spatial features then they could be related by a topological relationship. The same is true for temporal relationships, since a property semantic correspondence involving a temporal relationship can exist between these entity types.

The three mentioned types of semantic correspondences are not interdependent. An example could be a basement of a building from one

---

[5] in the case of complex attributes

schema and a building from another schema: they have the same geometry, but they are not the same objects, i.e., there is a spatial relationship but no population relationship. Generally, if a spatial or temporal PSC is caused by the spatiality or temporality of the entity types involved, there may be no population intersection for the same entity types. On the other hand, if a spatial or temporal PSC relates spatial or temporal attributes of two entity types[6], then there is a population intersection between these entity types.

Example. For our example schemas there are PSCs that are caused by the existence of SC, and there are those that are due to overlay of the location or time dependence of the objects modeled by the schemas.

S_1`.RoundAbout.Roads` = S_2`.Road.Name;`

S_1`.Road` ● S_2`.RoadSection;`

S_1`.FlowerBed` ● S_2`.RoundCross;`

S_1`.Park` ⊢ᴹ S_2`.RoundCross;`

The last two PSCs illustrate the situation when there is no population link between two entity types but there is a link between spatial and temporal attributes of these entity types. The spatial relationship between the `FlowerBed` and the `RoundCross` indicates that a flowerbed can lay inside a round about. The condition under which this assertion is true is defined by a corresponding matching rule shown in the example hereafter.

The last temporal relationship would correspond to a situation when for security reasons, the road administration decides to reconstruct a park surrounded by roads as a round about, since it is less dangerous then the previous layout or a crossroad.

On the next layer of the ICAs there are Matching Rules that allow to determine exactly which instances represent the same real-world objects via their key attribute values. The syntax of the MRs is the following:

`[Function]AttributePath Operator`
`[Function]AttributePath;,`

where `Function` is a pre-defined or user-defined function over the key attribute domain, `AttributePath` is composed of the name of a schema, the name of an entity type, and the attribute or attributes' name(s), and `Operator` is one of the following:

– equality of the domain values - {=},
– user-defined correspondence of the domain values - {↔},
– spatial ● or temporal ⊐ equality operator.

---

[6] not necessary spatial or temporal since MADS supports orthogonal concepts

The difference between PSCs and MRs assertions is that the MRs relate only key attributes whereas PSCs may deal with any attribute. For MRs it is also necessary to presume that the equality can not always be established directly with the = operator. For example, for different measurement systems a correspondence table must be used, for different attribute value types a function can be defined, and for ad-hoc correspondence some heuristics can be used.

The correspondence operator ↔ is used for such situations when the equality is not the equality in the mathematical sense. Spatial or temporal equality is used when there is no identification attribute other than geometry, location, or time.

Example. The MRs corresponding to the PSC are the following:

S₁.RoundAbout.RANum ↔ S₂.RoundCross.RouCId;

S₁.Road ● S₂.RoadSection;

S₁.InsideRA.RANum ↔ S₂.RoundCross.RouCId;

S₁.Park ● S₂.RoundCross;

For instances of types Road from S₁ and RoadSection from S₂ we do not have any other means for matching instances than to compare their geometry. The last relationship says that if the geometry of a park is equal to that of a round crossroad, then, according to the PCS stated for temporal attributes of these two instances, the park was rebuilt as the round crossroad.

4.2   Integration Goals

As we mentioned above in this section, we consider important to add one more step to the integration procedure: choosing an integration goal. The integration goal imposes the application of an integration technique for schema elements involved in the semantic correspondences. The choice is based on permissible characteristics of the resulting integrated schema element(s). There are three possible types of losses as the consequence of integration [7]:

- loss of information;
- loss of precision;
- reversibility of the integrated schema, meaning that all the information stored in component schemas is deducible from the integrated one.

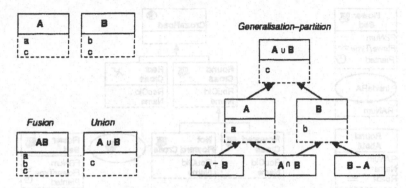

Figure 10. Sample Integration Patterns

Figure 10 shows several ways to integrate two entity types *A* and *B* with one common attribute *c*. The *Fusion* approach preserves the information, i.e., neither attribute values nor instances are lost. The cardinalities of the attributes *a* and *b* are set to be minimal, e.g., if an attribute was multivalued, its domain is reduced to a single value. Depending on the application this might be counted as loss of precision. Concerning the reversibility of the fused entity type, it is reversible if there exists a one-to-one attribute value mapping function.

Under the *Union* approach, information is not preserved because only the common attribute is retained in the resulting entity type. Obviously if integration under this approach is not reversible, the values of the attributes *a* and *b* cannot be reconstructed.

The last approach, *Generalization-partition*, preserves the information as well as precision, and it is reversible. Integration techniques such as those presented in Figure 10 can be applied to a whole schema. This means, all the schema elements are integrated according to the chosen technique or, for each schema element a particular, the most suitable integration technique is applied.

Example. Using our example and assuming that we need to make an integrated schema based on the two input schemas, we can obtain significantly different results. They depend on the purpose of usage of the integrated schema. If the integrated view is created for park administration, we might keep minimal information about the crossroads and the resulting entity type would be modeled as shown in Figure 11. This entity type is obtained with the fusion technique, with loss of information, (the spatial features are dropped); with loss of precision, (the cardinality of the link between RoundAbout and FlowerBed is *0:1)*; and finally with no precise way to reconstruct geometry of crossroads, (geometry can be approximately derived from the geometry of flower beds). Still, such a representation suits the user needs.

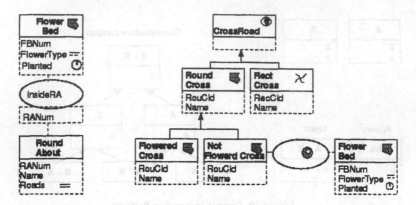

Figure 11. Fusion Technique Applied *Figure 12.* Generalization-Partition Technique Applied

If, on the other hand, the integrated schema would be used by road administration or for both the divisions, we might want to preserve all the information and maybe enrich a resulting schema with new entity or relationship types. Figure 12 shows the result obtained with the generalization-partition technique. Regarding the temporal PSC between Park and RoundCross, it can be modeled with an additional temporal transition relationship between these entity types. We did not present this type of relationship in the paper, but it is supported in MADS data model.

We believe that it is important to present clearly to the integrated schema designer both the possible structural solutions and the features, or loss of those, that the resulting schema will possess. Formalization of the possible structural solutions, on the one hand, limits the designer in the choice of the structural solutions[7] by those that are proposed to him/her. On the other hand, a formal definition of the structural solutions makes the goal of designing a semi-automatic integration tool close to feasible.

5.   SUMMARY AND FUTURE DEVELOPMENTS

In this paper we deductively presented the notion of interoperability in application to the spatio-temporal domain. We also presented a generic architecture of an interoperable system as the most general means of interoperability. Then we specialized the structure of the mediation component that is intended to provide the interoperable functionality of the system. Considering our domain of interest, we presented MADS conceptual data model and MADS spatial and temporal domain ontologies.

---

[7] for federating two entity types there exists at least 15 choices, see [7], we believe that a designer would hardly come up by him/herself with that many variants.

We then considered the conceptual level of data representation, for which we presented a provisory integration methodology comprising four phases: pre-integration, correspondence formulation, choosing an integration goal and generating an integrated schema.

Finally, we gave a preliminary syntax for formulating the interschema correspondence assertions which are basically the rules defining the common elements found in heterogeneous spatio-temporal data sources.

Our ambitions are to formalize the syntax of inter-schema correspondence assertions for spatio-temporal domain, to add a viable way to manage heterogeneous integrity constraints, and finally to design a tool which would enable us to achieve our research proposals.

REFERENCES

1. Abel D., Ooi Beng Chin, Tan Kian-Lee, and Tan Soon Huat, Towards Integrated Geographical Information Processing, International Journal of Geographical Information Science, 12(4):353-371, June 1998.
2. Aslan G., and McLeod D., Semantic Heterogeneity Resolution in Federated Databases by Metadata Implantation and Stepwise Evolution. VLDB Journal, (8):120-132, 1999.
3. Balovnev O. T., Bergman A., Breunig M., Gremers A. B., and Shumilov S., A CORBA-Based Approach to Data and System Integration for 3D Geoscientific Application, in Proceedings of the 8th International Conference on Spatial data Handling (SDH'98), pages 396-407, Vancouver, Canada, July 1998.
4. Bergamaschi S., Castano S., Vincini M., and Benevantano D., Semantic Integration of Heterogeneous Information Sources, Data & Knowledge Engineering, (36):215-249, March 2001.
5. Chomicki J., and Revesz P. Z., Constraint-Based Interoperability of Spatio-Temporal Databases. GeoInformatica, 3(3):211-244, September 1999.
6. Online Dictionary of Computer Science. http://burks.bton.ac.uk/burks/foldoc/.
7. Dupont Y., Une Méthode Flexible pour l'Intégration de Schémas dans les Bases de Données à Objets Complexes, PhD thesis, Ecole polytechnique fédérale de Lausanne, 1996.
8. Fowler J., Perry B., Nodine M., and Bargmeyer B., Agent-Based Semantic Interoperability in InfoSleuth. ACM SIGMOD Records, 28(1):60-67, March 1999.
9. Goodchild M., Egenhofer M., Fegeas R., and Kottman C., (Eds), Interoperating Geographic Information Systems. Kluwer Academic Publishers, 1999.
10. Guarino N., Information Extraction: A Multidisciplinary Approach to an Emerging Information Technology, chapter Semantic Matching: Formal Ontological Distinctions for Information Organization, Extraction, and Integration, pages 139-170. Springer-Verlag, 1998. M.T. Pazienza.

11. Guarino N., and Welty C., Ontological Analysis of Taxonomic Relationships, in Lander A., and Storey V., (Eds), Proceedings of ER-2000: The 19th International Conference on Conceptual Modeling., LNCS. Springer-Verlag, October 2000.

12. Guarino N., and Welty C., Towards a Methodology for Ontology Based Model Engineering, in J. Bezivin and J. Ernst, editors, Proceedings of the ECOOP-2000 Workshop on Model Engineering, June 2000.

13. Gupta A., Marciano R., Zaslavsky I., and Baru C., Integrating GIS and Imagery through XML-Based Information Mediator, in P. Agouris and A. Stefanidis, (Eds), International Workshop on Integrated Spatial Databases: Digital Images and GIS (ISD'99), volume 1737 of Lecture Notes in Computer Science. Springer, Portland, Maine, USA, June 1999.

14. Juristo N., and Moreno Ana M., Introductory Paper: Reflection on Conceptual Modeling. Data & Knowledge Engineering, (33):103-117, July 2000.

15. OpenGIS consortium. http://www.opengis.org.

16. Papazoglu M. P., Spaccapietra S., and Tari Z., (Eds), Advances in Object-Oriented Modeling, chapter Database Integration, The Key to Data Interoperability, The MIT Press, 2000.

17. Parent C., Spaccapietra S., and Zimanyi E., Spatio-Temporal Conceptual Models: Data structures + Space + Time, in 7th ACM Symposium on Advances in GIS, Kansas City, Kansas, Kansas City, Kansas, November 5-6 1999.

18. Qian X., and Lunt Teresa F., Semantic Interoperation: A Query Mediation Approach. Technical Report SRI-CSL-94-02, Computer Science Laboratory, SRI International, April 1994.

19. Sheth Amit P., Changing Focus on Interoperability in Information Systems: from System, Syntax, Structure to Semantics, chapter in [9]. Kluwer Academic Publishers, 1999.

20. Spaccapietra S., Parent C., and Vangenot C., GIS databases: From Multiscale to Multirepresentation, in B.Y.Choueiry and T.Walsh, (Eds), Proceedings 4th International Symposium, SARA-2000, volume 1864 of LNAI, Horseshoe Bay, Texas, USA, July 26-29 2000. Springer-Verlag.

21. Tan J., Zaslavsky A., and Bond A., Meta Object Approach to Database Schema Integration, in Proceedings of the International Symposium on Distributed Objects and Applications, 2000.

22. Wiederhold G., Mediators is the Architecture of Future Information Systems. The IEEE Computer Magazine, March 1992.

Chapter 4

TIME : A Translator Compiler for CIS

Christophe Nicolle
LE2I – Université de Bourgogne - B.P. 47870, 21078 DIJON Cedex – FRANCE
Email: cnicolle@u-bourgone.fr

Abstract: To build a Cooperative Information System, a first step is to collect schemas of each local database. All the schemas exported from databases are translated and integrated into a cooperative schema, which is used by the final user to query the cooperation "transparently". In this article, we focus on the definition of tools that are used to build and manage cooperative information systems. These tools enable the automatic or semi-automatic generation of specific translators. The first step of our methodology is a knowledge acquisition step that allows for the data model description of each local database. The second step is to compare all these descriptions in order to organize the corresponding concepts in a metatype hierarchy. The third step consists of the definition of transformation rules. Thus, from the specifications of a source data model and a target data model, our solution allows translators to be built automatically.

Key words: Interoperability, metamodel, translators generation, cooperative information system

1.   INTRODUCTION

Recently, new multi-database architectures have emerged, including *federated databases*, *cooperative information systems*, and *interoperable systems*. These new architectures enable the interoperation of a set of independent information systems that exchange data over distributed networks. In this paper, we will use the terms *multi-database* and *interoperable information systems* interchangeably to refer to the above systems. Heterogeneity, which may concern structural representation, semantics and data formats, can greatly hinder data exchanges between different information systems.

H. Bestougeff et al. (eds.), Heterogeneous Information Exchange and Organizational Hubs, 59–72.
© 2002 *Kluwer Academic Publishers.*

To combine, integrate or share information from existing databases, several important issues must be addressed:

1. Resolution of semantic differences between heterogeneous sources,
2. Translation of schema and queries from one data model to another,
3. Translation of data and data format between systems.

Several approaches have been proposed for building multi-database systems from heterogeneous sources of information. A classical approach for managing multi-database systems uses global federated schema to span multiple information systems [5,9]. Schema integration techniques are required for building the global schema and for mapping local schema to the federated schema. Sheth et al [9] present a good survey of federated databases. They distinguish two types of federation.

Tightly coupled federations are based on global schema that merge the external schema of all participating information systems.

Loosely coupled federations are based on "local federated schema" which combine the external schema of a subset of the participating information system.

The wrappers/mediators approach models heterogeneous federations at two levels of granularity and interoperation. First, wrappers are used at the low level to encapsulate functionality and services of the information sources [4]. At the next level, mediators are used to unify and combine the low level functionality.

Another approach to interoperable information systems is based on the ontology concept. Ontology defines a common vocabulary which represents shared information, concepts, or knowledge among heterogeneous systems [2]. To achieve interoperation of information systems, the component systems define their export and import schema with respect to the shared ontology.

At various levels, the above approaches require translators and related tools for resolving semantic differences, mapping information, and translating queries between information systems [3].

Previous work in data model translation has focused to a significant extent on defining universal canonical metamodels capable of spanning all possible data models. Typically, canonical metamodels are used as *pivot models* to which data models are mapped before their final translations to target models. A major drawback of this approach is the difficulty of defining an adequate maximal metamodel [6]. Furthermore, the canonical metamodel approach is not appropriate for meeting interoperable system requirements such as scalability, extensibility and dynamic composability.

Issues related to data model translation in multi-database systems have received little attention from database researchers in recent years. Torlone et al [1] define a multiple-data-model tool for managing heterogeneous information systems. Their solution enables a user to define database schema in a super model in order to perform translations from one model to another. The supermodel contains a limited set of meta-constructs to cover all possible models. Papazoglou et al in [8] have proposed a translation-based methodology for resolving semantic conflicts between heterogeneous information systems. They propose a semantic translation protocol which provides a commonly agreed upon set of abstractions for modeling concepts found in diverse models.

In this article, we present a case tool to help in the building of cooperative information systems (CIS). We address a different aspect of data and query translation in the project TIME, an ongoing research at the "Université de Bourgogne" for the design of tools to support the management of interoperable information systems.

Our concern is not with the definition of a static one-on-one data model translation approach [10]. Instead, we focus on an adaptable and semantic oriented data model and query translation approach that takes into account several important characteristics of interoperable information systems including: extensibility and composability.

Extensibility requires a translation solution that can easily integrate new data models into the system while composability, which is the ability of an application to dynamically define the subset of data sources it accesses, requires on demand translation among a subset of data models. To meet these requirements, we propose a multi-data-model translation approach based on an extensible metamodel containing a set of metatypes. These metatypes act as meta-level semantic descriptors of modelling concepts found in existing data models. They are organized in an OO-like generalization hierarchy that captures semantic similarities among them. The metatype hierarchy, which initially contains five kernel metatypes, can be extended to include new model specific metatypes that are defined by specializing existing metatypes.

2.   OVERVIEW OF OUR METHODOLOGY

To build a Cooperative Information System (CIS), a first step is to collect schemas of each local database. In CIS, all schemas exported from databases are translated and integrated into a cooperative schema, which is used by final users to query the cooperation "transparently". TIME defines a CASE tool environment to support the management of interoperable information systems. The theoretical foundation of TIME is provided by abstract metatypes representing data modelling constructs. The key component of the methodology is a metatype generalization hierarchy that is used to unify and correlate the constituent data models of interoperating systems. Multi-data-model translation based on the TIME metatype hierarchy consists of two main phases.

The first phase is devoted to the construction of the metatype hierarchy. This is carried out by the XEditor and the Strategic Hierarchy Building tool that take as input the formal specification in description logic of the appropriate metatypes.

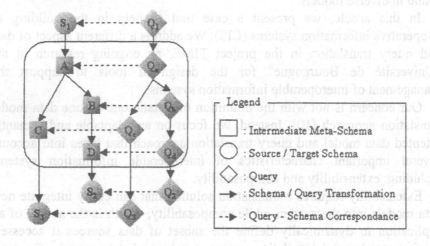

Figure 1. Schema and Query Translation Process

The second phase is devoted to the generation of translators between the various data models composing the cooperation. It is composed of three steps. First, the source schema is converted to an intermediate meta-schema by replacing syntactic structures of source modelling concepts by the syntax of the corresponding metatypes.

Next, the intermediate meta-schema is converted to one or more equivalent meta-schema. This is carried out by transformation rules that allow translation of metatype instances between two metatypes directly linked in the hierarchy.

Each application of the rules generates a new intermediate meta-schema (e.g. meta-schema A → meta-schema B in Figure 1) composed of metatypes semantically closer to the concepts of the target data model. Note that some or all of the intermediate translation steps can be shared when a source model is translated to several target data models, thus reducing the overall cost of the multi-model translation process. Finally, the resulting meta-schema is mapped to the target data models (see the mapping of schema C, D to the respective target schema S3 and S2 in Figure 1).

Query translation based on the metatype hierarchy follows the same steps as above. A query on a source schema is mapped into a corresponding intermediate meta-query (meta-query Q1 $\rightarrow$ meta-query Qa in Figure 1). Next, query transformation rules are applied on this meta-query to obtain a set of meta-queries (Qa $\rightarrow$ Qb, Qa $\rightarrow$ Qc, Qb $\rightarrow$ Qd). These rules are defined according to the schema transformation rules. At the end, target meta-queries are mapped into corresponding queries described in target data manipulation languages (Qc $\rightarrow$ Q3, Qd $\rightarrow$ Q2). In this article, we focus on the presentation of the metamodel construction and transformation rules specification. The management of queries is beyond the scope of this paper.

3. BUILDING THE METAMODEL

The extensible metamodel of TIME consists of a set of metatypes and transformation rules which map or convert metatype occurrences. As stated above, a metatype is an abstract description of a modeling concept. It captures the expressive power or capacity with which modeling concepts describe real world entities.

3.1 Metatype Definition

A metatype M is defined by a tuple $M = (A_M, C_M, P_M)$, where A_M models syntactic elements used to describe the structures of real world entities. C_M represents a set of constraints on the structural descriptors of A_M, and P_M is a (possibly empty) set of operations associated with M.

The extensible metamodel contains two groups of metatypes. The kernel of the metamodel is made up of five basic generic metatypes: META, MComplex-Object, MSimple-Object, MNary-Link and MBinary Link.

The second group contains a set of metatypes that are specific to data models. They are used to extend the metamodel when new data models are introduced in the multi-database system. The metatypes can be classified into two categories: Object metatypes and Link metatypes.

- **Object Metatypes:** Two basic object metatypes are included in the kernel of the metamodel to represent modelling constructs which can be used to describe real world entities: for example, the concepts Object, Entity, Records, and Relation of the Object, Entity-Relationship, Codasyl and Relational models respectively. Metatype MComplex-Object characterizes concepts used to model the complex and multi-valued structures of the real world while the metatype MSimple-Object categorizes the simple or flat structures such as the table concept of the relational data model. The set of attribute descriptors associated with Object metatypes allows the representation of concepts used to model primitive types (integer, string, char) and complex types defined by complex structure constructors (set, list, …)

- **Link Metatypes:** To model links which abstract different relationships or associations among real world entities, the kernel provides two basic link metatypes. The metatype MNary-Link represents the category of modelling types for N-ary relationships. The metatype MBinary-Link represents modelling concepts that are used to express binary relationships between two real world entities. The relationship types of the ER model and the generalization links found in ER and OO models are some examples of these metatypes. In addition, link metatypes can also model 1) cardinalities associated with objects participating in relationship and 2) specific attributes of relationship types.

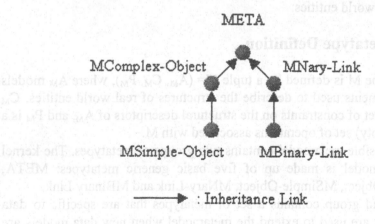

Figure 2. Initial Hierarchy of Metatypes

The metatypes are organized in a hierarchy represented by a directed non-cyclic graph. This hierarchy is used to capture semantic similarities between directly connected nodes. Figure 2 shows the initial hierarchy graph composed of the basic metatypes of the kernel metamodel. The nodes of the graph correspond to the metatypes, and the arrows model OO-like inheritance links between metatypes.

This "meta-inheritance" structure is used to extend the metamodel by specializing existing metatypes to define new metatypes. To define a new metatype, new constraints are added to the definition inherited from one or more existing meta-types. For example in Figure 2, the metatype MSimple-Object is derived from the metatype MComplex-Object by adding constraints to state the fact that an occurrence of MSimple-Object has a simple flat structure. As in object-oriented models, an inheritance link between two metatypes allows the reuse of both structural properties and metatype constraints.

META is the highest metatype in the hierarchy. Its purpose is to define meta-constraints that model the most common characteristics shared by all metatypes. For example, it contains a general identification function that can be specialized to define specific identity functions such as the primary key of the relational models and the OID concepts of the OO models. The Figure 3 shows a metatype hierarchy that extends the kernel metamodel depicted in Figure 2. In addition, it contains metatypes generalizing the concepts of Relational, Codasyl and OO data models.

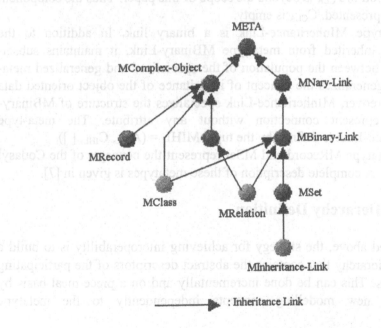

Figure 3. Hierarchy Extension to Three Data Models Concepts

The metatype MRelation (REL) represents the concept RELATION of the Relational data model. It is defined by $REL=(A_{REL}, C_{REL}, P_{REL})$. MRelation shares several characteristics such as a flat and simple structure with the metatype MSimple-Object. Thus, it represents a specialization of MSimple-Object. The structure A_{REL} of MRelation is derived from the structure of A_{SO} of MSimple-Object. MRelation refines the ID function inherited from the generic metatype META corresponding to the precise definition of the relational primary key; namely, a set of attribute labels that uniquely identifies the tuples of a relation. Moreover, since a relation may represent a relationship between two or more real world entities, MRelation also specializes the metatype MBinary-Link. Therefore, a specialization link is added between metatypes MRelation and MBinary-Link. The corresponding constraints inherited from metatype MBinary-Link are added to the component C_{REL} of MRelation.

The meta-type MClass specializes meta-type MComplex-Object and MBinary-Link. It is defined by MCLA = $(A_{CLA}, C_{CLA}, P_{CLA})$. The structure A_{CLA} is a mixed between the structure of A_{CO} and the structure of A_{BL}. The inheritance from A_{BL} allows the representation of reference attributes. The meta-type MClass refines the component P_{CO} to introduce the behavioural aspect of the objects. A detailed and formal description of the representation of OO method in P_{CLA} is beyond the scope of this paper. Thus the component P_{CLA} is not presented. C_{CLA} is empty.

The meta-type MInheritance-Link is a binary link. In addition to the constraints inherited from meta-type MBinary-Link, it maintains subset-constraints between the population of the specialized and generalized meta-types that generalizes the concept of inheritance of the object oriented data model. Moreover, MInheritance-Link specializes the structure of MBinary-Link to represent connection without any attribute. The meta-type MInheritance-Link is defined by the tuple MIHL = $(A_{IHL}, C_{IHL}, [\ ])$.

The metatype MRecord and MSet represent the concepts of the Codasyl data model. A complete description of these metatypes is given in [7].

3.2   Hierarchy Definition

As stated above, the strategy for achieving interoperability is to build a metatype hierarchy that contains the abstract descriptors of the participating data models. This can be done incrementally and on a piece-meal basis by connecting new modelling concepts independently to the metatype hierarchy.

Furthermore, the metatype hierarchy can be constructed on demand and specifically for groups of information systems. The order in which different metatypes are introduced and placed on the metatype hierarchy may change the definition of existing metatypes and thus increase the constructing cost of the hierarchy. The placement strategy may also increase the cost of defining and associating translation rules to the edge of the hierarchy.

For example, placing a new metatype between two initially coupled metatypes M1 and M2 forces the sub-metatype M1 to inherit from a new super-metatype, changing its definition. Moreover, schema and query transformation rules associated to the edge from M1 to M2 must be redefined.

To help a designer to reduce the above construct costs, we have developed a tool called Strategic Hierarchy Builder that can build the hierarchy from a set of formal descriptions of the constituent metatypes. The purpose of the Strategic Hierarchy Builder (SHB) is to help in the description and classification of new data model features in a hierarchy. To realize the addition of a new data model, it is necessary to describe its features in terms of metatypes. The SHB helps to define these metatypes and to place them in the metatype hierarchy of TIME. It allows a designer to specify the features of the new data model in Description Logic without referring to already existing metatypes.

First, specializing the generic metatype definition proposed in the SHB does the description of the new data model. Then, this description is compared using the subsumption mechanism with already existing metatype data model definitions. Last, the new hierarchy is re-constructed integrating the definition of the new data model. TIME translator uses this hierarchy and the simplified definitions of data model metatypes generated by the SHB. The metatype hierarchy and the simplified definitions are the results of the SHB used by TIME to define transformation rules.

4.   BUILDING TRANSFORMATION RULES

To carry out schema translation, transformation rules are coupled with generalization links of the metatype hierarchy. These rules are used to convert instances between two connected metatypes.

The building of these rules is made using a tool called Translation Rule builder (TRB). The TRB helps to build transformation rules that allow instance transformations between two metatypes.

Transformation rules are expressed in first order logical predicate of general form $R(I_1, M_1, I_2, M_2)$, where I_1 is the source meta-schema, I_2 is the target meta-schema, and M_1 and M_2 are metatypes. This rule produces the target meta-schema I_2 from I_1 by converting all instances of metatype M_1 in the source meta-schema I1 into one or more instance(s) of metatype M_2.

For example, $R(IMS_s, CO, IMS_t, SO)$ is a basic oriented rule which translates all the MComplex-Object instances (CO) of a source Intermediate Meta-Schema (IMS_s) to MSimple-Object instances (SO) to obtain a target Intermediate Meta-Schema (IMS_t). This rule is called basic because it handles basic metatypes. A rule is called extended when it handles at least one non-basic metatype.

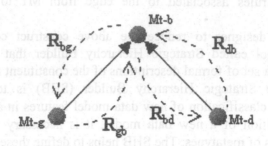

Rxy : transformation rule
- - ->: Sense of transformation

Figure 4. Rules and Hierarchy of Metatypes

The knowledge of both hierarchy and deducted descriptions of metatypes reduces the cost of the rule definition process:

1. Transformation rules are defined to transform instances between directly coupled metatypes in the hierarchy. Thus the number of transformation rules is reduced. Without the hierarchy, the translation between the five basic metatypes would need 20 transformation rules (4+3+2+1 couples of metatypes * 2 orientations). With the hierarchy, the translation between all metatypes can be done with only 8 transformation rules (4 couples of directly linked metatypes * 2 orientations). In this case, to translate non-directly coupled metatypes, the TRB composes a new rule (called composed rule) with existing rules.

2. Next, the definitions of directly coupled metatypes are very closed. The deducted descriptions of metatypes point out which part of the description must be translated. For example, the transformation rule that translates instances of MComplex-Object to MSimple-Object works only on the attribute type to get only simple attribute type.

Rules are not limited to converting a structure into others structures or constraints into other constraints. In some specific cases, rules can convert a structure into programs or constraints and inversely. Thus, the translation of a relational schema with key constraints into an object-oriented model yeilds an object schema with encapsulated methods [7]. Figure 4 shows an example of transformation rules. The rule noted R_{db} ensures the transformation of instances from concept MT-d to concept MT-b.

The construction of translators is accomplished in three steps. The first step determines transformation paths. A transformation path joins two distant metatypes in the metamodel. For example, Figure 5 depicts a combination of transformation rules from MT-h to MT-g and MT-f. Transformation path and the resulting meta-schema transformation are stored in a schema translation library. Many studies have shown that using a combination of translation rules to map data models can reduce the cost or complexity of translation. Moreover, a translation path between two concepts can be reused partially or totally. The construction of transformation paths is achieved using Dijkstra's algorithm.

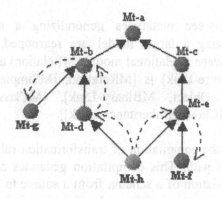

Figure 5. Translation Paths

The second step consists in regrouping transformation paths to create a translation path. This step is achieved by successive amalgamations of transformation paths. First, transformation paths that possess the same source metatype and the same target metatype are regrouped. For example, as depicted in Figure 6, a first meta-schema transformation path from MT-h to MT-g is partially reused for a second meta-schema transformation form MT-h to MT-i.

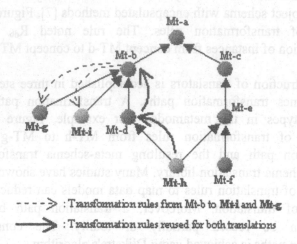

---▷ : Transformation rules from Mt-b to Mt-i and Mt-g

────▷ : Transformation rules reused for both translations

Figure 6. Reusing a Translation Path

Next, paths between metatypes generalizing a source model and metatypes generalizing a target model are regrouped. In Figure 3, the translation path between a relational model (MRelation) and an object model (MClass, MInheritance-Link) is [MRelation, [MSimple-Object, MBinary-Link], [MComplex-Object, MBinary-Link], [MClass, MBinary-Link], [MClass, MSet], [MClass, MInheritance-Link]].

The last step is the compilation of transformation rules according to the resulting translation path. This compilation generates a specific translator that allows the translation of a schema from a source to a target data model and inversely. An association of the code of every rule is done to obtain this translator. Then an optimization of this code is made. The Translator Compiler provides the java source code of the translator. Therefore, it is possible to build the corresponding executable file on the various platforms composing the cooperation.

Using the metatype hierarchy and transformation rules for database interoperation makes the definition of new transformation rules easier because the definitions of two metatypes directly linked are closed. This method of transformation is independent from the number of heterogeneous models in the federation. Transformations are defined between concepts and not between models.

5. CONCLUSION

In this paper, we have presented a methodology for translating multiple data models. We addressed the problem by defining tools that allow for the construction of specifics metamodels. The dynamic construction of the metamodel allows having a metamodel adapted to information systems that want to make part of the cooperation.

Moreover, it makes the addition of a new information system in the cooperation easier. The addition of a new model in the cooperation is done locally by a description of local data models concepts using XEditor. The resulting definitions allow for both a new metamodel building adapted to the new cooperation as well as specific translators. The specialization hierarchy allows a definition reusing of every metatype by a mechanism of inheritance and simplifies their definition.

The TIME method permits the creation of extensible and dynamic cooperations. It provides a minimum set of metatypes that capture the semantics of different concept categories found in the data models that compose the cooperation. It also achieves extensibility by organizing the metatypes in a specialization hierarchy. Thus, a new metatype is defined by specializing an existing metatype. It achieves translation by defining a set of transformation rules, translation paths, and translators. It enables transformation rules to be reused and translation steps to be shared both of which reduce the work of translators building.

Our future objectives are to extend the above results, and to define a formal methodology and algorithm for heterogeneous query processing. This will allow us to define a query interface for the interoperation or migration of existing systems.

REFERENCES

1. Atzeni P., Torlone R., MDM: A Multiple-Data-Model Tool for the Management of Heterogeneous Database Schemes, Proceedings of the SIGMOD International Conference, pp 538-531, 1997.
2. Benslimane D., Leclercq E., Savonnet M., Terrasse M.N., Yétongnon K., On the definition of Generic Multi-Layered Ontologies for Urban Applications, International Journal of Computers, Environment and Urban Systems, Volume 24 (2000), pp 191-214, Elsevier Science Ltd, England.
3. Cluet S., Delobel C., Siméon J., Smaga K., Your Mediator Need Data Conversion!, Proceedings of ACM SIGMOD International conference on Management of Data, June 2-4, 1998, Seattle, Washington, USA.

4. Garcia-Molina H., Hammer J., Ireland K., Papakonstantinou Y., Ullman J., Widow J., Integrating and Accessing Heterogeneous Information Sources, in TSIMMIS, Proceeding of the AAAI Symposium on Information Gathering, pp. 61-64, Stanford, March 1995.
5. Gardarin G., Finance B., Fankhauser P., Federating Object-Oriented and Relational Databases: The IRO-DB Experience, Proceeding of the 2nd International Conference on Cooperative Information systems (COOPIS 97), Kiavah Island, South Carolina, June 24-27, 1997.
6. Hong S., Maryanski F., Using a Meta Model to Represent Object-Oriented Data Models, Proceedings 6th International Conference on Data Engineering, Los Angeles, CA, USA, February 5-9 1990.
7. Nicolle C., Jouanot F., Cullot N., Translation Tools to Build and Manage Cooperative Heterogeneous Information Systems, Proceeding of the 18th International Conference on Database, DATASEM'98, Brno, Czechoslovakia, October 4-6, 1998.
8. Papazoglou M., Russel N., Edmond D., A Translation Protocol Achieving Consensus of Semantics between Cooperating Heterogeneous Database systems, Proceeding of the First IFCIS International Conference on Cooperative Information Systems, COOPIS 96, pp 78-89, June 19,21, 1996, Brussels, Belgium.
9. Sheth A.P., Larson J.A., Federated Database Systems for Managing Distributed, Heterogeneous, and Autonomous Databases, ACM computing surveys, vol. 22, No 3, 1990.
10. Yan L.L., Ling T.W., Translating Relational Schema with Constraints Into OODB Schema, Proceedings of the IFIP WG2.6 Database Semantic Conference on Interoperable Database Systems (DS-5), Lorne, Victoria, Australia, pp 69-85, 16-20 November, 1992.

Chapter 5

An Implementation of Database Integration Strategies

Kemmel da Silva Scopim, Renato Katsuragawa, Marcos Sunye

Department of Computer Science, Federal University of Paraná – UFPR81531-970 Curitiba – Paraná, Brazil.

Email: {kemmel,renatok,sunye@inf.ufpr.br}

Abstract: Today's modern organizations commonly use different databases to accomplish their operational data management functions. These numerous and heterogeneous database systems were designed to run in isolation, and thus do not cooperate with each other. In order to operate successfully, organizations require interoperability among these databases. Improvements in productivity will be gained if the systems can be integrated so as to cooperate with each other and to support global applications, accessing multiple databases. This work proposes the implementation of an heterogeneous database integration. Through the input of a set of databases, the process produces, as an output, a unified description of the initials schemas which are called integrated schema. This process also implements the interschema mapping strategy that supports the access to the data stored in the initial databases via the integrated schema.

Key words: Heterogeneous database integration, implementation strategies, schema integration, ERC+ data model.

1.   INTRODUCTION

Many organizations use numerous and diverse databases to accomplish their day-to-day data management functions. Typically, these databases are heterogeneous in that they were implemented using different data models, database technologies, and hardware platforms. Organizations may have several of such databases accomplishing a portion of their data management functions.

Research on heterogeneous database management has emphasized the development of mechanisms that provide access to data from multiple databases while preserving the local autonomy of the databases, (i.e. without

73

H. Bestougeff et al. (eds.), Heterogeneous Information Exchange and Organizational Hubs, 73–86.
© 2002 Kluwer Academic Publishers.

making changes to the existing databases and preserving their integrity and initial investments).

It is becoming increasingly important to develop mechanisms that allow for interoperability among these databases. One approach to providing interoperability among heterogeneous databases is to define one or more schemas that represent a coherent view of the underlying databases. The process of generating these schemas is known as *schema integration* [2].

Since the schema integration allows for heterogeneous database integration, several data models can be used to represent the schemas to be integrated. We should represent all database schemas in a unique data model to facilitate the integrated schema specification, even though the initial databases are based on different data models.

The data model chosen, in this work is the Extended Entity Relationship Complex data model (or ERC+). Because ERC+ supports the relativist semantic, it is able to express in a more complete way the relationship between an object's meaning in the real world and its representation in a database. The ERC+ data model is an extended Entity Relationship data model (ER) that was defined to support a complex object description and its manipulation. We also adopted this data model because it is applied in the main integration methodology used in this work.

Our goal is to relate the use of proposed methodologies with the practical implementation of the integration process, contributing to a better knowledge of this process.

The development environment of this work uses the following systems of the Federal University of Paraná (UFPR); System of University Automation, which is composed of the following distinct databases: Management of Human Resources (SAU-02), Academic Controls (SAU-05) and Protocols System (SAU- 01) based on the hierarchical model and DMS II DBMS; Library System (SIBI) based on the relational model using MS ACCESS; and the System of Research and Masters Degree Control (PRPPG) based on the relational model and Oracle DBMS.

In the next section we describe the ERC+ data model, which meets database application requirements by merging features of traditional semantic data models with object-oriented capabilities, such as structural object orientation, inheritance, and object identity.

The rest of this paper is organized as follows according to the four implementation phases. Section 3 describes the pre-integration task and the database systems studied in this work. Section 4 presents the correspondences identification and the verification of the schemas conformity. Section 5 provides a description of the process that generate the integrated schema and Section 6 describes the generation of the mapping from integrated schema to the initial databases. Finally, in the last section, we present some conclusions about this work.

2.   THE ERC+ DATA MODEL

The ERC+ (Extended Entity Relationship Complex [5]) is an extended entity-relationship model, specifically designed to support complex objects. Its goal is to closely represent real-world objects. It uses the concept of entity type to describe objects, and the concept of relationship type to represent relationship among objects.

An entity type is defined by its name, its schema (which is the set of the structures of its attributes), its generic entity type, the set of the entity types which are in conjunction, and its population, which is a set of occurrences (entities) with their object identity (*oids*) and values.

A relationship type is defined by its name, the set of entity types it links with the description of the characteristics of the links (role names and cardinalities), the set of structures of its attributes (which constitutes its schema), and its set of occurrences.

An attribute is defined by the object to which it is attached, its structure, and its values for each occurrence of its object.

Domains define the set of all possible values for an attribute, an entity, or a relationship type. Values may be either atomic, like Brazil or 2000, or complex - i.e., composed by other values. A complex value is a set of pairs <attribute name, v> where v is either a value or a multiset of values.

The concept of structures bears the recursiveness necessary for describing complex objects. This concept conveys the characteristics of an attribute (its name and cardinalities, its composition and domain) independently from its association to the object it describes. This arrangement allows different attributes (representing similar properties for different object types) to share the same structure. A shared structure simplifies the formal definition of the algebraic operators, whose action often includes creating a new attribute with the same structure as the attribute it is derived from.

An *oid* is associated with each entity. A real-world object, regardless of its complexity, may be modeled as an occurrence of a single-entity type. Entity types may comprise any number of attributes that may, in turn, recursively, consist of other attributes. Attributes, entities and relationship may be valued in multisets (i.e., allowing duplicates).

In diagrams, a relationship type is represented by a lozenge with the name of the relationship inside it. A simple continuous line identifies a monovalued and mandatory relationship (1:1); a simple dashed line represents an optional monovalued relationship (0:1); a double dashed line represents an optional multivalued relationship (0:n) and a dashed line with a continuous line represents a mandatory multivalued relationship (1:n).

A relationship type may link several (two or more) entity types. Like entity types, a relationship type may have attributes. Relationship types may be cyclic, that is, they may bind the same entity type twice or more, each time with a different role.

Furthermore, ERC+ supports two other kinds of links between entity types: the *is-a link* and the *may-be-a* link. Both are used to relate two entity types that to some extent represent the same real world objects, each with a different point of view. Entities representing the same real-world object share the same *oid*, which is associated with the real-world object.

The classical is-a link (or generalization link) specifies that the population of entity type ES is a subclass (specialization) of another entity type EG (generalization). Thus, every *oid* contained in ES is also an *oid* of EG. This link is depicted in ERC+ diagrams by an arrow: ES →EG. No cycle is allowed in the generalization graph. It is a lattice.

The may-be-a link (or conjunction link) between two entity types E1 and E2 is used to specify that some (possibly all) entities of E1 describe the same real-world objects as entities of E2 do, and vice versa, i.e., the population of E1 and E2 may share *oids*. A dashed line between E1 and E2 graphically represents the may-be-a link: E1- - -E2.

The *is-a* and *may-be-a* links allow us to model three situations that may arise between the sets of *oids* of two entity types E1 and E2:

Both *is-a* and *may-be-a* links allow for the inheritance of properties from one entity type to another.

3.   PRE-INTEGRATION

In this phase, schemas that correspond to the individual databases being integrated are translated into schemas using a common model.

The purpose is to change the schemas to be integrated into a more homogeneous schema, both syntactically and semantically. This change facilitates the integrated schema specification, even when the initial databases were modeled using a different data model.

This is a complex problem that costs a lot of time, primarily because most schematic representations cannot capture the intended semantics of the databases completely. Hence, the process of integration requires extensive interaction with database designers and administrators to understand the semantics of the databases and ensure that the semantics of the integrated schema do not violate the semantics of the initial databases.

Traditionally, a semantic model, such as the entity-relationship model, was used in this phase. In our case, all the initial databases were modeled using a common data model: the ERC+. We decided to adopt this model because it meets database application requirements by merging features of traditional semantic data models with object-oriented capabilities, such as structural object orientation, inheritance, and object identity.

The Federal University of Paraná (UFPR), the study site of this work, has a high grade of heterogeneity related to database management systems, which are structured in different platforms. In this case, the following systems were studied for this phase:

- System of University Automation (SAU). It is based on the hierarchical model and uses, as DBMS, the DMS-II. This system is composed by three databases:

    - **Protocols System** (SAU-01): created to manage the document or developing process. It has transactions that allow for the process to open, to assist its developing and localization. It enables a decentralization of the protocol and the archive.

    - **Human Resource Management** (SAU-02): developed to support the activities of human resource management of the UFPR, enclosing all the inherent transactions to the legislation for servers. The SAU-02 allows for the control of all human resource areas.

    - **Academic Controls** (SAU-05): The SAU-05 records personal information about the students and their school records, including the performance on the entrance exams, courses for which they are or were registered, the grades and the obtained credits. The courses' coordination is answerable for, mainly, the personal data of the students, their registration and the credits registration.

- System of Research and Masters Degree Control (PRPPG). It is based on the relational model and uses the Oracle DBMS. This database contains important information about research developed at UFPR or with the official participation of the university. This system also stores researchers' information and that of their staff, i.e., the collaborators who are graduate or post-graduate students, professors, technicians or specialists, visiting professors, university staff and other people who have some relationship with the UFPR.

- Library System (SIBI). This system is also based on the relational model and uses the MS SQL Server DBMS. It is composed by the Central Library (Administrative Headquarters) and many others units distributed geographically throughout the university campus. The SIBI controls the users of library services and has approximately 35,000 registered users.

The main difficulties for the conclusion of this phase are the complexity of the studied systems and the lack of information on the databases. For these reasons, this phase demanded a lot of time to acquire adequate knowledge for the semantic comprehension of the objects in question. Thus, the presence of each systems analyst was indispensable to obtain the necessary information. In addition, because this phase was completely manual, the development cost became high.

4.   CORRESPONDENCE IDENTIFICATION

The goal of this phase is to identify those objects in the initial schemas that may be related, or in conflict (i.e., entities, attributes, and relationships) and to classify the relationships among them. This is done by examining the semantics of the objects in the different databases and identifying relationships based on their semantics.

The semantics of an object can be ascertained by analyzing schematic properties of entity classes, attributes, and relationships in the schema, as well as by interacting with designers and exploiting their knowledge and understanding of the application domain.

The main objective of this step is the generation of a reliable set of relationships among database objects. It is important that these relationships be accurate because they are used as input for the integrated schema generation phase.

Two tasks were performed in this phase. First, we identified objects that were related within the databases. Initially we identified eleven related objects that are represented in Table 1.

Once a potential set of related objects was identified, the second task was to classify the relationships among these objects into various categories. To classify the relationships, we used the set of techniques and processes described in [4]. As not all the cases of our application could be solved by this methodology, we also used, as a back up, the methodology described in [1].

By this phase, the semantic, descriptive and structural conflicts were identified.

We found eleven conflicting objects among the initial schemas. These objects had resulted in fifteen correspondences that were classified in five different types.

SAU-1	SAU-2	SAU-05	SIBI	PRPPG
Sector	Employee	Professor-Class	Library-User	Collaborator
	Sector	Student		Researcher
	Dependent	Sector		Allotment

Table 1. Conflicting objects

- **Correspondence 1**: Student (SAU-05) and Employee (SAU-02) entities. These entities are *disjoint* with 27 related attributes.

- **Correspondence 2**: Employee (SAU-02) and Professor-Class (SAU-05) entities. The set of oids of Professor-Class entity is *included* in the Employee entity set.

- **Correspondence 3**: Employee (SAU-02) and Researcher (PRPPG) entities. Employee and Researcher entities *share* some oids.

- **Correspondences 4**: Employee (SAU-02) and Student (SAU-05) entities. There is a *conflicting data type* in the attribute *phone*.

- **Correspondences 5**: Sector (SAU-01) and Sector (SAU-02) entities. These entities are *similar*.

5. GENERATION OF THE INTEGRATED SCHEMA

In this phase, the interschema relationships generated previously lead to the generation of an integrated representation of the initial schemas.

The generation of the integrated schema is the process of generating one or more integrated schemas from the existing schemas. These schemas represent the semantics of the databases being integrated and are used as inputs to the integration process.

The output of this process is one or more integrated schemas representing the semantics of underlying schemas.

These integrated schemas are used to formulate queries that may possibly be spanned over several databases.

5.1   Integration Rules

The integration rules are created to resolve various forms of heterogeneity identified among conflicting objects in initial schemas. For each kind of correspondence classified in the correspondence identification phase we create a matching integration rule. Below, are shown four integration rules that were created:

Rule 1: Disjunct Rule

Description: A generic entity must be created with the related attributes between the two entities with this kind of correspondence. An *is-a link* must be used starting from conflicting entities to a generic entity:

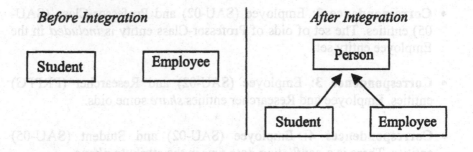

Figure 1. Integration Rule: Disjunction

Rule 2: Inclusion Rule

Description: A *may-be-a* link must be used between the entity types with this kind of correspondence.

Rule 3: Intersection Rule

Description: A *may-be-a* link must be used between the entity types with this kind of correspondence.

Rule 4: Equivalent Rule

Description: A entity type must be created to represent the entity types with this kind of correspondence.

5.2 Intermediate Schema Generation

After all initial schemas have been modeled and the correspondences among the objects have been identified and classified, and after the integration rules have already been specified, the schema integration phase is ready to be performed.

We have selected the *binary ladder technique*, as recommended by the methodologies used as the basis for this study, where the intermediate schemas are used as the source for the integration with the next ones.

The order of the integration of the underlying schemas was defined as followed:

Step	Input Schema 1	Input Schema 2	Output Schema
1	SAU-05	SAU-02	Intermediate schema 1
2	PRPPG	Intermediate schema 1	Intermediate schema 2
3	SIBI	Intermediate schema 2	Intermediate schema 2
4	SAL-01	Intermediate schema 3	Integrated schema

Table 2. Intermediate Schemas

Two input schemas, the interschema correspondences identified previously and the integration rules, are the inputs in each step of the intermediate schema generation. As the output, we have an intermediate schema that represents the semantic among the underlying schemas.

The integration process not only generated the integrated schema but also enabled us to collect schema-mapping information. It accompanies the generation of the integrated schema step and involves storing information about mappings among objects in the transformed (integrated) schema and objects in the local schemas. Such mappings are important for query transformation.

In the process of obtaining the integrated schema we resolved all the correspondences previously found that represented the structural, semantic and descriptive conflicts as well as the initial database heterogeneity.

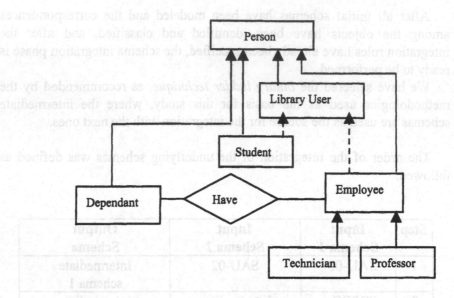

Figure 2. A Part of the Integrated Schema

The final integrated schema has resulted in 44 entity types, 35 association types, 7 *is-a link* and 5 *may-be-a link*.

6.   IMPLEMENTATION OF THE INTERSCHEMA MAPPING

This phase represents the mapping implementation between the integrated schema and the initial schemas. With respect to this phase, the first decision to be made concerns how the connections among the databases will be accomplished and in which DBMS the integrated schema will be implemented.

6.1   Establishing Connections Among the DBMS

In our environment, we have adopted the strategy depicted in Figure 3 because it provides the lowest answer time for querying in the integrated schema. This is so because all the data are stored in the same kind of DBMS. The integrated schema has been implemented in a debian 2.1 linux operation system with Oracle 8.0.5 server DBMS.

In order to establish the connection between the integrated schema and the initial schemas of SAU-01, SAU-02, SAU-05 and SIBI, it was necessary to create two database mirrors (a replication of an instance of DMSII database and ACCESS database), one for the DMS II DBMS and another for MS ACCESS.

One way to directly establish a connection between Oracle and non-Oracle systems is by using specific gateways to non-Oracle system. In our case, we could not adopt this strategy because there is neither a specific gateway for DMSII DBMS nor for MS ACCESS, and moreover one extra layer will remain between integrated schema and DMSII, slowing down the answer time for queries in the integrated schema. Consequently, we did not adopt this strategy.

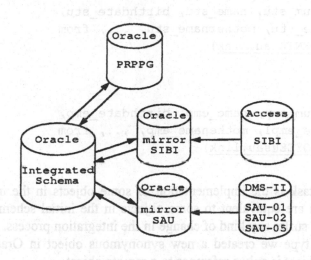

Figure 3. Strategy of the Interschema Connection Adopted

The connection between the integrated schema and the initial schema of the PRRPG, as well as between the integrated schema and the database mirrors uses Oracle's networking software, Net8, which makes the inter-database communication easier across the network.

6.2 Implementation of the Schema Mapping Information

The second step of mapping implementation can be divided into two tasks. One of these is the implementation of existing objects in the integrated schema that suffered any kind of change during the integration process.

For each object of this type we created a new view object in Oracle with the mapping information collected in the integration schema phase. Below is presented the view person object that solves the correspondence number one described in the previous sections.

```
create view person

(id,  name, birthdate, fathername, mothername, ...) as

(select num_stu, name_stu, birthdate_stu,
fathername_stu, mothername_stu, ..., from
prod.STUDENT@sau.link)

UNION

(select num_emp, name_emp, birthdate_emp,
fathername_empl, mothename_emp, ..., from
prod.EMPLOYEE@sau.link)
```

The other task is the implementation of some objects in the integrated schema, which are equivalent to some objects in the initial schema. These objects did not suffer any kind of change in the integration process. For each object of this type we created a new synonymous object in Oracle. This synonymous object is only a reference to a remote object.

Example:

```
create synonym research for
thales.research@prppg.link;
```

With the creation of views and the creation of synonyms, the location transparency was solved too. This feature hides the physical location of database objects from applications and users.

One point that should be stated about this schema mapping strategy is that any change in the initial database structures of SAU-01, SAU-02, SAU-05 or SIBI does not imply changes in the integrated schema.

The changes will occur only in the software that offloads data from the initial databases onto the database mirrors.

On the other hand, some cases of changes in the PRPPG database objects could result in changes on the DBMS object repository where the integrated schema was implemented. But an object that does not belong to any correspondences cases and which suffers some kind of structural change, will not cause changes in the integrated schema because there exists only a reference between the integrated schema and an object of this type.

7. CONCLUSION

In this work, we presented an implementation of two approaches of heterogeneous distributed database integration.

We used the methodologies described in [3] and [4] because, after analyzing other methodologies, we considered them, with a group of rules, more feasible for our case.

The first methodology was usable in almost all parts of this work. However in certain specific cases, the latter methodology could be used to simplify the work of the person integrating the databases.

In this implementation, the main difficulty came from the understanding of the objects included in each initial system. The presence of each systems' analyst who could explain in more detail the conceptual assumptions of each system was very important to the success of this implementation.

The ERC+ data model was adopted because it has some features that could be suited with the methodologies adopted such as inclusion, intersection and disjoint semantic among the objects.

Nowadays, there is a prototype of this implementation running for tests purposes.

The most important benefits of this integration process include:

- dissemination of knowledge of distributed and heterogeneous applications;
- unified vision of data;
- possibility of construction of support decision systems and data warehouses with better semantic definition due to a bottom-up construction;
- new databases derived from the integrated schema;
- applications migration.

REFERENCES

1. Batini M., and Lenzerini C., A Methodology for Data Schema Integration in the Entity Relationship Model. IEEE Transactions on Software Engineering, 1984.
2. Ram S., and Ramesh V.., Schema Integration: Past, Present and Future. Management of Heterogeneous and Autonomous Databases Systems, Morgan Kaufmann Publishers, 1999.
3. Rodacki A., Aplicação de Estratégias de Integração de Banco de Dados: Um Estudo de Caso, Master Degree Thesis UFPR, 2000.
4. Spaccapietra S., Parent C., and Dupont Y., Independent Assertions for Integration of Heterogeneous Schemas. Very Large Database Journal, Vol 1(1), 1992.
5. Spaccapietra S., Parent C., Sunye M., and Leva A., ERC+: An Object+ Relationship Paradigm for Database Applications. IEEE Computers Science Press, 1995.

Chapter 6

An Architecture for Data Warehouse Systems Using a Heterogeneous Database Management System – HEROS

Diva de S. e Silva[1], Sean W. M. Siqueira[2], Elvira Mª A. Uchôa[2], Mª Helena L. B. Braz[3], and Rubens N. Melo[2]

[1] IBGE, Av. Chile 500, 8º andar, Centro, Rio de Janeiro, Brazil
Email: divasouz@ibge.gov.br
[2] PUC-Rio, Rua Marquês de São Vicente, 225, Gávea, 22453-900, Rio de Janeiro, Brazil
Email:{sean, elvira, rubens}@inf.puc-rio.br
[3] DECivil/ICIST, Av. Rovisco Pais, Lisboa, Portugal

Abstract: One of the most challenging prospects facing the Data Warehouse (DW) project is the integration of heterogeneous data from different sources. The database community has spent years researching the integration of heterogeneous and distributed data. Heterogeneous Database Management Systems (HDBMS) have been presented as one of the solutions to this problem. In this paper, we propose an architecture for DW systems using a HDBMS as the middleware for data integration. This architecture uses a subset of Common Warehouse Metamodel (CWM) specification in order to provide more semantic to data integration according to a standard proposal. A case study presenting the use of the proposed architecture is also shown.

Key words: Heterogeneous data base systems, data warehouse architecture, common warehouse metamodel

1. INTRODUCTION

Nowadays, it is very difficult for users to find the information they seek, in a fast and consistent manner. The data is generally heterogeneous and high in volume, and is usually distributed on the production systems of the company. Moreover, this data often fails to reflect the managerial perspective, which is essential for decision support.

Data warehousing technology has been employed to facilitate decision support. Data from the production systems of the enterprise and from

87

H. Bestougeff et al. (eds.), Heterogeneous Information Exchange and Organizational Hubs, 87–104.
© 2002 *Kluwer Academic Publishers.*

external sources are combined, with the objective of facilitating analysis under the managerial prism. However, the complexity of such data integration has caused the failure of many Data Warehouse (DW) systems [7].

In the database community, a possible solution for heterogeneous data integration is the use of heterogeneous database management systems (HDBMS). In specific group of such systems the data from several sources, which are interconnected by communication networks, are accessed with no heterogeneity and in a manner that is transparent to the end user. This integration process assures the high quality of the resulting information.

This paper proposes an architecture for DW systems that uses a HDBMS (HEROS) for data integration. A metamodel is used in order to provide a DW semantic to the integration process. This metamodel is a subset of the Common Warehouse Metamodel (CWM) [5]. A case study demonstrates the systematic use of this architecture to create DW systems.

The remainder of this paper is organized as follows. Section 2 presents some DW and HDBMS concepts, in particular HEROS. Section 3 describes the proposed DW architecture and its components. In Section 4, a systematic use of the architecture is presented. In Section 5, the proposed architecture is compared to related works. Finally, in Section 6, some final remarks are emphasized.

2.   CONCEPTS

This section introduces the essential concepts for understanding the proposed architecture.

2.1   Data Warehouse

According to William H. Inmon [8], DW has the following characteristics:
- It is subject oriented (data are stored according to business areas or specific subjects/aspects of interest to the company).
- It is integrated (i.e., it integrates data coming from several data sources and many inconsistencies are treated and solved).
- It is a non-volatile collection of data (data are loaded and accessed, but are generally not updated in the DW environment).
- It is time-variant (the time horizon for DW is significantly longer than that of production systems; data are a sophisticated series of snapshots, taken at one moment in time; and the key structure of the DW always contains some temporal elements).

– It is used in support of management's decisions.

In general, an architecture for DW systems involves the integration of current and historical data. Data sources can be internal (production systems of the company) or external (containing complementary data from outside the company, such as economic indicators). Generally, data integration deals with different data models, definitions and/or platforms. This heterogeneity forces the existence of extraction and transformation applications in order to allow for data integration. Once integrated, the resulting data are stored in a new database – DW – that combines different points of view for decision support. This database is used for data analysis by end-user applications.

A DW can be divided into several databases, called Data Marts (DM) [9]. These DM contain information that may be useful to the different departments of a company. They are thus considered departmental DW. DM/DW can be accessed through OLAP (Online Analytical Processing) tools, Data Mining applications and/or EIS (Executive Information Systems). These tools allow for data navigation, managerial analysis and knowledge discovery.

Techniques for DW/DM development are described in [8] and [9]. In [3], concepts, components and tools of Data Warehousing, OLAP and Data Mining are introduced. Finally, topics on planning and designing a DW can be found in [1].

2.2 Heterogeneous Database Management System

In database community, HDBMS are one of the solutions for integrating heterogeneous and distributed data. HDBMS ([6], [12], [13], [15] and [16]) is a layer of software for controlling and coordinating heterogeneous, autonomous and pre-existing data sources connected by communication networks. Heterogeneity refers not only to technological differences (hardware and software), but also to differences in data models, database management systems (DBMS) and semantics.

The analysis of the level of integration that exists among the component systems allows heterogeneous database systems (HDBS) to be classified into tightly coupled or loosely coupled HDBS [15]. In loosely coupled HDBS, the end-user must know the locations and paths of the data sources he/she wishes to access. The HDBMS just supply mechanisms to facilitate the access. In tightly coupled HDBS, the end-user has an integrated view, in which there is no heterogeneity. Thus, this HDBS gives the illusion of accessing a single system.

In the Computer Science Department of PUC-Rio, a HDBMS called HEROS – HEteRogeneous Object System [11] has been developed ([21] and [22]). HEROS is a tightly coupled HDBMS. It allows for the integration of a federated set of HDBS. In this cooperative yet autonomous HDBMS, queries and updates can be executed with transparency in relation to location of data, access paths and any heterogeneity or redundancy [21].

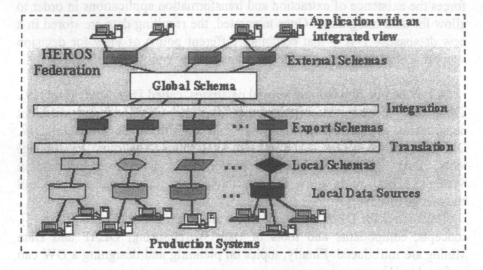

Figure 1. Schema Architecture Used by HEROS

The schema architecture used by HEROS is shown in Figure 1. In this architecture, each data source has a local schema that is represented in its own data model. This local schema is translated to HEROS' object oriented data model, resulting in an export schema. All export schemas must be integrated, resulting in a single global schema, with no heterogeneity. Finally, the end user's views can be created from this global schema, generating external schemas. A HEROS' federation consists of an integrated set of autonomous component systems.

3.   PROPOSED ARCHITECTURE

The proposed architecture for DW systems emphasizes data integration. This architecture is organized in four layers, as presented in Figure 2: Data Sources, Integration Middleware, DW Materializer and Data Visualization/Analysis Tools. More details can be found in [18].

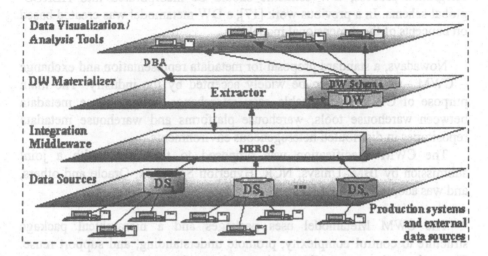

Figure 2. Proposed Architecture for DW systems

3.1 Data Sources

In the proposed architecture, the "Data Sources" layer refers to data from production systems of the company, as well as from external sources. It comprises only relevant data to the DW. External sources are important to complement the information of the company.

This layer also includes the schema of the component systems. These schemas are expressed using the concepts of the data model used by the local DBMS. However, if it is not a DBMS, a specific model could be used to represent the data structure. A local schema can be the conceptual schema of the local data source or a view, which is defined for an application or users' class, specific to the component system.

3.2 Integration Middleware

The integration middleware layer is composed of HEROS HDBMS, where data extraction, cleaning transformations and integration processes are executed.

This layer allows a group of autonomous but cooperative data sources, to be integrated in a federation, such that queries and updates can be executed transparently to data location, heterogeneity and redundancy.

In order to provide easier understanding of the resulting data from the integration process, DW semantic should be incorporated into HEROS' global schema. In a previous work [17], a DW metamodel was created based on concepts of the dimensional model [9].

Nowadays, a standard proposal for metadata representation and exchange – CWM – is expected to be widely accepted by the industry. The main purpose of CWM is to enable easy interchange of warehouse metadata between warehouse tools, warehouse platforms and warehouse metadata repositories in distributed heterogeneous environments.

The CWM specification was proposed to the OMG with a joint submission by IBM, Unisys, NCR, Hyperion Solutions, Oracle and others, and was adopted as an OMG standard in June 2000 [5].

The CWM Metamodel uses packages and a hierarchical package structure to control complexity, promote understanding, and support reuse. The main packages are: Foundation package, Resource package, Analysis package and Management package.

This work considers the CWM proposal in the definition of HEROS' global schema. A standard proposal provides clearer understanding of the main concepts, which are formally defined. The use of a standard also improves interoperability.

The purpose of this work is to define an architecture for DW systems. As DW systems provide better data analysis through the use of OLAP tools, a subset of the OLAP package (a sub-model of the Analysis package) is used to define HEROS' global schema. This semantic makes it easier for any analytical application or tool to explore the resulting data, and also facilitates the configuration of OLAP tools that are CWM compliant.

The OLAP package defines not only general concepts of multidimensional modeling (such as cube and dimension) but also navigational concepts (such as hierarchy). Navigational concepts address application requirements that are more volatile and user-dependent, so they were not considered in the proposed metamodel. The chosen subset resulted in a more generic metamodel.

Using the UML notation [24], a DW can be represented as a class (schema) composed of cubes and dimensions (Figure 3).

A cube is composed of one or more dimensions and a single dimension can belong to one or more cubes. This metamodel must first be instantiated in HEROS' global schema in order to incorporate DW semantics into HEROS' federations. Later it must be specialized in order to represent specific characteristics of each particular DW [18].

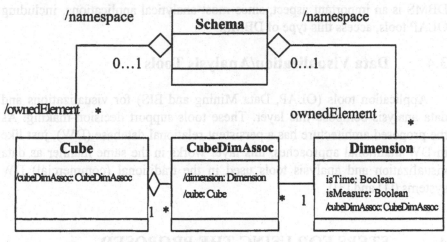

Figure 3. DW Metamodel

3.3   DW Materializer

HEROS provides access to the component systems with no data materialization. Therefore, the DW materializer layer is responsible for supplying data persistence after an integration process. This persistence provides better performance since a query, which is submitted to a stored DW (where integrated data were previously stored), executes much faster than doing the whole integration process on the fly. The execution of the integration process increases network traffic and processing time in the local systems which must also execute local applications. Furthermore, a persistent DW stores historical data, which is one of the DW requirements for trend analysis.

In order to materialize data resulting from HEROS' processing, it is necessary to use an extractor program. This program sends requests to HEROS for extraction/integration of local data and stores the results in a persistent database. This is one of the most important components of the proposed architecture.

The DW database administrator (DBA) requires data extraction/load for a specific DW, thereby activating the extractor. So, the extractor sets HEROS into action, which makes the access and data integration. The results are then returned to the extractor. Then, the extractor analyzes the DW catalog to determine the table of the persistent DW database in which it should insert the data.

After being inserted in their respective tables, the business data are ready to be accessed through data visualization/analysis tools. The DW catalog is stored in the persistent DW database, a relational DBMS. Using a relational

DBMS is an important aspect, since most analytical applications, including OLAP tools, access this type of DBMS.

3.4   Data Visualization/Analysis Tools

Application tools (OLAP, Data Mining and EIS) for visualizations and data analysis compose this layer. These tools support decision-making. As the proposed architecture has a persistent relational database (DW), just like in DW traditional approaches, this layer works in the same manner as data visualization and analysis tools used in the traditional (commercial) DW systems ([1] and [3]).

4.   STEPS FOR USING THE PROPOSED ARCHITECTURE

To use the proposed architecture, it is necessary to follow three steps: the DW construction, the DW load, and the DW use through data visualization and analysis tools.

In order to evaluate the architecture, a case study is used. This case study was adapted from a real case, but was simplified to facilitate the understanding of the architecture's functionality. The case study is as follows:

A Non-Governmental Organization (NGO), called *Rivers and Lakes* (fictitious name), wants to control predatory fishing, by integrating and consolidating information on fishing landings. The information comes from several landing locations in the municipal districts of the Amazon basin.

Each landing location has an administrative structure and its own information system, according to local needs. With the financial support from an important international corporation, it was possible to install a communication network connecting landing locations and the NGO.

The NGO will use the proposed architecture to create a DW, called Fish-DW whose main objective is to monitor the predatory fishing. This control is needed because the local environmental laws have become more and more rigorous. Consequently, companies, fishermen colonies and even the fishermen themselves have been involved in controlling and monitoring fishing activities and their environmental impact. Information about fishing activities must be available in an integrated way with easy access in order to provide this control.

The development of a new DW system – using the proposed architecture follows five steps [18]:

1. Business interviews and data gathering for identifying and understanding the data sources.

2. Creation of a HEROS' federation for the new DW system. In order to execute this step it is necessary to:

– define a new HEROS' federation and to explain the data semantic of each local system on HEROS' data dictionary.
– create an export schema for each local schema. At present, this activity is needed because HEROS' active rules mechanism has not been developed yet. This mechanism would create the export schemas automatically from the local schemas.
– create the global schema. To do so, it is necessary to specialize the DW metamodel classes, considering the integration of the export schemas and to define command trees achieving data semantic integration and consolidation. The global schema integrates all the export schemas organizing the integrated information according to the proposed DW metamodel.

3. Creation of tables for storing data in the persistent DW.

4. Creation of a mapping catalog between HEROS' outputs and the tables, which compose the persistent DW.

5. Definition and configuration of visualization and analysis tools.

In Fish-DW system, the existence of two types of data sources was noticed through interviews with users and data gathering. These data sources are:

Fishing system – there is a fishing system, which controls fishing data, running on several landing locations. Even though there are several Fishing systems as data sources, this case study considers only one in order to make the steps easier to understand.
Research system – relative to data of reproduction periods of the fish species. This system is used only in the NGO.
Figure 4 details the local schemas of these two component systems with some simplifications.
For the creation of a federation, in HEROS, it is necessary to follow the steps proposed in [23]. Considering these steps, a new DW federation - RL-

NGO - was created. This federation is composed of three component systems:

Fishing System – on Oracle DBMS, version 7.3;

Research System – on Postgres DBMS version 4.0;

HEROS – HEROS' own database, used as a working area during the integration process.

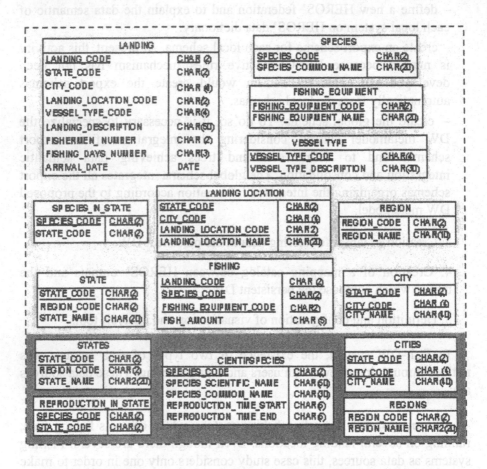

Figure 4. Local Schemas of the Fishing System and Research System Respectively

For the creation of export schemas, it is necessary to represent the local schemas in HEROS' data model.

Figure 5 presents the classes of the export schemas concerning the simplified case study. The methods of these classes represent the data mappings from the export schema to the local schema. For each method of an export schema, local procedures must be implemented to extract data from local component systems.

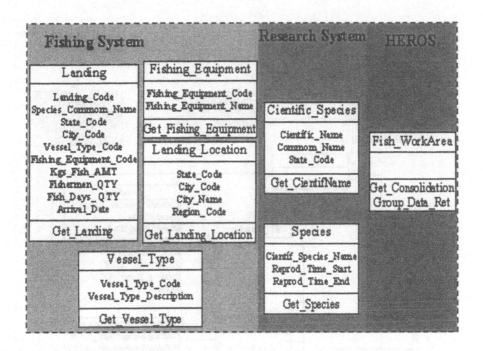

Figure 5. Export Schemas of the Component Systems

Finally, the DW metamodel is specialized in HEROS' global schema, according to the semantic of the case study (Figure 6). A global query relative to global classes may be decomposed to sub-queries for other classes in the global schema, and afterwards to sub-queries for classes in the export schemas.

Once the federation of DW is created, in HEROS, the next step is the creation of the necessary tables of the DW, in the persistent database. In the case study, the created tables are *Cube*, *Landing_Location*, *Vessel_Type*, *Species*, *Species* and *Landing*.

Then, it is necessary to create a catalog for mapping between HEROS' outputs and the DW tables. This catalog enables the extractor to load the persistent DW database from the integrated result of HEROS' data processing. Figure 7 represents the catalog for the case study.

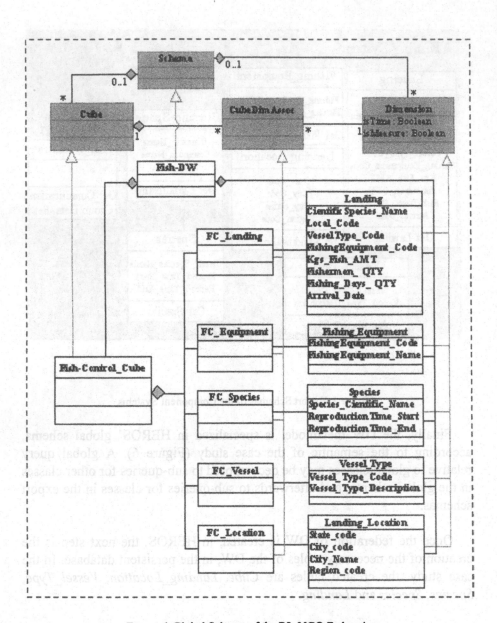

Figure 6. Global Schema of the RL-NGO Federation

Corp. Unity	DW	Output Position	Table Name	Attribute Name
RL-NGO	Fish-DW	01	Cube	Cube_name
		02	Landing_Location	Cube_name
		03		State_code
		04		City_code
		05		City_Name
		06		Region_code
		07		IsTime
		08		IsMeasure
		09	Vessel_Type	Cube_name
		10		VesselType_code
		11		VesselType_Description
		12		IsTime
		13		IsMeasure
		14	Fishing_Equipment	Cube_name
		15		FishingEquipment_code
		16		FishingEquipmentName
		17		IsTime
		18		IsMeasure
		19	Species	Cube_name
		20		Species_Cientific_Name
		21		ReproductionTime_Start
		22		ReproductionTime_End
		23		IsTime
		24		IsMeasure
		25	Landing	Cube_name
		26		State_code
		27		City_code
		28		CientificSpecies_Name
		29		VesselType_code
		30		FishingEquipment_code
		31		ArrivalDate
		32		Kgs_Fish_AMT
		33		Fishermen_QTY
		34		Fishing_Days_QTY
		35		IsTime
		36		IsMeasure

Figure 7. Catalog of Mappings between HEROS' Output and DW Persistent Tables

In the proposed architecture, the last step for the development of a DW system refers to the choice (and/or settings) of data visualization and analysis tools. Although commercial OLAP tools would have been suitable as well, a specific application (FishA – Fishing Analysis) was developed to access/analyze data from the resulting database. One of the screens of FishA is shown in Figure 8.

Finally, the DW is loaded via the activation of the extractor by the DBA.

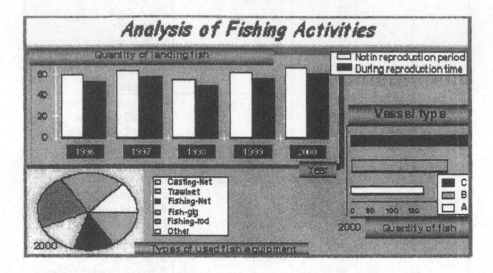

Figure 8. Screen from the Application FishA

5. RELATED WORKS

This section evaluates the merits of the proposed architecture, by comparing it to alternative proposals. This discussion is focused on the data integration technique. In Figure 9, a table summarizes the considered alternative proposals: WHIPS project [10], TIC96-6903 project [14] and some commercial products such as: Virtual DB ([4]), SynopSys&trade [19] and InterViso [20].

Commercial products generally behave as "black" boxes. The integration procedures are hidden from the users who are responsible for the DW definition. This fact obscures the user's perception about extraction and cleansing processes, increasing the risk of errors in the integrated data. Moreover, these commercial products do not consider the semantic heterogeneity. This must be treated through other programs/procedures, in a phase prior to the use of these products.

The use of HEROS to integrate heterogeneous data assumes that local data-schemas and translation processes are well known to the person responsible for the DW definition. Since this knowledge is encoded in

HEROS, it will treat the heterogeneity automatically and will carry out the data integration process. In order to include a new data source, the user (DBA) needs only to specialize some classes in HEROS' data model. This approach contributes to a more organized and transparent process.

HEROS supports the development of a DW without the need for external programs. The DW metamodel's concepts, which were specified in HEROS, allow DW data to be analyzed according to business reality. Thus, the integration process becomes less liable to errors, reducing the possibility of failure of the DW project.

Projects/Products	Commercial/Academic	Integration Technique
Virtual DB, InterViso e SynopSys&trade	Commercial	Proprietary Programs
WHIPS Project	Academic (Stanford University)	Mediators and Wrappers
TIC96-6903 Project - DEXA'98	Academic (Universitat Politècnica da Catalunya)	HDBMS [2]
Proposed Architecture	Academic (PUC-Rio)	HDBMS (HEROS)

Figure 9. Related Works

Some commercial projects, like Virtual DB, InterViso and SynopSys&trade, use the idea of a virtual DW, where there is no data materialization. The adopted integration mechanism generally is similar to loosely coupled HDBS. By contrast, the proposed architecture considers the existence of a materialized DW. It contributes to better performance, as data integration does not need to be accomplished every time a new query is executed. Furthermore, using a tightly coupled HDBS provides integration transparency to the end-user.

The WHIPS project is based on wrappers and mediators for data extraction and transformation to the DW. Wrappers and mediators are software programs, which are developed to assist a specific class of problems. They work as black boxes and do not allow the access to their logic. The proposed architecture uses HDBMS HEROS for data extraction, transformation and integration. The use of a HDBMS allows any system, even a non-conventional one, to be integrated in an easy way. It is only required to do the specialization of some classes in its data model.

The TIC96-6903 project described an idea that is similar to our work. However, until now, no literature was found mentioning the adopted solution or any ensuing evolution.

By contrast, the proposal that is presented in this paper details the use of an HDBMS in the architecture of DW systems and defines the steps for its use. Moreover, the work described in this paper specifies a metamodel of DW systems that forms the basis for the definition of HEROS' global schema. The existence of the metamodel facilitates data integration in DW systems. In addition, the use of a subset of the OLAP package (a proposed standard) in the metamodel improves interoperability. As CWM specification is a recent proposal (june/2000), no other work using it has been found.

6.   FINAL REMARKS

In the highly competitive business world, it is very important to access the right information in order to make the best decision. DW systems intend to present the information according to managerial needs. However, one of the biggest challenges in the development of DW systems is related to data integration, because the necessary data are usually distributed and heterogeneous.

In order to contribute to the solution of these problems, an architecture for DW systems using a HDBMS – HEROS – was proposed. A simplified case study in the environmental domain was developed to demonstrate the steps for the use of the proposed architecture.

These steps guide the development of the DW systems. The use of a HDBMS improves data quality. Therefore, DW projects based on the proposed architecture are more reliable, flexible and have more semantics. The end-user employs DW semantics that are supported by the DW metamodel's definition, and accesses integrated information without noticing heterogeneity.

Even though the idea of using an HDBMS as an integration middleware for the development of DW systems was also discussed in [14], the architecture proposed in this paper is more detailed, and its feasibility was supported by a case study.

Furthermore, the work presented in this paper uses a metamodel that is a subset of CWM specification, which is expected to be an industrial standard. Using a metamodel facilitates data integration, while using a standard increases interoperability.

Suggestions for future work include the implementation of a monitor which activates the extractor to automatically load the DW. This application could be a set of agents monitoring inserts and updates in the local data sources and activating the extractor.

REFERENCES

1. Barquin R., Edelstein H., Planning and Designing the Data Warehouse, Prentice Hall, Inc., 1997.
2. Beck K., Johnson R., Patterns Generate Architectures, European Conference on Object Oriented Programming (ECOOP'94), Springer-Verlag, Bologna, Italy, July 1994.
3. Berson A., Smith S. J., Data Warehousing, Data Mining & OLAP, McGraw-Hill Companies, Inc., 1997.
4. Callaghan, D., Virtual DB Breaks Down Data Barriers; Data Management & Analysis; Web Site: http://www.midrangesystems.com/archive/1997/oct10/dm101603.htm
5. Common Warehouse Metamodel (CWM) Specification, Object Management Group, http://www.omg.org/technology/cwm/index.htm
6. Conrad S., Eaglestone B., Hasselbring W., et al. Research Issues in Federated Database Systems, Report of EFDBS'97 Workshop, SIGMOD Record, Vol. 26, N. 4, December 1997.
7. Dresner H., Lett B., Evaluating Executive Information Systems. An Gartner Group Strategic Analysis Report. September 1995.
8. Inmon W. H., Building the Data Warehouse, John Wiley & Sons, Inc., 1996.
9. Kimball R., The Data Warehouse Toolkit, John Wiley & Sons, Inc., 1996.
10. Labio W. J., Zhuge Y., Wiener J. L., Gupta H., Molina H. G., Widow J., The WHIPS Prototype for Data Warehouse Creation and Maintenance; Proc. ACM SIGMOD Conf. AZ, USA, 1997.
11. Pacitti E., Silva S. D., Duarte C. H. C., Melo R. N., HEROS: An Object Oriented Heterogeneous Database System, VIII Brazilian Database Symposium, Campina Grande, PB, 1993 (in Portuguese).
12. Pitoura E., Bukhres O., Elmagarmid A., Object Orientation in Multidatabase Systems, ACM Computing Surveys, Vol. 27, N. 2, June 1995.
13. Ram S., Guest Editor's Introduction: Heterogeneous Distributed Database Systems, in: IEEE Computer, Vol.24, N.12, December 1991.
14. Samos J., Saltor F., Sistac J., Bardés A., DataBase Architecture for Data Warehousing: An Evolutionary Approach; DEXA Conference and Workshop Programme, Vienna, Austria, 1998.
15. Sheth A. P., Larson J. A., Federated Database Systems for Managing Distributed, Heterogeneous, and Autonomous Databases; ACM Computing Surveys, Vol. 22, N. 3, September 1990.
16. Silberschatz A., Zdonic, S., Database Systems – Breaking Out the Box, SIGMOD Record, Vol. 26, N. 3, September 1997.
17. Silva D., Siqueira S., Uchôa E., Braz M., Melo R. N., An Architecture for Data Warehouse Systems Using an Heterogeneous Database Management System, XV Brazilian Database Symposium, João Pessoa, PA, October 2000.
18. Silva D. S., An Architecture for Data Warehouse Systems using HEROS: an Heterogeneous Database Management System. Computer Science Department –

Pontifícia Universidade Católica do Rio de Janeiro (PUC-Rio). M.Sc. Thesis, 1999 (in Portuguese)

19. SynopSys™ White Paper, Web Site: http://www.themis.co.uk/WhtPaper1.html, January 1998.
20. Templeton M., Metadata Challenges in Federating Databases; Web Site: http://computer.org/conferences/meta96/templeton/templeton.html
21. Uchôa E. M. A., Lifschitz, S., Melo R. N., HEROS: A Heterogeneous Object-Oriented Database System; DEXA Conference and Workshop Programme, Vienna, Austria, 1998.
22. Uchôa E. M. A., Melo R. N., HEROS[fw]: a Framework for Heterogeneous Database Systems Integration; DEXA Conference and Workshop Programme, Florence, Italy, 1999.
23. Uchôa E. M. A., A Framework for Heterogeneous Database Systems. Computer Science Department – Pontifícia Universidade Católica do Rio de Janeiro (PUC-Rio). Ph.D. Thesis, 1999 (in Portuguese)
24. Unified Modeling Language (UML), Object Management Group http://www.omg.org/uml/

Chapter 7

Developing an Active Data Warehouse System

Shi-Ming Huang[1], Yu-Chung Hung[2], Irene Kwan[3], Yuan-Mao Hung[2]
[1]Department of Information Management, National Chung Cheng University, Taiwan
[2]Department of Information Management, Tatung University, Taiwan
[3]Department of Information Systems, Lingnan University, Hong Kong
E-mail: smhuang@mis.ccu.edu.twn

Abstract: Although many data warehouse systems have been developed in recent years, the practice of data warehouse is still immature. Most current systems are limited in terms of flexibility, efficiency and scalability. Furthermore, the contents of data warehouses are fast becoming a large and messy jungle, with data that is increasingly difficult to maintain and analyze. Much research has been done in data marts to solve these problems. Unfortunately, the solutions only isolate the information into an independent data cube. Users will retrieve the knowledge from one single angle, but not from a global view. This is because:
- The presented data warehouse models lack human involvement, particularly in the form of guidance and user control.
- The presented data warehouse systems do not allow users to define the relationship within data marts.
To deal with the above problems, this study intends to design a novel architecture for a data warehouse augmented with an active rule technique. The proposed architecture focuses on a uniform metadata model and an active monitor conditions triggered in the data warehouse, which employs inference engine for further analysis or warning.

Key words: Data warehouse, active rules, active data warehouse system, OLAP, multi - dimensional query

1. INTRODUCTION

Since the mid 90's data warehousing has been an emerging technique for data retrieval and integration from distributed, autonomous, and possibly heterogeneous systems [2, 8, 10, 12]. Data warehousing refers to a collection of technologies aimed at improving decision-making.

105

H. Bestougeff et al. (eds.), Heterogeneous Information Exchange and Organizational Hubs, 105–122.
© 2002 Kluwer Academic Publishers.

It is an architectural construct of information systems that provides users with current and historical decision support information that is often hard to access or present in traditional operational databases.

It is also a cornerstone of the organization's ability to do effective information processing. Among other things such processing enables the organization to explore, discover and share important business trends and dependencies that otherwise would have gone unnoticed.

Active rules have been used in databases for several years [6, 7, 9]. The aim of an active database is to perform automatic monitoring of conditions defined over the database state, and then to enable an action to take place (possibly subject to time constraints) when the state of the underlying database changes (i.e. transaction-triggered processing). Most active database rules are defined as production rules. These databases use the event-based rule language, in which a rule is triggered by events such as insertion, deletion or modification of data.

The general form of an active database rule is represented as follows:

On event
If condition
Then action

Recently, many active rules have also been integrated into data warehouse architecture to maintain data consistency of the materialized views [1, 13].

This paper describes a novel architecture for an Active Data Warehouse System (ADWS) that integrate active rule technology and data warehouse technology.

In our definition, an Active Data Warehouse System (ADWS) is a data warehouse system, which provides active rule's functionality in order to monitor the multi-dimensional query events and to go a step further with analysis or warning.

The traditional data warehouse systems are passive; they execute queries or transactions only when explicitly requested to do so. However, in our proposed data warehouse system, it is possible to build up the hypotheses that add active rules.

In our novel architecture the data warehouse will become alive when augmented with active rules. In this framework, when an event occurs, an active rule is triggered and the associated condition is checked.

If the condition is satisfied, the corresponding action of the rule is executed.

2. SYSTEM ARCHITECTURE

This section describes our novel architecture for an ADWS. Figure 1 illustrates the basic architecture of our system. In this data warehouse, there are two repositories and three basic process modules. The two repositories are (1) a metadata repository and (2) an active rule repository. The metadata repository stores the translated database schemas of source databases, the global database schema, the star schema of the data warehouse application, and system information of the data warehouse. The active rule repository stores the active rules of data warehouses.

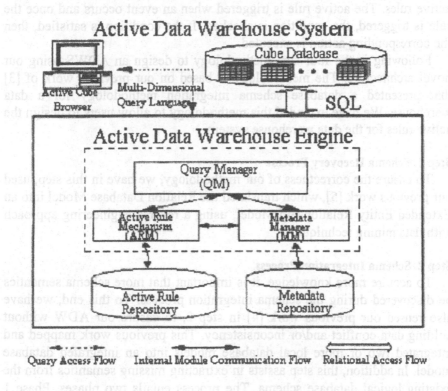

Figure 1. Active Data Warehouse System

Three basic procedure modules are considered: (1) a Query Manager (QM) module, which analyses multi-dimensional queries from active cube browsers, (2) a Metadata Manager (MM) module, which contains the communication mechanism to manage the metadata repositories, and (3) an Active Rule Mechanism (ARM) module with an inference engine to activate step by step the triggered rules and infer the correct result. The detailed mechanisms of each module are discussed in the following sections.

The working environment of this ADWS entails three parts, i.e. the active cube browser treated as a user interface, a cube database, and an active data warehouse engine. The physical data of the data warehouse is stored in the cube database which is implemented on relational databases. The active cube browser will send a request to the active data warehouse engine. The request is represented by our multi-dimensional query language which includes the events information.

The QM module of the active data warehouse engine will process the query request and translate it to SQL. It will also pass the event information to ARM. The ARM may trigger the event information and procced with further analysis or warning. The data warehouse becomes dynamic with active rules. The active rule is triggered when an event occurs and once the rule is triggered, the condition is checked. If the condition is satisfied, then the corresponding action is executed.

Following is the four step methodology to design an ADWS using our novel architecture. The methodology is based on our previous work of [3] that presented a database schema integration methodology for a data warehouse. We have extended this methodology to allow users to design the active rules for the data warehouse system.

Step 1. Schema Recovery Process

To ensure the correctness of our methodology, we have in this step, used our previous work [5], which translated the Relation Database Model into an Extended Entity Relationship Model, using a reverse engineering approach with data mining technique.

Step 2. Schema Integration Process

To acquire more knowledge, it is important that more schema semantics be discovered during the schema integration process. To this end, we have also reused our previous work [4] in step 2, to ensure our ADW without holding data conflict and/or inconsistency. This previous work mapped and integrated two or more local database models into an integrated database model. In addition, this step assists in extracting missing semantics from the existing logical database schema. The process entails two phases. Phase 1 identifies and resolves schema conflicts among local databases. Phase 2 merges the reconciled local database schemas into an integrated database schema. This procedure is repeated until the schemas of all databases have been integrated into a single global schema. The global schema is then stored in our metadata repository.

Step 3. Cube Database Creation

With the readiness of the global schema, the system would then allow users to design the cube schemas through the global database schema. It would then use the database gateway to convert the local data into the cube databases. Since the star schema is used to represent the cube database, the designer could then choose the dimension and measurement of the star schema from the global database schema in order to design the cube.

Step 4: Active Rule Creation

Upon the complete construction of the cube databases, the designer can then design active rules for the cube databases. The active rules are represented in ECA format: inference can be performed by our active rule mechanism. The detailed active rule syntax can be found in section 3.

Once these steps are completed, the user can use our ADWS browser to retrieve data from a cube database. The active rules of ADWS may entail inference during the query process.

2.1   Metadata Repositories

2.1.1   Global Database Schema Metadata

Multi-database users view the global schema as the definition of a single database. The heterogeneity of local DBMSs are masked by the global database schema. The global database schema approach requires a total integration at the schema level. In this approach, all local DBSs are translated into EER models. These EER models will be integrated into a reconciled EER model as a global database schema. The meta-data of our global database schema need to represent the EER model. Figure 2 displays our global database schema metadata using the OMT [11] model.

2.1.2   Star Schema Metadata

Data warehouses can be implemented on standard or extended relational database management systems, called Relational OLAP (ROLAP) servers. These servers assume that data is stored in relational databases, with special database designs (i.e. star or snowflake schemas) to represent the multidimensional data model, and use special access methods and query processing techniques to efficiently map OLAP operations on the underlying relational database. Alternatively, multidimensional OLAP (MOLOP) servers may be used.

These are specialized servers that directly store multidimensional data in special data structures (e.g., arrays) and then implement the OLAP operations over these special data structures. Since the data warehouse is constructed in a relational database, the star schemas are a good choice for the data cube.

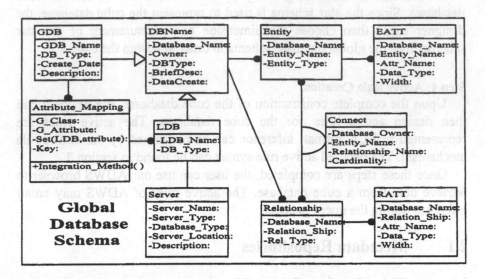

Figure 2. The OMT Model of Global Database Schema Metadata

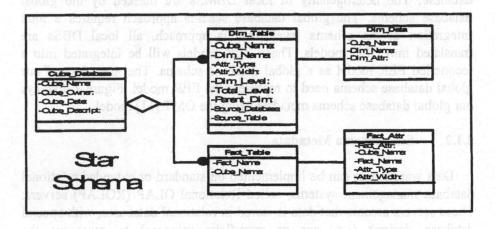

Figure 3. The OMT Model of Star Schema

The most popular design technique used to implement a data warehouse is that of the star schema. Due to its structure, the star schema takes advantage of typical decision support queries by using one central fact table for the subject area, as well as multi-dimension tables containing de-normalized descriptions of the facts. After the fact table is created, OLAP tools can be used to pre-aggregate commonly accessed information. Figure 3 displays the OMT model of star schema metadata.

2.2   Active Rule Schema Metadata

There are many useful semantics presented in this active rule schema metadata. The active rule schema can be expressed in two parts: a rule body table and a coupling model table. The rule body table describes the ECA base active rules schema, and the coupling model table describes how the active rules can be integrated into the MDQ. Figure 4 presents the OMT model of the active rule schema.

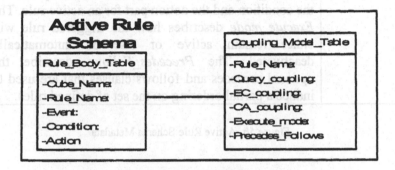

Figure 4. The OMT Model of Active Rule Schema

In addition, Figure 5a and 5b below define the semantic of the terminology that we applied in developing our active rule schema metadata.

Active Rule Schema Metadata	
Rule_ Body_ Table	The Rule_Body_Table class describes the ECA base active rules information about the active rule schema. It includes Cube_Name, Rule_Name, Event, Condition, and Action. The Cube_Name and Rule_Name describe the cube name and rule name, respectively. The Event controls rule triggering; the Condition specifies an additional predicate that must be true if a triggering rule is to automatically execute its Action.

Figure 5a. Active Rule Schema Metadata

Coupling_ Model_ Table	The Coupling_Model_Table class describes the different execution attributes to determine semantic of an active rule in our ADWS. It includes Query_coupling, EC_coupling, CA_coupling, Execute_mode, and Precedes_Follows. The *Query_coupling* describes the RQ whether triggered or not. The *EC_coupling* defines the execution sequence of the event and the condition part for an active rule. The *CA_coupling* defines the execution sequence of the condition and the action part for an active rule. The *Execute_mode* describes how the triggered rule will either remain active or else be automatically deactivated. The *Precedes_Follows* describe the optional precedes and follows clauses that are used to induce a partial ordering on the set of defined rules.

Figure 5b. Active Rule Schema Metadata

3.   ACTIVE RULE MECHANISM

Figure 6 depicts the architecture of the active rule mechanism for our ADWS. When the *Rule Activation* module receives an event, it retrieves the related active rules from the active rule repository. The *conflict resolution* module deals with the rule conflict situation. Finally, an active rule is executed and a new event occurs.

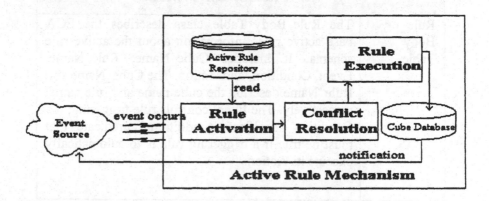

Figure 6. Architecture of Active Rule Inference Engine

3.1   Data Warehouse Event

Figure. 7 shows the event hierarchy, which we have developed to depict the event classification of a multi-dimensional query data warehouse.

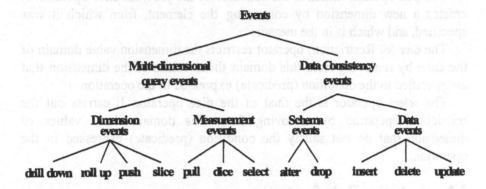

Figure 7. Event Classification

Events can be broadly classified into:

- *Multi-dimensional query events* – events which act as the basic building blocks and for each of which a detector need to be associated and embedded in the system
- *data consistency events* – in which case the event is raised by an operation on some piece of structure (e.g., insert a tuple, update a tuple, update a schema, and drop a schema).

The OLAP operators defined in the literature [10] and considered in this paper are drill-down, roll-up, push, slice, pull, dice, and select. Our approach focus on multi-dimensional query events, which can be in turn classified into two categories: *Multi-Dimensional events* and *Measurement events*.

1- Multi-Dimensional events include:

The **drill-down** operator, a binary operator that considers the aggregate cube joined with the cube that has more detailed information and that increases the detail of the measure going to the lower level of the dimension hierarchy.

The **roll-up** operator decreases the detail of the measure, aggregating it along the dimension hierarchy. Roll-up involves computing all of the formula-based relationships of data for one or more dimension.

The **push** operator is used to convert a dimension into the relative measure in order to manipulate it or to consider it as new measure. Combining with the Pull operator, it can exchange measure and dimension and then, is able to treat them both uniformly.

The **slice** (or Destroy Dimension) operator deletes one dimension of the cube, so that the sub-cube derived from all the remaining dimensions is the slice result that is specified.

2- Measurement events includes:

The **pull** operator which is the converse of the previous slice operator. It creates a new dimension by converting the element, from which it was specified, and which is in the measure.

The **dice** (or Restriction) operator restricts the dimension value domain of the cube by removing from this domain those values of the dimension that are specified in the condition (predicate) expressed in the operation.

The **select** operator is the dual of the dice operator. It carries out the restriction operation by removing from this domain those values of dimension that do not satisfy the condition (predicate) expressed in the operation.

3.2   Active Rule Syntax

Active Data Warehouse Management Systems couple database technology with rule-based programming to achieve the capability of reaction to database stimuli, called events. An ADWS consists of a data warehouse and a set of active rules; the most popular form of active rules is the so-called event-condition-action (ECA) rule, which specifies an action to be executed upon the occurrence of one or more events, provided a condition is held. In this section, we provide our active rule syntax, which extends the standard ECA rule format.

Figure 8 shows the syntax of our active rule. The syntax has two parts: a rule body and a coupling model. The rule body describes the ECA (Event-Condition-Action) base active rules, and the coupling model describes how the active rules can be integrated into the database query. The rule body is composed of three main components: a query predicate, an optional condition, and an action. The query predicate controls rule triggering; the condition specifies an additional predicate that must be true if a triggered rule executes automatically its action. Active rules are triggered by database state transitions – i.e., by execution of operation blocks. After giving a transition, rules whose transition predicate holds with respect to the effect of the transition are triggered. By using a coupling model, database designers have the flexibility of deciding how the rule query integrates within the Multi-Dimensional Query (MDQ). There are five different execution attributes that determine the semantic of an active rule in our ADWS:

– *Query_coupling*: the execution of a rule is treated as a query in our ADWS, i.e. rule query. If the Query_coupling is set to **'same'**, then the MDQ is committed only when the RQ (Rule Query) and DQ (Data

Query) are both committed. If the Query_coupling is set to 'separate', then the committed MDQ will only depend on the DQ. It is suggested that the *Query_coupling* is set to 'Separate', when the active rule does not have any effect on the DQ. This will enhance system performance in terms of query execution time.

- *EC_coupling*: This attribute defines the execution sequence of the event and condition part for a relational active rule. The 'before' *EC_coupling* means that the rule condition is evaluated immediately before the DQ is executed. The 'after' *EC_coupling* means that the rule condition is evaluated after the DQ is in the prepare-to-commit state.
- *CA_coupling*: This attribute presents the execution sequence of the condition and action part for an active rule. The 'immediate' *CA_coupling* means that the rule action is executed immediately after the rule condition is evaluated and satisfied. The rule action executed after DQ is in the prepare-to-commit state, when *CA_coupling* is specified to 'deferred'.
- *Execute_mode*: The triggered rule will automatically be deactivated after it is committed, when its *Execute_mode* is specified to 'once'. On the other hand, the rule is always active if *Execute_mode* is specified to 'repeat'.
- *Precedes_Follows*: The optional 'precedes' and 'follows' clauses are used to induce a partial ordering on the set of defined rules. If a rule r_1 specifies a rule r_2 in its 'precedes' list, or if r2 specifies r1 in its 'follows' list, then r_1 is higher than r_2 in the ordering.

Rule Body:	*Coupling Model:*
Define Rule <rule name>	Query_coupling = Same | Separate
On <query_predicate>	EC_coupling = Before | After
[if <conditions>]	CA_coupling = Immediate|
then	Deferred
[evaluate query-commalist]	Execute_mode = Repeat | Once,
execute <action>	[Precedes <rule_names>]
query_predicate ::= event	[Follows < rule_names>]
[,event [,event]]	
event ::= drill down |roll up |	
push| slice| pull| dice| select	
condition ::= query_commalist	
query_commalist ::= query	
[,query]*	
query ::= table_expression	

Figure 8. The Syntax of Our Active Rule

3.3   Active Rule Inference Engine

In our ADWS, the rule activation process flow is delineated in the following steps:

Step 1: Query coupling evaluation:

If *Query_coupling* is *separate*, the system will submit the triggered rule to QM (query manager) as a new query. Otherwise, the system will continue the following steps.

Step 2: Event-Condition coupling evaluation-- *before:*

2a.   Reasoning rules, which *EC_coupling* is equal to *before*.

2b.   If the condition evaluation result is true, the following two possible situations may occur.

    2b.1.   The action part is executed immediately if its *CA_coupling* is equal to *immediate*.

    2b.2.   The action part is saved into a queue if its *CA_coupling* is equal to *deferred*.

2c.   Steps 2a, 2b are repeated until no more rules are reasoned by step 2a.

Step 3: Execution of the data query.

Step 4: Execution of the queued rules, which are stored by step 2b.2.

Step 5: Event-Condition evaluation--*after:*

5a.   Reasoning rules, which *EC_coupling* is equal to *After*.

5b.   If the condition evaluation result is true, the following two possible situations may occur.

    5b.1.   The action part is executed immediately if its *CA_coupling* is equal to *immediate*.

    5b.2.   The action part is saved into a queue if its *CA_coupling* is equal to *deferred*.

5c. Steps 5a, 5b are repeated until no more rules are reasoned by step 5a.

Step 6: Execution of the queued rules, which are stored by step 5b.2.

Step 7: Commitment of the query if and only if all sub-queries are committed.

4.   MULTI-DIMENSIONAL QUERY LANGUAGE

Data analysis applications look for unusual patterns in data. They categorize data values and trends, extract statistical information, and then contrast one category with another. The active cube browser will send a query to our ADWS. The protocol of the query is our Multi-Dimensional Query Language (MDQL) which includes the events information.The Query

Manager (QM) module of the active data warehouse engine will process the MDQL and translate to *SQL*.

In relational data warehouse systems, users (or application programs) submit streams of multi-dimensional query operations for execution. The operations in a model of system behavior are grouped into various operation blocks.

By generalization, the operation blocks (rather than individual operations) may permit formalism that adapts easily to most relational database languages and assumes some familiarity with SQL.

This is why, the SQL-like syntax is used to implement the MDQL. That can enable the users to easily implement the multi-dimension query in the ad hoc application. In addition, the SQL like syntax can reduce users' effort to learn the new syntax. Then the *X_DIMENSION* and *Y_DIMENSION* fields are designed to match for our output format.

The query language syntax is illustrated in Figure 9

```
SELECT
[Alias.] Select_Item [AS Column_Name]
          [, [Alias.] Select_Item [AS Column_Name]
...]
FROM GlobalTableName/StarSchemaName [Alias]
          [, GlobalTableName [Alias] ...]
Operation_Block := sql-op; seq-op; .......; sql-op
Sql-op := X_DIMENSION  | Y_DIMENSION
[X_DIMENSION BY Column_Name[OLAP_OPERATOR][LEVEL
Number]
[, Column_name  [OLAP_OPERATOR] [LEVEL
Number]...]]
[Y_DIMENSION BY Column_Name[OLAP_OPERATOR][LEVEL
Number]
[, Column_name  [OLAP_OPERATOR] [LEVEL
Number]...]]
OLAP_OPERATOR =
[RollUp/DrillDown/Push/Pull/Slice/Dice/Select]
[WHERE condition expression]
```

Figure 9. Multi-Dimensional Query Language Syntax

Example: Let us consider the data cube represented in Figure 10., where its "multidimensional" view is illustrated.

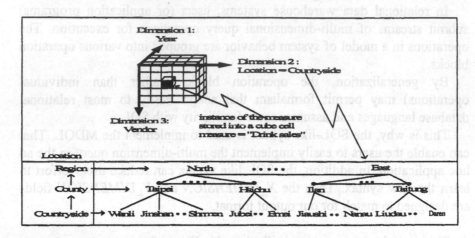

Figure 10. Example of a Data Cube with Hierarchy

Let us suppose a user is browsing the cube data in the countryside level and that a new query is defined as below.

"Select Vendors for which the total sales is > 37000 units in each County of the North"

Using our MDQL we can represent this query as follows:

```
SELECT County, Vendors, Drink Sales

FROM Sales_Cube

X_DIMENSION: = Roll-Up from Countryside to Region,
Select Region = North, Drill-Down from Region to
County

Y_DIMENSION: = Push Vendors, Pull # of sales, Dice #
of sales > 37000
```

5.   SYSTEM IMPLEMENTATION

We have discussed thus far the theoretical research direction in the paradigm of data warehouse architecture, multidimensional query language, and active rule mechanism. In this section, the practical implementation issues for our prototype system - TADWS (Tatung Active Data Warehouse System), is presented to prove our hypothesis. TADWS system is based on a multi-tier environment. The client is an active cube browser system, which is written in Java. The middle tier is the ADW engine, which is built in Visual Basic. The cube database is designed in MS-SQL. The Figure 11 depicts the TADWS architecture:

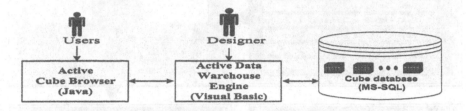

Figure 11. The architecture of Our Prototype System.

5.1   Active Cube Browser

The active cube browser provides an OLAP function for users' enqueries. Several events occur when users interact with the browser. The Active Data Warehouse Engine receives the event and uses an active rule mechanism to go a step further to analyze and return back a warning to the active cube browser. Figure 12 shows the Active Data Warehouse Engine in the process of detecting a dimension drill down event; the rule of Great_Sales is triggered to make decisions about next month's market and material supply chain relationship.

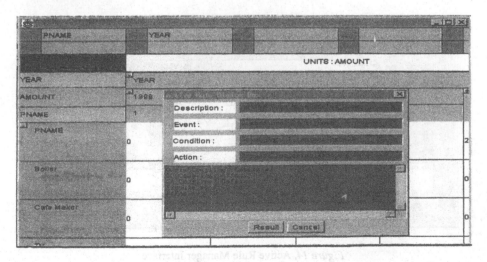

Figure 12. Active Cube Browser

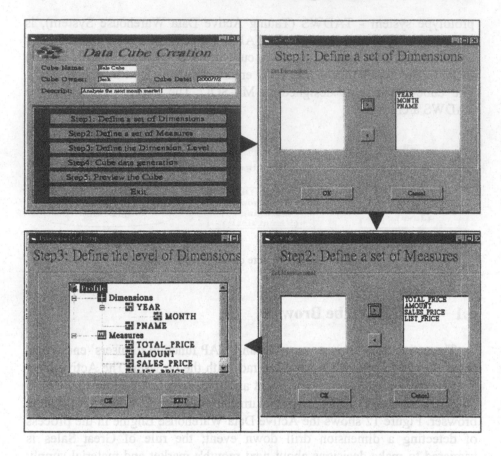

Figure 13. The Sequence of Data Cube Creation Interface

Figure 14. Active Rule Manager Interface

5.2   Active Data Warehouse Engine

The operational process flow of the data cube creation in our prototype system is intuitively demonstrated in Figure 13. We first choose to define the set of dimensions, then choose the option for defining a set of measurements before defining the dimension's hierarchy, and finally, the cube data generation. Users can also preview the data cube that they have just created by selecting Step 5 on the Data Cube Creation menu, as shown in Figure 13. Figure 14 shows the interface of the active rule manager in our system. Users can employ the system to create, update, or drop the active rules.

6.   CONCLUSIONS

In summary, this paper has discussed:

- The creation of an active data warehouse architecture and the relational metadata for global database schema, star schema, and active rule schema to represent the ADWS metadata.
- The process of the data integration for a cube.
- Our active rule syntax and its activation mechanism in detail.
- The design of a multi-dimensional query language for active cube browser.

In addition, a case study operated on our prototype TADWS has been investigated in order to evaluate the correctness of our approach. As we have explained, schema integration is one of the core problems in data warehousing. An effective data warehouse requires integrated schema from multiple distributed databases for storing cleaned, summarized and analytical data. We have presented here a novel methodology to integrate different database schemas into a global database schema for a data warehouse system.

As the traditional data warehouse systems are basically passive, they execute queries or transactions only when explicitly requested to do so by a user or an application program. In this paper, we explored the integration of active rules into the data warehouse system. The result of this successful integration is that the data warehouse becomes actively dynamic. It is thus able to proactively analyze the related data automatically anytime the user's query triggers the related active rules.

ACKNOWLEDGEMENTS

The National Science Council, Taiwan, under Grant No. NSC 89-2213-E-194-041 has supported the work presented in this paper. We greatly appreciate their financial support and encouragement.

REFERENCES

1. Ceri S., et. al, Automatic Generation of Production Rules for Integrity Maintenance, ACM Transactions on Database Systems Vol. 19, No. 3, 1994, pp.367-442.
2. Han J., et. al, Constraint-Based, Multidimensional Data Mining, Computer, 1999.
3. Huang S., et. al, A Database Schema Integration Methodology for A Data Warehouse, 9th International Database Conference (IDC'99), 1999, ISBN: 962-937-046-8, pp415-418.
4. Huang S., et. al, Conflict Resolution and Reconciliation in Multidatabase Systems, International Journal of Information and Management Sciences, Vol. 11, No. 3, 2000, ISSN:1017-1819, pp.31-56.
5. Huang S., et. al, Translate Relation Database Model Into Extended Entity Relationship Model: A Reverse Engineering Approach, Tatung Journal, Vol: 26, 1997, ISSN: 0379-7309, pp.175-186.
6. Huang S., Huang C., A Semantic-Based Transaction Model for Active Heterogeneous Database Systems, The Proceeding of 1998 IEEE International Conference on Systems, Man, and Cybernetics, IEEE Press, 1998.
7. Huang S., Liu J., Developing an Active Heterogeneous Database System, Proceedings of Intelligent Information Systems, 1997, pp.415-419.
8. Linda D. P., Data Quality: A Rising e-Business Concern, IT Professional, Volume: 2 Issue: 4, 2000, pp. 10-14.
9. Paton W., Diaz O., Active Database Systems, ACM Computing Surveys, Vol. 31, No. 1, 1999.
10. Pourabbas E., Rafanelli M., Hierarchies and Relative Operators in the OLAP Environment. ACM SIGMOD, Vol. 29, Num. 1, 2000.
11. Rumbaugh J., et. al, Object-Oriented Modeling and Designing, (Prentice-Hall, Inc.), A Division of Simon & Schuster Englewood Cliffs, 1991.
12. Venkatrao M., et.al, Data Cube: A Relational Aggregation Operator Generalizing Group-By, Gross-Tab, and Sub-Totals, Data Mining and Knowledge Discovery, 1997, pp.29-53.
13. Widom J., et. al, The STRIP Rule System for Efficiently Maintaining Derived Data, Proceedings of the ACM SIGMOD International Conference on Management of Data, 1997, pp.147-158.

Chapter 8

Building Secure Data Warehouse Schemas from Federated Information Systems

Fèlix Saltor[1], Marta Oliva[2], Alberto Abelló and José Samos[3]
[1]U. Politècnica de Catalunya (UPC), Dept. de Llenguatges i Sistemes Informàtics (LSI)
Email: {saltor, aabello}@lsi.upc.es
[2]U. de Lleida (UdL), Dept. d'Informàtica i Enginyeria Industrial (IEI)
Email: oliva@eup.udl.es
[3]U. de Granada (UGR), Dept. de Lenguajes y Sistemas Informáticos (LSI)
Email: jsamos@ugr.es

Abstract: There are certain similarities between architectures for Federated Information
Systems and architectures for Data Warehousing. In the context of an
integrated architecture for both Federated Information Systems and Data
Warehousing, we discuss how additional schema levels provide security, and
operations to convert from one level to the next.

Key words: Federated information systems, data warehousing, security policies, data
marts, multidimensional schema.

1.   INTRODUCTION

Heterogeneity is widespread among preexisting information sources, such as Databases (DBs). Such heterogeneity must be overcome in order to build either a *Federated Information System* (FIS) or a *Data Warehouse* (DW), upon these preexisting information sources, which may present *systems*, *syntactic* and *semantic* heterogeneities. We have chosen to focus on semantic heterogeneities (see our chapter "Semantic Heterogeneities in Multidatabase Systems" ([11 in 3], or [22]).

Within an integrated schema architecture for both FIS and secure Data Warehousing, two important issues emerge, concerning:

- The relationship between schema levels and security (section 3).
- The operations on schemas to convert from level to level (section 4).

123

H. Bestougeff et al. (eds.), Heterogeneous Information Exchange and Organizational Hubs, 123–134.
© 2002 *Kluwer Academic Publishers.*

Section 2 presents our terms of reference, while conclusions, in section 5, acknowledgments and references close this paper.

2. TERMS OF REFERENCE

This paper is developed around some terms of reference such as security policies, FIS architecture, DW. It also draws upon our previous work that is explained in the following subsections.

2.1 Multi Level Security (MLS)

With respect to security policies, we shall assume that some of the preexisting information sources use *Mandatory Access Control* (MAC), more specifically *Multi Level Security* (MLS), or its equivalent in *Role Based Access Control* (RBAC). This assumption does not preclude that some other sources use *Discretionary Access Control* (DAC). Rather, it necessitates that at the level of the whole FIS the most strict security policy, i.e. MLS, is used (for an explanation of these terms, see for example, [4], or the proceedings of the IFIP WG 11.3 Working Conferences on Database Security listed at [7]).

2.2 Federated Information Systems (FIS)

The area of Federated and Interoperable Databases and FIS has already been researched for a number of years (for concepts, see for example [3], [8], [24]). We will use a 7-level schema architecture, depicted in Figure 1. There is a software *processor* for each line between schemas, omitted in the Figure.

This architecture is presented in [17], as an extension of the 5-level schema reference architecture introduced in [20], in order to separate different issues in different processors (*separation of concerns*). A relevant difference from the reference architecture is the inclusion of two additional schema levels.

One of the two additional levels contains *Authorization Schemas*, representing derivations (subsets) of the Federated Schema, for a class of federated users with a certain Clearance Level.

On the other hand, the schema level called "External Schema" in [20] is split into two: an *External Schema* defines a schema for a class of users/applications; it is still expressed in the *Canonical Data Model* (CDM). A *User External Schema* is the conversion of an External Schema from the CDM to the user data model.

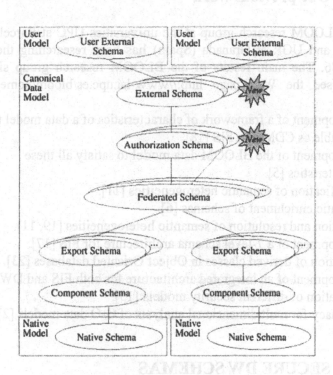

Figure 1. Seven levels schema architecture

2.3 Data Warehousing and Data Marts

We will be using Inmon's definitions:

– A *Data Warehouse* is a subject-oriented, integrated, time-variant, nonvolatile collection of data in support of management's decision-making process.

– *Data Mart* is a subset of a DW that has been customized to fit the needs of a department or subject area.

For further explanations of DW concepts, see [13, 12].

Another frequently used term in the field is *Multidimensional Schema*. The main purpose of having Multidimensional Schemas defined is to ease the presentation, navigability, and access to the data by distinguishing two kinds of entities: those that are to be analyzed (central *facts*), and those used to analyze (i.e. surrounding *analysis dimensions*).

2.4   Our previous work

The BLOOM research group at the universities UPC at Barcelona, UdL at Lleida and UGR at Granada (Spain) has been researching these topics since 1986. The main results of the BLOOM research group since 1986 include (see the Web page http://www-lsi.upc.es/bloom/home.html for details):
- Development of a framework of characteristics of a data model that make it suitable as CDM of a FIS [18].
- Development of the BLOOM data model to satisfy all these characteristics [5].
- Classification of semantic heterogeneities [11].
- Semantic enrichment of schemas [6].
- Detection and resolution of semantic heterogeneities [19, 11].
- Development of a 7-level schema architecture for FIS [17].
- Definition of derived classes in Object Oriented databases [23].
- Development of an integrated architecture for both FIS and DW [1].
- Integration of different security models [15].
- Adequacy for multidimensional analysis of O-O data models [2].

3.   SECURE DW SCHEMAS

3.1   Authorization DW Schemas

Authorized access in a DW is scantily studied. However we think that the set of data, stored in a DW, that is needed to support the decision-making process, has to be protected from unauthorized accesses, just as any other information system, because data involved in decision making is probably very confidential.

Authorization Schemas help federated databases in MLS data protection, because each Authorization Schema defines the subset of information that a class of users/applications can access. In our integrated architecture (see section 3.2), Authorization DW Schemas help Data Warehousing in the same way.

The process to obtain Authorization Schemas (and Authorization DW Schemas in the integrated architecture) from a Federated Schema (from a DW Schema, respectively) takes into account the security policy of the federation itself. In our case the security policy is based on a MLS system, so Authorization Schemas assist the fulfillment of the Simple Property and *-Property rules. The existence of an Authorization Schema for each security level of the partial ordered set of the federation itself is necessary. The set of data included in an Authorization Schema is classified either at the same level or at a lower level, than that corresponding to the Authorization Schema.

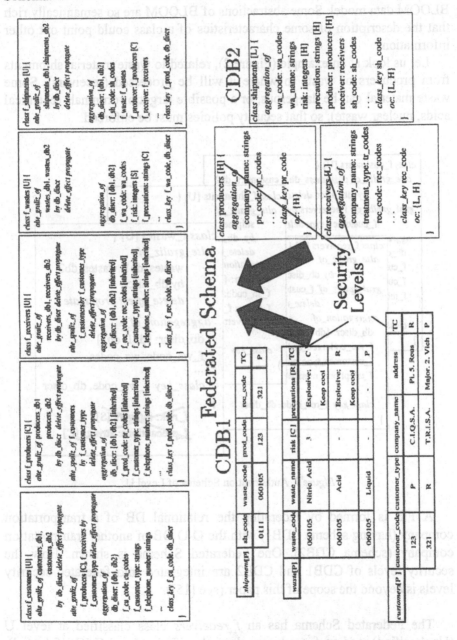

Figure 2. Data Schema and Security Policies Integration

Another characteristic of Authorization Schemas is that they are also used to assist information inference control. In our case the inference problem worsens because the use of the semantic abstractions of the BLOOM data model. Some abstractions of BLOOM are so semantically rich that the description of some characteristics of a class could point out other information.

Let us look at an example (Figure 2), related to waste material shipments from producers of waste to where it will be processed (receivers). Some waste material can be dangerous, or a possible target of criminals (chemical acids, nuclear waste), so that security policies must be enforced.

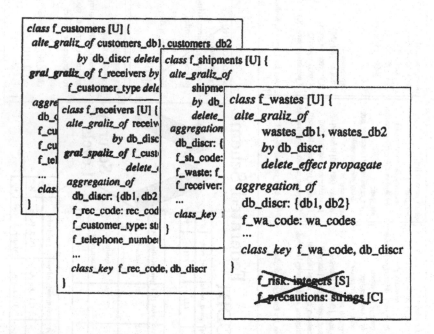

Figure 3. Authorization Schema of Level U.

A FIS is formed by federating the relational DB of a transportation company (having schema CDB1) with the O-O DB of another transportation company (schema CDB2). One Federated Schema is shown. How the security levels of CDB1 and CDB2 are integrated into federated security levels is beyond the scope of this paper (see [15]).

The Federated Schema has an *f_receivers* class classified at level U (Unclassified), and an *f_producers* class classified at level C (Confidential). Since class *f_customers* is an *alternative generalization* of classes f_receivers and f_producers, a user with Clearance Level U cannot see the f_producers class. Yet the property *alternative* suggests the existence of at least one unauthorized class (it is a *covert channel*).

The Authorization Schema corresponding to level U is shown in Figure 3. Some properties have been modified (in bold) to solve the inference problem.

3.2 Our Integrated Architecture

An integrated architecture, which combines our 7-level schema levels architecture with the schemas needed to produce a secure DW and its Data Marts, was presented in [1]. It is shown in Figure 4.

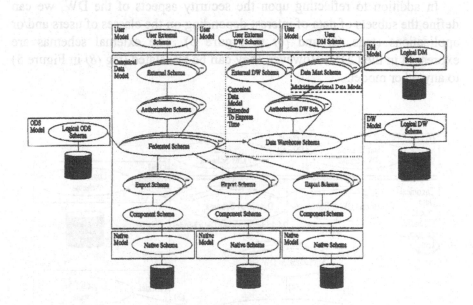

Figure 4. Integrated FIS + DW Architecture

It is important to notice the location of the DW Schema. If we assume that the presence of a processor (performing changes either in data model, in semantics, or in UoD) forces the appearance of a new level, the DW should be placed in between the Federated Schema and the Authorization Schemas. However, the DW Schema is placed at the same level as the Federated Schema, because they play equivalent roles. If the Export Schemas were expressed in a temporal CDM, and we had an integration processor for it, then Federated Schema and Data Warehouse Schema would collapse into a single schema.

On the other hand, the double storage system (DW-DM) should not be avoided. The DW is data-driven designed, and will contain data that may not ensure its future usefulness (which worsen performance). The DM is query-driven designed (in a multidimensional data model), oriented to optimize response times. Thus, what we will likely have is a temporal, or relational database that supports time, incrementally designed and populated, as data is generated. From this huge, central DW, we will define and feed smaller DMs, on an as needed basis. Note that we are not suggesting a methodology, but an architecture. Defining a methodology is absolutely beyond the scope of this paper, and the architecture does not impose it.

3.3   External DW and Data Mart Schemas

In addition to reflecting upon the security aspects of the DW, we can define the subsets of data of interest depending on the classes of users and/or applications (tags *(5)* and *(6)* in Figure 5). The external schemas are expressed in the CDM. However, they can be translated (tag *(8)* in Figure 5) to any other model.

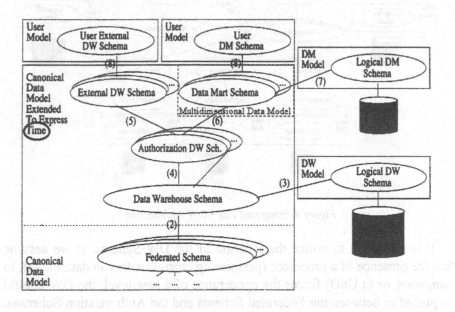

Figure 5. DW Schemas Architecture from the Federated Schema

At this point, the strength is not in the data itself, but in the needs of the users. Here, we will have a query-driven design, where what really matters is the vision the user has. If the users have a multidimensional vision of the data, we will obtain Star External Schemas (by *(6)* in Figure 5). If most of the users have that vision, what we likely get is a set of stars sharing some of their dimensions. Sometimes, this is called a "Star Constellation" or "Data Warehouse Bus" [14].

Due to performance, most of these Star Schemas are materialized (represented by *(7)* in Figure 5), giving rise to DM built with either ROLAP (*Relational On-Line Analytical Processing*) or MOLAP (*Multidimensional On-Line Analytical Processing*) techniques. However, other External Schemas used for Data Mining or solving some sporadic queries would not need to be materialized.

4. OPERATIONS ON SCHEMAS

We need different kinds of operations in the CDM (BLOOM in our case) in order to perform the following functions:

1. *Conforming* operations to transform the (export) schema of one DB to a form more suitable for integration into a Federated schema [16]. These operations are also useful in other contexts, in particular in deriving external schemas (views) in O-O DBMSs.

2. *Generalization* of classes from different DBs to a superclass in a Federated schema. The schema integration process, which produces a Federated schema from several Export schemas, can be considered as a two-step process: first, conforming operations change the form of the Export schemas into a common form, and then these are generalized. *Discriminated* generalization is preferred, because of the reasons explained in [10], in particular the support of "multiple semantics" [20] and no loss of information, because each (virtual) object in a Federated schema is given a tag (*discriminant*) indicating which component DB it comes from.

3. *Object identification function* (oif) to assert when an object O_1 in one DB represents the same real world object as an object O_2 in another DB. Different users may use different *oif*s, as explained in [21].

4. *Collapse* two objects into one using a particular *oif* [9]. If all users share the same *oif* for a Federated class, or if integrity constraints among the component databases (interdependencies) must be enforced, then the

collapsing operation may take place during the process of schema integration; otherwise, the derivation of each External schema may collapse using a different *oif*.

5. *Dealing with value discrepancies*, preserving all values by having multivalued attributes in Federated schemas. External schemas may use different options, such as giving preference to the value coming from a particular DB (shown by its discriminant), or by "aggregation by reduction" operations (sum, average, maximum,…) [21].

6. *Protecting security* by hiding relationships between abstractions that could reveal confidential information, as exemplified in section 3.1.

7. *Transform* into the Data Mart model the structures of the DW data model. O-O models are preferred, as discussed in [2].

5.   CONCLUSIONS

We have explained how an integrated architecture may preserve MultiLevel security, when that architecture is built upon a number of component databases, and when it supports both a Federated Information System and a Data Warehouse. We have also discussed the kinds of operations needed in this architecture.

We are currently working on the conforming operations, on security level integration, and on O-O data models supporting time in the way required by Data Warehouses and Data Marts.

ACKNOWLEDGEMENTS

This work has been partially supported by the Spanish Research Program PRONTIC under projects TIC2000-1723-C02-01 and TIC2000-1723-C02-02, as well as the grant 1998FI-00228 from the Generalitat de Catalunya.

REFERENCES

1. Abelló A., Oliva M., Samos J., Saltor F., Information System Architecture for Data Warehousing from a Federation, in Roantree et al. (Eds), Engineering Federated

Informations Systems (Proc 3rd. Workshop on EFIS'00, Dublin, June 2000). Infix/IOS Press, 2000, pp 33-40.

2. Abelló A., Samos J., Saltor F., Benefits of an Object-Oriented Multidimensional Data Model. In Dittrich et al. (Eds), Objects and Databases International Symposium (Sophia-Antipolis, June 2000), Springer-Verlag, LNCS 1944, 2001, pp. 141-152.

3. Bukhres O.A., Elmagarmid A., (Eds), Object-Oriented Mutidatabase Systems: A Solution for Advanced Applications, Prentice-Hall, 1996.

4. Castano S., Fugini M.G., Martella G., Samarati P., Database Security. Addison-Wesley, 1995.

5. Castellanos M., Saltor F., Garcia-Solaco M., A Canonical Model for the Interoperability among Object-Oriented and Relational Databases, in: Ozsu, Dayal & Valduriez, (Eds), Distributed Object Management (Proceedings, Int. Workshop on Distributed Object Management, IWDOM, Edmonton, Canada, August 1992). Morgan Kaufmann 1994, pp.309-314.

6. Castellanos M., Saltor F., Garcia-Solaco M., Semantically Enriching Relational Databases into an Object Oriented Semantic Model, in: D. Karagiannis (Ed.), Database and Expert Systems Applications (5th International Conference DEXA'94, Athens, Sept.1994). Springer Verlag, LNCS 856, 1994, pp 125-134.

7. http:// www.informatik.uni-trier.de/ ley/db/index.html

8. Elmagarmid A., Rusinkiewicz M., Sheth A.P., (Eds), Management of Heterogenous and Autonomous Database Systems, Morgan Kaufmann, 1999.

9. Garcia-Solaco M., Castellanos M., Saltor F., A Semantic-Discriminated Approach to Integration of Federated Databases, in: Laufmann et al. (Eds), Proc. of the 3rd International Conference on Cooperative Information Systems (CoopIS'95, Vienna, May 1995). Univ. Toronto, 1995, pp. 19-31.

10. Garcia-Solaco M., Saltor F., Castellanos M., A Structure Based Schema Integration Methodology, in Proc. 11th Int. Conference on Data Engineering (ICDE'95, Taipei, March 1995). IEEE-CS Press, 1995, pp 505-512.

11. García-Solaco M., Saltor F., Castellanos M., Semantic Heterogeneity in Multidatabase Systems. In [3], pp 129-202.

12. Inmon W.H., Imhoff C., Sousa R., Corporate Information Factory, Wiley Computer Publishing, 1998.

13. Inmon W.H., Buiding the Data Warehouse (2nd ed.), John Wiley & Sons, 1996.

14. Kimball R., The Data Warehouse Toolkit, John Wiley & Sons, 1996.

15. Oliva M., Saltor F., Integrating Multilevel Security Policies in Multilevel Federated Database Systems, in Proceedings of the 14th IFIP 11.3 Working Conference in Database Security, Schoorl, The Netherlands, August 2000.

16. Rodríguez E., Abelló A., Oliva M., Saltor F., Delgado F., Garví S., Samos J., On Operations along the Generalization/Specialization Dimension. Engineering Federated Informations Systems (Proc 4rd. Workshop on EFIS'01, Berlin, October 2001). To appear.

17. Rodríguez E., Oliva M., Saltor F., Campderrich B., On Schema and Functional Architectures for Multilevel Secure and Multiuser Model Federated DB Systems, in Conrad et al. (Eds), Proceedings of the Int. CAiSE'97 Workshop, Barcelona, Otto-von-Guericke-Universität Magdeburg, June 1997, pp. 93-104.

18. Saltor F., Castellanos M., García-Solaco M., Suitability of Data Models as Canonical Models for Federated DBs. ACM SIGMOD Record vol 20(4), pp 44-48 (special refered issue: A. Sheth (Ed.): Semantic Issues in Multidatabase Systems, December 1991).

19. Saltor F., Campderrich B., Rodríguez E., Rodríguez L.C., On Schema Levels for Federated Database Systems, in Yetongnon & Hairiri (Eds), Proceedings of the ISCA International Conference on Parallel and Distributed Computing Systems, Dijon, France, pages 766-771, September 1996.

20. Sheth A.P., Larson J.A., Federated Database Systems for Managing Distributed. Heterogeneous and Autonomous Databases, ACM Computing Surveys, 22(3):183-236, September 1990.

21. Saltor F., Rodriguez E., On Intelligent Access to Heterogeneous Information in: Jeusfeld et al (Eds.), Proceedings, 4th Int. Workshop on Knowledge Representation meets DataBases (KRDB'97, Athens, August 1997). CEUR-WS Vol 8-1997, pp 15.1-15.7.

22. Saltor F., Rodriguez E., On Semantic Issues in Engineering Federated Information Systems (Extended Abstract), in: Conrad, Hasselbring & Saake (Eds.), Engineering Federated Information Systems (Proc. 2nd Int. Workshop EFIS'99, Kuehlungsborn, May 1999). infix, Sankt Augustin, 1999, pp 1-4 (ISBN 3-89601-013-1).

23. Samos J., Saltor F., External Schema Generation Algorithms for Object Oriented Databases, in: Patel et al (Eds.), Proceedings, Int. Conf. on Object Oriented Information Systems (OOIS'96, London, December 1996), Springer, 1996, pp 317-332.

24. Thuraisingham B., Data Management Systems: Evolution and Interoperation, CRC Press, 1997.

Chapter 9

Conceptual MetaCube
Metadata for Multidimensional Cube

Nguyen Thanh Binh

*Institute of Software Technology, Vienna University of Technology,Favoritenstrasse 9-
11/188, A-1040 Vienna, Austria*
Email: binh@ifs.tuwien.ac.at

Abstract: OLAP applications have very special requirements from the underlying
multidimensional data that differ significantly from other areas of application
(e.g. the existence of highly structured dimensions). In this paper we propose a
conceptual multidimensional data model that facilitates a precise rigorous
conceptualization for OLAP. First, our approach bears a strong relation with
mathematics by applying some mathematics concepts, i.e. *partial order,
partially ordered set* or *poset*. Afterwards, this mathematical soundness
provides a foundation on which to handle natural hierarchical relationships
among data elements within dimensions that have many levels of complexity
in their structures. Hereafter, the multidimensional data model organizes data
in the form of metacubes, which is a generalization of other cube models. In
addition, a metacube is associated with a set of groups, each of which contains
a subset of the metacube domain, which is a hierarchical set of data cells.
Furthermore, metacube operators (e.g. *jumping, rollingUp* and *drillingDown*)
are defined in a very elegant manner.

Key words: Formal multidimensional data model, OLAP, metacube model, metacube
operators.

1.   INTRODUCTION

"*...On-Line Analytical Processing (OLAP) is a category of software
technology that enables analysts, managers and executives to gain insight
into data through fast, consistent, interactive access to a wide variety of
possible views of information that has been transformed from raw data to
reflect the real dimensionality of the enterprise as understood by the user.
OLAP functionality is characterized by dynamic multidimensional analysis*

135

H. Bestougeff et al. (eds.), Heterogeneous Information Exchange and Organizational Hubs, 135–148.
© *2002 Kluwer Academic Publishers.*

of consolidated enterprise data supporting end user analytical and navigational activities including calculations and modeling applied across dimensions, through hierarchies and/or across members, trend analysis over sequential time periods, slicing subsets for on-screen viewing, drill-down to deeper levels of consolidation, rotation to new dimensional comparisons in the viewing area etc. ...". [26].

OLAP tools are frequently used as front-end tools in data warehouse environments. They allow for the interactive analysis of multidimensional data. Consequently, multidimensional database technology is gaining considerable attention by vendors and researchers. Independent from the different possible architectures concerning data storage and query processing, they all present the data to the user in a multidimensional data model and queries are formulated using the multidimensional paradigm.

The research community in different areas of applications has proposed several formal multidimensional models and corresponding query languages. But each approach presents its own view of multidimensional analysis requirements, terminology and formalism. This is why there is no commonly accepted formal multidimensional data model. Such a model is necessary to serve as a foundation for standardization and future research. This is the main motivation for us to invest in and focus on a new multidimensional data model that is suitable for OLAP applications, since these applications have very special requirements to the underlying multidimensional data that differ significantly from other areas of application (e.g. the existence of highly structured dimensions).

In this paper, we present a suitable mutidimensional data model for OLAP. The main contributions are:

(a) the application of some mathematical concepts, i.e. partial order, partially ordered set or poset [10] that provide a foundation for defining multidimensional components, (i.e. dimensions, measures and metacubes);

(b) the introduction of a formal multidimensional data model, which is used for handling dimensions with any complexity in their structures;

(c) the very elegant manner of defining three metacube operators, namely jumping, rollingUp and drillingDown.

The remainder of this paper is organized as follows. In Section 2, we discuss related works. In Section 3, we introduce a conceptual data model that begins with the introduction of *poset* concepts and ends with the definition of metacube concepts. The paper concludes with Section 4, which presents our current and future works.

2. RELATED WORKS

The concept of multidimensionality (or n-dimensionality) of these datasets, and in particular, of aggregate data [27], as well as the concepts of dimension (often called category attribute, descriptive variable, character) and of measure (often called summary attribute, quantitative data, variable) have been already discussed [15, 27].

Recently, in the literature, many authors proposed multidimensional data models and query languages.

Gray et al. in [8] proposed the data cube operator as an extension of SQL, which generalized the histogram, cross-tabulation, roll-up, drill-down, and sub-total constructs found in most reports.

In [12] the authors formalized a multidimensional data model for OLAP, and developed an algebra query language called Grouping Algebra. The relative multidimensional cube algebra is proposed in order to facilitate the data derivation.

Gyssens et al. in [9] presented a tabular database model and discussed a tabular algebra as a language for querying and restructuring tabular data.

Lehner in [11] discussed the design problem that arose when the OLAP scenarios became very large, and they proposed a nested multidimensional data model which is useful during schema designing and multidimensional data analysis phases.

During the past few years, many commercial products, like Arborsoft (now Hyperion) Essbase, Cognos Powerplay or MicroStrategy's DSS Agent have been introduced on the market [4]. But unfortunately, sound concepts were not available at the time the commercial products were being developed.

The scientific community struggles to deliver a common basis for multidimensional data models ([4], [6], [9], [12], [21], [22], [19]). The data models presented so far differ in expressive power, complexity and formalism. However, the need for a formal model for OLAP that explicitly incorporates the notation of different and independent views on dimensions while also offering a logical way to compute summary information has become apparent.

In [12], a multidimensional data model is introduced based on relational elements. Dimensions are modeled as "dimension relations", practically annotating attributes with dimension names. The cubes are modeled as functions from the Cartesian product of the dimensions to the measure and are mapped to "grouping relations" through an applicability definition.

In [11] n-dimensional tables are defined and a relational mapping is provided through the notation of completion. Multidimensional databases are considered to be composed from tables forming denormalized star schemata. Attribute hierarchies are modeled through the introduction of functional dependencies in the attributes of dimensions.

Cabibbo and Torlone [5] have proposed a multidimensional data model based on the notations of dimensions and f-tables. Dimensions are partially ordered categories that correspond to different ways of looking at the multidimensionsal information. F-tables are repositories for the factual data functionally dependent on the dimensions. Data are characterized from a set of roll-up functions, mapping the instance of a dimension level to instances of other dimension levels.

In [4], a framework for Object-Oriented OLAP is introduced. Two major physical implementations exist today: ROLAP and MOLAP, and their advantages and disadvantages due to physical implementation are introduced. The paper also presents another physical implementation called O3LAP model. [19] takes the concepts and basic ideas of the classical multidimensional model based on the Object-Oriented paradigm. The basic elements of their Object Oriented Multidimensional Model are dimension classes and fact classes.

3. CONCEPTUAL DATA MODEL

In our approach, a multidimensional data model is constructed based on a set of dimensions $\mathcal{D} = \{D_1,..,D_x\}, x \in N$, a set of measures $\mathcal{M} = \{M_1,..,M_y\}, y \in N$ and a set of metacubes $C = \{C_1,..,C_z\}, z \in N$, each of which is associated with a set of groups $Groups(C_i) = \{G_1,..,G_p\}, p, i \in N, 1 \le i \le z$. The following sections formally introduce the descriptions of dimensions with their structures, measures, metacubes and their associated groups.

3.1. Mathematical Concepts

To bring the power of mathematics to bear on real-world problems, one must first model the problem mathematically. First we define partial relations, then *POSETs*. Afterwards, a partial order on a finite set is often represented by a simplified graph, called a Hasse diagram.

notation: Throughout the rest of this subsection, the symbol $\prec$ is used to denote the relation under discussion.

Definition 3.1.1. [*Partial order relation*]
A relation $\prec$ on a set S is called *a partial order* if $\prec$ is reflexive, antisymmetric and transitive.

Definition 3.1.2. [*POSET*]

A pair $<S, \prec>$ is called *poset (partially ordered set).*

Definition 3.1.3. [*Hasse diagram*]

Let $\prec$ be a partial order on a finite set S. A H*asse diagram* representing the poset $<S, \prec>$ is a graph defined as follows:

- $V = S$. A vertex represents each element of the set S.
- $E \subseteq S \times S$. If $x \prec y$ for distinct elements x and y, then a vertex for x is positioned higher than the vertex for y; and if there is no z different from both x and y such that $x \prec z$ and $z \prec y$, then an edge is drawn from the vertex x downward to the vertex y.

Definition 3.1.4. [*Directed path*]

Let G be a Hasse diagram representing a *poset* $(S, \prec)$. A *directed path* in G is a nonempty sequence $p = (v_0, .., v_n)$ of vertexes such that $(v_i, v_{i+1}) \in E$ for each $i \in [0, n-1]$. This path from v_0 to v_n and has length n. defined as follows:

Definition 3.1.5. [*Partition*]

Let G be a Hasse diagram representing a *poset* $<S, \prec>$. A collection of distinct non-empty subsets of S, denoted by $\{S_1, .., S_l\}, l \in \mathbf{N}$, is a *partition* of S if the three following conditions are satisfied:

- $S_i \cap S_j = \phi, \ \forall i, j \in \mathbf{N}, 1 \le i < j \le l,$
- $\bigcup_{i=1}^{l} S_i = S,$
- $\forall S_i : (v_i, v_u) \in E$ for all $v_t, v_u \in S_i$

3.2. Multidimensional Concepts

3.2.1. Dimension concepts

First, we introduce hierarchical relationships among dimension members by means of one hierarchical domain per dimension.

A hierarchical domain is a *poset* of dimension elements, organized in a hierarchy of levels, corresponding to different levels of granularity. It also allows us to consider a dimension schema as a poset of levels.

In this concept, a dimension hierarchy is a *path* along the dimension schema, beginning at the root level and ending at a leaf level. Moreover, the definitions of two dimension operators, namely $O^{ancestor}$ and $O^{descendant}$, provide abilities to navigate along a dimension structure.

As a consequence, dimensions with any complexity in their structures can be captured with this data model.

Definition 3.2.1.1. [*Dimension Hierarchical Domain*]
A dimension hierarchical domain is a *partially ordered set* or *poset*, denoted by $< dom(D), \prec_D >$,

where:

- $dom(D) = \{dm_{all}\} \cup \{dm_1,..,dm_n\}$: $\{dm_1,..,dm_n\}$ is a set of dimension elements of the dimension D, e.g. *1999, Q1.1999, Jan.1999,* and *1.Jan.1999,* etc. are dimension members within the dimension *Time* (Figure 1).
- There exists only an *all* that is the *root* or the *minimal element* of the poset.
- The relation $\prec_D$ on the set $dom(D)$ is a *partial order*, such that the graph (Hasse diagram) $G_D = (V_D, E_D)$, defined as the representation over the *partial order* $\prec_D$ over the $dom(D)$, is a tree and is defined as follows:

$V_D = dom(D)$,
$E_D \subset dom(D) \times dom(D) . \forall (dm_i, dm_j) \in E_D : dm_i \prec_D dm_j$ is an edge in G_D. The edge is given when there is an ordered relationship in the sense of hierarchy.

- And the two operators $\{+,-\}$: $\forall dm_i \in dom(D)$:
$$-(dm_i) = \{dm_j \in dom(D) : dm_j \prec_D dm_i\}$$
$$+(dm_i) = \{dm_k \in dom(D) : dm_i \prec_D dm_k\}$$
- The *all* or *root* member:
$$(\exists! all \in dom(D))(\neg \exists dm \in dom(D) : dm \prec_D all).$$
- Leaf members:
$$(\forall dm_i \in dom(D))(\neg \exists dm_j \in dom(D), i \neq j : dm_i \prec_D dm_j).$$

Example 3.2.1.1. Figure 1 shows a representation in tree term of the dimension *Time*. Hereafter, we have:

- dom(Time)={all,1999,Q1.1999,...,3.Mar.1999},
- all $\prec_D$ 1999,1999 $\prec_D$ Q1.1999,...,Mar.1999 $\prec_D$ 3.Mar.1999,
- -(1999)=all; +(1999)={Q1.1999,W1.1999,W5.1999,W9.1999}.

Definition 3.2.1.2. [*Dimension Levels*]
Let a dimension D have a hierarchical domain $< dom(D), \prec_D >$, a finite set of levels of the dimension D is defined as $Levels(D) = l_{All} \cup \{l_0,..,l_h\}$,

where:
- $\forall l_i \in Levels(D), l_i = < Lname, dom(l_i) >$:

- *Lname* is the name of the level l_i,
- $dom(l_i) \subset dom(D)$. Furthermore, a family of sets $\{dom(l_0),.., dom(l_h)\}$ is a *partition* of $dom(D)$.
- l_{All} is the *root level* and $dom(All) = \{dm_{all}\}$

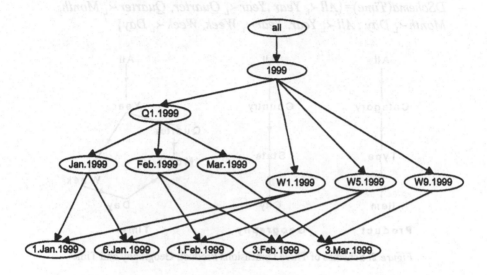

Figure 1. Instance of the Dimension Time with Unbalanced and Hierarchical Sstructure

Example 3.2.1.2. The dimension *Time* has six levels: *Levels(Time)*={*All ,Year, Quarter, Month, Week, Day*}. And:

- dom(All)= {all}, dom(Year)={1999}, dom(Quarter)= {Q1.1999}
- dom(Month)= {Jan.1999,Feb.1999,Mar.1999},
- dom(Week)={W1.1999,W5.1999,W9.1999},
- dom(Day)= {1.Jan.1999,6.Jan.1999,1.Feb.1999,3.Feb.1999,3.Mar.1999}

Definition 3.2.1.3. [*Dimension Schema*]
A schema of a dimension D, denoted by:
DSchema(D)=$\langle$*Levels*(D), $\prec_L$$\rangle$, is a partially ordered set of levels.

where:
- *Levels*(D) is a finite set of dimension levels,
- And $\prec_L$ is an ordered relation over the levels and satisfies the following condition:
- $l_i \prec_L l_j$ if ($\exists dm_t \in dom(l_i)$) *and* ($\exists dm_u \in dom(l_j)$): $dm_t \prec_D dm_u$.

Example 3.2.1.3. Figure 2 is used to describe schemas of three dimensions *Product, Geography*, and *Time*.

- *DSchema(Product)=\{All ≺$_L$ Category, Category ≺$_L$ Type, Type ≺$_L$ Item\}*
- *DSchema(Geography)=\{All ≺$_L$ Country, Country ≺$_L$ State, State ≺$_L$ City\}*
- *DSchema(Time)=\{All ≺$_L$ Year ,Year ≺$_L$ Quarter, Quarter ≺$_L$ Month, Month ≺$_L$ Day , All ≺$_L$ Year, Year ≺$_L$ Week, Week ≺$_L$ Day\}*

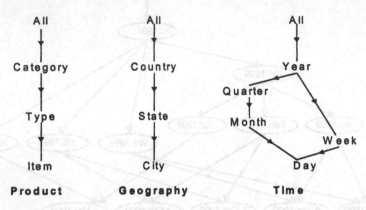

Figure 2. Schemas of Three Dimensions Product, Geography and Time

Definition 3.2.1.4. [*Dimension Hierarchy*] A hierarchy is defined by a *path(All, l$_{leaf}$)* within the schema of a dimension D. The path begins at the *root* level and ends at a leaf level.

Let $H(D) = \{h_1,..,h_m\}, m \in N$ be a set of hierarchies of a dimension D. If *m=1* then the dimension has a single hierarchical structure, otherwise the dimension has multihierarchical structure.

Definition 3.2.1.5. [*Dimension Operators*]

Two dimension operators (*DO*), namely $O^{ancestor}$ and $O^{descendant}$, are defined as follows: $\forall l_c, l_a, l_d \in Levels(D), \forall dm_i \in dom(l_c)$:

$$O^{ancestor}(dm_i,l_a) = \begin{cases} dm_j \in dom(l_a): dm_j \prec_D dm_i & \text{If } (l_a \prec_L l_c) \\ \text{} & \text{Else} \\ undefined \end{cases}$$

$$O^{descendant}(dm_i,l_d) = \begin{cases} \{dm_i \in dom(l_d) \mid dm_i \prec_D dm_i\} & \text{If } (l_c \prec_L l_d) \\ \text{} & \text{Else} \\ undefined \end{cases}$$

Example 3.2.1.5.

- ancestor(Q1.1999,Year,Time)=1999,
- descendant(Q1.1999,Month,Time)= {Jan.1999,Feb.1999,Mar.1999}.

3.2.2. The Concepts of Measures

In this section we introduce the concept of measures, which are the objects of analysis in the context of the multidimensional data model. First, we introduce the notion of measure schema, which is a tuple $MSchema(M) = \langle Fname, O \rangle$. If a measure O is "NONE", then the measure stands for a fact, otherwise it stands for an aggregation.

Definition 3.2.2.1. [*Measure Schema*]
A schema of a measure M is a tuple $MSchema(M) = \langle Fname, O \rangle$,

where:
- *Fname* is a name of a corresponding fact,
- $O \in \Omega \cup \{NONE, COMPOSITE\}$ is an operation type applied to a specific fact [3]. Furthermore:
  $\Omega = \{SUM, COUNT, MAX, MIN\}$ is a set of aggregation functions.
  COMPOSITE is an operation (e.g. average),
  NONE measures are not aggregated. In this case, the measure is the fact.

Definition 3.2.2.2. [*Measure Domain*]
Let $\mathcal{N}$ be a numerical domain where a measure value is defined (e.g. $\mathcal{N}$, Z, $\mathcal{R}$ or a union of these domains). The domain of a measure is a subset of $\mathcal{N}$. We denote this by $dom(M) \subset \mathcal{N}$.

3.2.3. The Concepts of MetaCubes

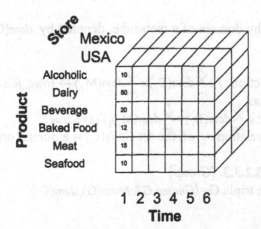

Figure 3. Sales Metacube is Constructed from Three Dimensions: Store, Product and Time and One Fact: Total Sale.

First, a metacube schema is defined by a triple of a metacube name, an x tuple of dimension schemas, and a y tuple of measure schemas. Afterwards, each data cell is an intersection among a set of dimension members and measure data values, each of which belong to one dimension or one measure.

Furthermore, data cells of within a metacube domain are grouped into a set of associated granular groups, each of which expresses a mapping from the domains of x-tuples of dimension levels (independent variables) to y-numerical domains of y-tuples of numeric measures (dependent variables).

Hereafter, a metacube is constructed based on a set of dimensions, consists of a metacube schema, and is associated with a set of groups.

Let a metacube C be constituted from x dimensions $D_1,..,D_x, x \in N$, and y measures $M_1,..,M_y, y \in N$.

Definition 3.2.3.1. [*MetaCube Schema*]

The schema of a metacube is a tuple
$$CSchema(C) = \langle Cname, DSchemas, MSchemas \rangle :$$
where:
- *Cname* is the name of a metacube,
- *DSchemas* =< $DSchema(D_1),.., DSchema(D_x)$ > is an x-tuple of schemas of x dimensions $D_1,..,D_x, x \in N$ with $DSchemas(i) = DSchema(D_i), 1 \leq i \leq x$,
- *MSchemas* =< $MSchema(M_1),.., MSchema(M_y)$ > is a y-tuple of schemas of y measures $M_1,..,M_y, y \in N$ with $MSchemas(j) = MSchema(M_j), 1 \leq j \leq y$.

Definition 3.2.3.2. [*MetaCube Hierarchy Domain*]

The hierarchy domain of a metacube, denoted by $dom(C) = \langle Cells(C), \prec_c \rangle$ is a poset,
where:
- Given a function $f : \underset{i=1}{\overset{x}{\times}} dom(D_i) \times \underset{j=1}{\overset{y}{\times}} dom(M_j) \rightarrow \{true, false\}$, *Cells*(C) is determined as:
- $Cells(C) = \{c \in \underset{i=1}{\overset{x}{\times}} dom(D_i) \times \underset{j=1}{\overset{y}{\times}} dom(M_j) | f(c) = true\}$
- The binary relation $\prec_c$ on the set *Cells*(C) is a *partial order*.

Definition 3.2.3.3. [*Group*]
A group is a triple G= $\langle Gname, GSchema(G), dom(G) \rangle$

where:
- *Gname* is the name of the group,
- $GSchema(G) = \langle GLevels(G), GMSchemas(G) \rangle :$

$GLevels(G) = < l_{D_1},..,l_{D_x} > \in \overset{x}{\underset{i=1}{\bigtimes}} Levels(D_i)$ is an x-tuple of levels of the x dimensions $D_1,..,D_x, x \in N$.

$GMSchemas(G) = < MSchema(M_1),..,MSchema(M_y) >$ is a y-tuple of measure schemas of the y measures $M_1,..,M_y, y \in N$.

- $dom(G) = \{c \in \underset{i=1}{\bigtimes} dom(l_{D_i}) \times \underset{j=1}{\bigtimes} dom(M_j) \in Cells(C)\}$

Let h_i be a number of levels of each dimension D_i ($1 \leq i \leq x$). The total set of groups over a metacube C is defined as:

$Groups(C) = \{G_1,..,G_p\}, p = \prod_{i=1} h_i$ [18].

Definition 3.2.3.4. [*MetaCube Operators*]

Three basic navigational metacube operators (*CO*), namely *jumping*, *rollingUp* and *drillingDown*, which are applied to navigate along a metacube C, corresponding to a dimension D_i, are defined as follows:

Given a current groupby G_c, associated with a level l_c of a dimension D_i, and three other levels $l_j, l_r, l_d \in Levels(D_i)$.

- *Jumping:*

$$jumping(G_c, l_j, D_i) = G_j = < GLevels(G_j), GMSchemas(G_j) >$$

where:

$GMSchemas(G_j) = GMSchemas(G_c)$,

$GLevels(G_j)(i) = l_j$, $GLevels(G_j)(k) = GLevels(G_c)(k), \forall k \neq i$.

- *Rolling Up:*

$\forall dm \in dom(l_c)$, $G_r = jumping(G_c, l_r, D_i)$:

$rollingUp(G_c, dm, l_r, D_i) = G_r^{sub} = < GSchema(G_r^{sub}), dom(G_r^{sub}) >$

where:

$GSchema(G_r^{sub}) = GSchema(G_r)$,

$dom(G_r^{sub}) = \{c_r \in dom(G_r) \mid \exists c \in dom(G_c) : c.dms(i) = dm,$

$c_r.dms(i) = ancestor(dm, l_r, D_i)$, $c_r.dms(j) = c.dms(j), \forall j \neq i\}$

- *Drilling Down:*

$\forall dm \in dom(l_c)$, $G_d = jumping(G_c, l_d, D_i)$:

$drillingDown(G_c, dm, l_d, D_i) = G_d^{sub} = < GSchema(G_d^{sub}), dom(G_d^{sub}) >$

where:

$GSchema(G_d^{sub}) = GSchema(G_d)$,

$dom(G_d^{sub}) = \{c_d \in dom(G_d) \exists c \in dom(G_c) : c.dms(i) = dm,$

$$c_d.dms(i) \in descendant(dm, l_d, D_i), \ c_d.dms(j) = c.dms(j), \forall j \neq i\}$$

Definition 3.2.3.5. [*Metacube*]
A metacube is a tuple C = < *CSchema, D, Groups, CO* >,

where:
- *CSchema* is a metacube schema,
- $D = D_1, ..., D_x, x \in N$ is the set of dimensions,
- *Groups* is a total set of groups of the metacube.
- *CO* is a set of metacube operators.

4. CONCLUSION AND FUTURE WORK

In this paper, we have introduced the conceptual multidimensional data model, which facilitates even sophisticated constructs based on multidimensional data elements, such as dimension elements, measure data values and then cells.

The data model maintains a strong relationship with mathematics by using a set of new mathematical concepts, namely *poset*, to define its multidimensional components, i.e. dimensions, measures, and metacubes.

Based on these concepts, the data model is able to represent and capture natural hierarchical relationships among dimension members. Therefore, dimensions with complex structures, such as unbalanced and multi-hierarchical structures [14], can be modeled in an elegant and consistent way.

Moreover, the data model represents the relationships between dimension elements and measure data values by means of data cells. In consequence, the metacubes, which are basic components in multidimensional data analysis, and their operators are formally introduced.

For future work, we are currently investigating two approaches for implementation: pure object-oriented orientation and object-relational approach.

With the first model, dimensions and metacubes are mapped into an object-oriented database in terms of classes. In the alternative approach, dimensions, measure schema, and metacube schema are grouped into a term of metadata, which will be mapped into object-oriented database in term of classes.

Some useful methods built in those classes are used to give the required Ids within those dimensions. The given *Ids* will be joined to the fact table, which is implemented in the relational database.

REFERENCES

Conference Proceedings

1. Agrawal R., Gupta A., Sarawagi A., Modeling Multidimensional Databases. IBM Research Report, IBM Almaden Research Center, September 1995.
2. Albrecht J., Guenzel H., Lehner W., Set-Derivability of Multidimensiona Aggregates. First International Conference on Data Warehousing and Knowledge Discovery. DaWaK'99, Florence, Italy, August 30 - September 1.
3. Blaschka M., Sapia C., Höfling G., Dinter B., Finding your Way through Multidimensional Data Models. In 9th Intl. DEXA Workshop, Vienna, Austria, August 1998.
4. Buzydlowski J. W., Song II-Y., Hassell L., A Framework for Object-Oriented On-Line Analytic Processing. DOLAP 1998.
5. Cabibbo L., Torlone R., A Logical Approach to Multidimensional Databases. EDBT 1998.
6. Chaudhuri S., Dayal U., An Overview of Data Warehousing and OLAP Technology. SIGMOD Record Volume 26, Number 1, September 1997.
7. Codd E. F., Codd S.B., Salley C. T., Providing OLAP (On-Line Analytical Processing) to user-analysts: An IT mandate. Technical report, 1993.
8. Gray J., Bosworth A., Layman A., Pirahesh H., Data Cube: A Relational Aggregation Operator Generalizing Group-By, Cross-Tabs, and Sub-Totals. Proceedings of ICDE '96, New Orleans, February 1996.
9. Gyssens M., Lakshmanan L.V.S., A Foundation for Multi-Dimensional Databases, Proc.. VLDB'97.
10. Hurtado C., Mendelzon A., Vaisman A., Maintaining Data Cubes under Dimension Updates. Proc. IEEE/ICDE '99.
11. Lehner W., Modeling Large Scale OLAP Scenarios. 6th International Conference on Extending Database Technology (EDBT'98), Valencia, Spain, 23-27, March 1998.
12. Li C., Wang X.S., A Data Model for Supporting On-Line Analytical Processing. CIKM 1996.
13. Mangisengi O., Tjoa A M., Wagner R.R., Multidimensional Modelling Approaches for OLAP. Proceedings of the Ninth International Database Conference "Heterogeneous and Internet Databases" 1999, ISBN 962-937-046-8. Ed. J. Fong, Hong Kong, 1999.
14. Nguyen T.B., Tjoa A M., Wagner R.R., An Object Oriented Multidimensional Data Model for OLAP, in Proc. of First International Conference on Web-Age Information Management (WAIM'00), Shanghai, China, June 2000. Lecture Notes in Computer Science (LNCS), Springer, 2000.
15. Rafanelli M., Ricci F. L., Proposal of a Logical Model for Statistical Database, Proceedings 2nd International. Workshop on SDBM'83, Los Altos, CA, 264-272.
16. Samtani S., Mohania M.K., Kumar V., Kambayashi Y., Recent Advances and Research Problems in Data Warehousing. ER Workshops 1998.

17. Shoshani A., OLAP and Statistical Databases: Similarities and Differences. Tutorials of PODS 1997.

18. Shukla A., Deshpande P., Naughton J. F., Ramasamy K., Storage Estimation for Multidimensional Aggregates in the Presence of Hierarchies. VLDB 1996: 522-531.

19. Trujillo J., Palomar M., An Object Oriented Approach to Multidimensional Database. Conceptual Modeling (OOMD), DOLAP 1998.

20. Vassiliadis P., Modeling Multidimensional Databases, Cubes and Cube Operations, in Proc. 10th Scientific and Statistical Database Management Conference (SSDBM '98), Capri, Italy, June 1998.

21. Wang M., Iyer B., Efficient Roll-Up and Drill-Down Analysis in Relational Database, in 1997 SIGMOD Workshop on Research Issues on Data Mining and Knowledge Discovery, 1997.

Books

22. Connolly T., Begg C., Database System: A Practical Approach to Design, Implementation, and Management. Addison-Wesley Longman, Inc., 1999.

23. Gross J., Yellen J., Graph Theory and its Applications. CRC Press,1999.

24. Kimball R., The Data Warehouse Lifecycle Toolkit. John Wiley & Sons, Inc., 1998.

25. McGuff F., Kador J., Developing Analytical Database Applications. Prentice Hall PTR, 1999.

26. 19 OLAP Council. OLAP AND OLAP Server Definitions. 1997 Available at http://www.olapcouncil.org/research/glossaryly.htm

27. Shoshani A., Wong H.K.T., Statistical and Scientific Database Issues IEEE Transactions on Software Engineering, October 1985, Vol.SD-11, No.10.

28. Thomsen E., OLAP solutions: Building Multidimensional Information Systems. John Wiley& Sons, Inc., 1997.

Chapter 10

Integration of Keyword-Based Source Search and Structure-Based Information Retrieval

Gengo Suzuki, Yuichi Iizuka, Shiro Kasuga

NTT Cyber Space Laboratories
1-1 Hikari-no-oka Yokosuka-Shi Kanagawa, 239-0847 Japan
Email: {gsuzuki, iizuka, kasuga}@dq.isl.ntt.co.jp

Abstract: We propose a new method of accessing heterogeneous information sources such as Web pages and relational databases. In our method, users input only keywords. These keywords are then mapped to appropriate information resources such as values and data items, and then queries to information sources are generated. This approach is a mixture of keyword based web search engines and mediators. The proposed method is described along with a prototypical implementation.

Key words: Accessing heterogeneous information, keyword based search, mediators, information resource dictionary, conformity rate

1.   INTRODUCTION

As a result of the explosive spread of the Internet, we now have access to huge numbers of information sources. These sources include web home pages, relational databases, and image databases. Information retrieval has become the key technology of the Internet age.

Most information search services use keyword- based web search engines such as Yahoo and AltaVista. These engines accept free keywords as input and the outputs are the URLs of Web documents. Another approach, called "mediator" systems, has been developed in the database research area[1][4]. A mediator system can integrate several heterogeneous information sources. Mediators have expressive query language interfaces, such as SQL, but are not so easy to use.

H. Bestougeff et al. (eds.), Heterogeneous Information Exchange and Organizational Hubs, 149–158.

This paper proposes a new method of accessing heterogeneous information sources such as Web pages and relational databases. In our method, the keywords input by users are mapped to appropriate information resources such as values and data items, and then queries to information sources are generated. This method lies between keyword based web search engines and mediators.

Section 2 describes our motivation, and the proposed method is detailed in section 3. Section 4 introduces a prototype implementation. Conclusions are given in section 5.

2.   MOTIVATION

Table 1 compares the two most common tools for information retrieval. Dominating Internet information search is the URL search engine as used by Yahoo or Infoseek. If users input keywords, the tool looks through all indexed web pages and shows lists of relevant URL addresses.

Mediator systems, another search tool, were proposed by database researchers. Mediators are directed towards multi-database research activities. Users can access various information sources such as web pages or databases by posing query language requests. Retrieval results can return in either table form or object form. Retrieval conditions can, of course, be added. URL search engines are better in terms of input ease, while mediators are better at handling different information sources or structural retrieval.

Our proposed method offers both input ease and structural retrieval. It combines the approaches of full-text search and database retrieval.

	URL search engines	Mediators
Input ease	Good (Keyword)	Not good (Query Language)
Information source coverage	Not good (Only web)	Good (Web, Database,etc)
Structural retrieval support	Not good (Only URLs)	Good (Tables and Objects)
Examples	Yahoo, Infoseek	TSIMMIS (Stanford Univ.) Information Manifold (AT&T)

Table 1. Comparison of Existing Technologies

3. OUR METHOD: KEYWORD INPUT

We propose a retrieval method that offers the merits of both web search engines and mediators. The user interface of this method is keyword input.

The method maps keywords to "data" or "metadata" of information sources, as appropriate. It produces candidate queries that suit the known information sources. Candidate queries are ranked by conformity rates. In the case of web search engines, keywords are mapped only to "data"; in the case of mediators, users must determine whether the keywords map to "data" or "metadata". In our method, users need not be concerned as to whether keywords are "data" or "metadata".

For example, if a user enters the keywords "price" and "BMW", the user's requirement may be "to get the price of BMW cars".
The proposed method can determine that "price" is metadata and "BMW" is data.
If the information source is a relational database, the SQL query "select price from car where car_type like '%BMW%'" would be produced.

The features of our method are as follows:

– Automatic mapping from input keyword to database resources (values, columns, tables, etc.)

– Query candidates are ranked by conformity rate.

– Suitable query generation for each information source (SQL etc.)

When using URL search engines, keywords are mapped to only values. When using mediators, keywords are mapped to only columns and there is no conformity concept.

3.1 System Architecture

Figure 1. shows the system architecture of our method. The key to our method is the *Information Resource Dictionary*.

The *resource discovery module* uses the Keyword Index found in the Information Resource Dictionary.
The *format conversion module* uses the Schema Dictionary and the Domain Dictionary to handle expression differences.

The *query translation module* uses the Schema Dictionary and the Term Dictionary.

Differences in management systems such as DBMS, Web pages, or XML files are hidden by wrapper modules.

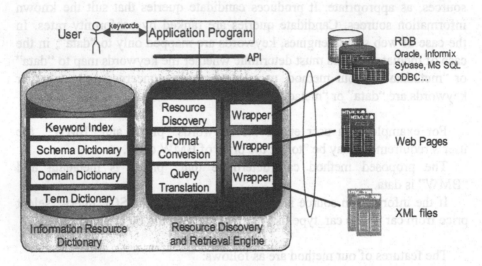

Figure1. System Architecture

3.2   Query Interpretation

The flow of the proposed method is described using the example shown in Figure 2.

The user inputs one or more keywords. In this example, the keywords are *name*, *Tiyota* and *price*.

First, this method decides whether each keyword is a value, a column name, or a table name. We call this process "resource discovery".

In this example, the keyword "name" matches the column "name", "Tiyota" matches a value in the column "Tiyota", while "price" matches the column "price".

As a result of resource discovery, many resource combinations are produced. We call each combination a "candidate".

The user is presented with candidate lists, he selects the relevant candidates, and executes them. A relevant query for each information source is generated, and the query is sent to the information source. The results are returned to the user.

In this example, the result is the record, Vits, Tiyota, 10000.

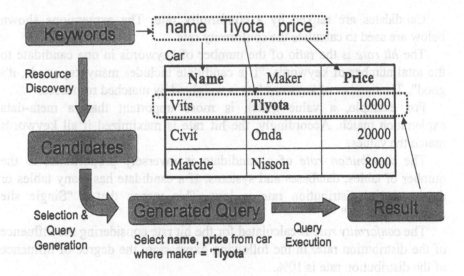

Figure 2. Example of Our Method

3.3   Index Dictionary

To determine keyword location, the index dictionary is used. The structure of the dictionary basically follows the usual inverted index file, but keyword location is described using database resources, not URLs.

Table 2 shows a simplified keyword index dictionary. The key to this table is "keyword". "Type", "Table", and "Column" show keyword location. For example "Tiyota" is one value in the column Maker, which is in the car table of the used-car database. This dictionary can be generated automatically.

Keyword	Type	Database	Table	Column
Tiyota	Value	used-car	car	Maker
Name	data-item	used-car	car	Name
Price	data-item	used-car	car	Price
...	...	...	...	...

Table2. Index Dictionary

3.4   Conformity Rate

Candidates are ranked by a conformity rate. The expressions shown below are used to calculate the conformity rate.

The *hit rate* is the ratio of the number of keywords in one candidate to the total number of keywords. "If a candidate includes many keywords, it's good". The number of keyword hits is weighted by matched resources.

For example, a value match is more important than a meta-data explanation match. Accordingly, the hit rate is maximized if all keywords match the values.

The *distribution rate* of a candidate is inversely proportional to the number of tables, databases and systems. If a candidate has many tables or databases, its distribution rate is low. This means that a "Single site candidate is good"

The *conformity rate* is calculated for the hit rate considering the influence of the distribution rate. In the following expression, the degree of influence of the distribution rate is 10%.

Hit Rate:

$$h = \frac{1}{n} \sum_{hit-keywords} r \qquad (1)$$

n: number of input keywords
r: resource parameter per hit keyword (0 to 1)
   if value match, then r = 1
   if metadata explanation match, then r = 0.15 etc.

– Distribution Rate:

$$d = \frac{6}{T + 2D + 3S} \qquad (2)$$

T: number of tables in one candidate
D: number of databases in one candidate
S: number of systems (database group) in one candidate.

– Conformity Rate:

$$c = h - \frac{1-d}{10} \qquad (3)$$

h: hit rate
d: distribution rate.

3.5   Heterogeneity Resolution

In this system, several heterogeneities among information sources are resolved [2, 3, 5].

– Structural heterogeneity:
If keywords are mapped to data items in several tables or information sources, relationships between tables in schema dictionary are located and added to query candidates.

– Data representation heterogeneity:
We use the concept of "domain", which means data representation of data item such as unit of price [2].
The domain dictionary manages domains of information sources and domains for users. For example, Japanese users want to use "yen" domain for price, while information source price domains are "dollars". The format conversion module can offset such domain differences.

– Naming heterogeneity:
Naming heterogeneities of data items are resolved by a synonym term dictionary.

4.   PROTOTYPE IMPLEMENTATION

We developed a prototype system based on our method.
This prototype can integrate, XML documents, HTML documents and relational databases such as Oracle, and Microsoft SQL Server.
It runs on Windows NT4.0 and IIS4.0. Microsoft SQL Server is used for dictionary management.

Figure 3 shows an input image of the prototype. The top area is for keyword input. Users input keywords in this area, and push the search button; candidates are shown in the bottom area. The conformity rate is shown on the left. Conditions such as "price is less than $40000" can be added using the text area. Candidate details can be shown by selecting a link. The query is executed when the execution button is pushed

Figure 4 shows details of a candidate. This shows that two information sources are related.
Figure 5 is a result table. In this example, BMWs whose prices are less than $40000 are shown.

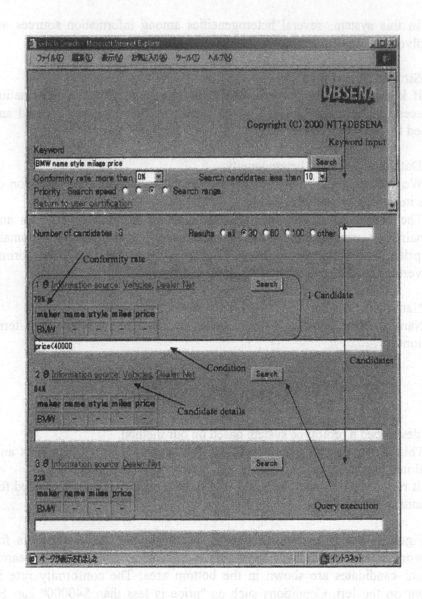

Figure 3. Prototype Image: Input & Candidates

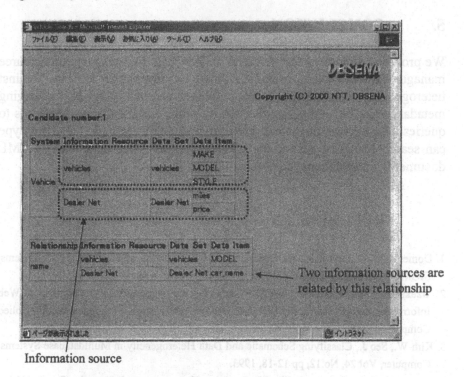

Figure 4. Prototype Image: Candidate Details

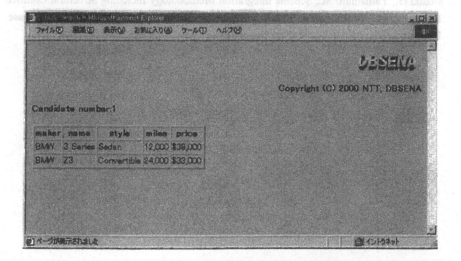

Figure 5. Prototype Image: Retrieval Results

5.   CONCLUSION

We proposed an information retrieval method based on information resource management. Our method enables flexible information retrieval against heterogeneous information sources. We developed ways of managing metadata and data, computing conformity rates, and translating keywords to queries. We have implemented a prototype of this method. This prototype can search and integrate various sources such as XML documents, HTML documents, and relational databases.

REFERENCES

1. Domenig R., Dittrich K.R., An Overview and Classification of Mediated Query Systems, SIGMOD Record vol 28, no 3, 1999.
2. Iizuka Y., Tsunakawa M., Seo S., Ikeda T., An Approach to Integration of Web Information Source Search and Web Information Retrieval, ACM Symposium on Applied Computing, 2000.
3. Kim W., Seo J., Classifying Schematic and Data Heterogeneity in Multidatabase Systems, Computer, Vol.24, No.12, pp 12-18, 1993.
4. Levy A.Y., Rajaraman A., Ordille J.J., Querying Heterogeneous Information Sources Using Source Descriptions, International Conference on Very Large Data Bases(VLDB'96), 1996.
5. Suzuki G., Yamamuro M., Schema Integration Methodology Including Structural Conflict Resolution and Checking Conceptual Similarity, in To-yat Cheung et al. (Eds.), Database Reengineering and Interoperability, Plenum Press, New York, pp 247-260, 1996.

Chapter 11

Knowledge Management for Heterogeneous Information Exchange

Bhavani Thuraisingham[1], Amar Gupta[2], Elisa Bertino[3], Elena Ferrari[3]
[1]*MITRE Corporation, Bedford MA, USA* [2]*Massachusetts Instiutute of Technology, USA*
[3]*University of Milano, Italy*
Email: thura@mitre.org

Abstract: This paper first examines knowledge management concepts. Then it will discuss the issues for heterogeneous information exchange. We first present what heterogeneous information exchange is, which includes exchanging information at all levels including heterogeneous database integration. Then we discuss each aspect of heterogeneous information exchange and the application of knowledge management. Essentially we discuss knowledge management applications for heterogeneous database integration, information management, e-commerce, XML, and the web. We also address security and data quality issues, and discuss ontologies and metadata. Finally we provide directions for knowledge management applications for heterogeneous information exchange.

Key words: Knowledge management, heterogeneous information exchange, heterogeneous databases integration, information management, e-commerce, collaboration, XML, web, security, data quality, ontologies, metadata

1. INTRODUCTION

During the past two decades there has been a lot of work on integrating heterogeneous databases. Organizations are now collaborating with each other and therefore the databases have to interoperate. Integrating heterogeneous databases is still a challenge. The different schemas, models and techniques have to be integrated so that the databases can operate in a seamless fashion.

In the past few years there has also been much interest in knowledge management. Organizations may want to share the knowledge and

159

H. Bestougeff et al. (eds.), Heterogeneous Information Exchange and Organizational Hubs, 159–168.
© 2002 *Kluwer Academic Publishers.*

experiences so that the tasks and activities are more manageable. Knowledge management is being applied to all aspects of organizational management.

This paper examines knowledge management concepts as well as the challenges to integrating heterogeneous databases as well as heterogeneous information exchange. Then it shows how knowledge management can be applied to integrating heterogeneous databases. The applications of knowledge management for e-commerce will also be discussed. Finally we discuss other aspects such as security, data quality, ontologies and metadata for knowledge management and heterogeneous information exchange.

2.   KNOWLEDGE MANAGEMENT

Knowledge management is the process of using knowledge as a resource to manage an organization. It could mean sharing expertise, developing a learning organization, teaching the staff, learning from experiences, as well as collaboration. Essentially knowledge management will include data management and information management. However this is not a view shared by everyone.

Various definitions of knowledge management have been proposed. A good text on knowledge management is that by Davenport [3]. Knowledge management is a discipline invented mainly by business schools. The concepts have been around for a long time. But the word knowledge management was coined as a result of information technology and the web.

In the collection of papers on knowledge management by Morey et. Al. [7], knowledge management is divided into three areas. These are strategies such as building a knowledge company and making the staff knowledge workers; processes such as techniques for knowledge management including developing a method to share documents and tools; and metrics that measure the effectiveness of knowledge management. In the Harvard Business Review on knowledge management there is an excellent collection of articles describing a knowledge creating company, building a learning organization, and teaching people how to learn [5]. Organizational behavior and team dynamics play major roles in knowledge management.

Knowledge management essentially changes the way an organization functions. Instead of competition it promotes collaboration. This means managers have to motivate the employee for sharing ideas and collaborating by giving awards and other incentives. Team spirit is essential for knowledge management. People often get threatened with imparting knowledge as their jobs may be on the line. They are reluctant to share expertise. This type of behavior could vary from culture to culture. It is critical that managers eliminate this kind of behavior not by forcing the issue but by motivating the staff and educating them of all the benefits that can occur to everyone with good knowledge management practices.

Teaching and learning are two important aspects of knowledge management. Both the teacher and the student have to be given incentives. Teacher can benefit by getting thank you notes and write-ups in the company newsletter. Student may be rewarded by certificates, monetary awards and other similar gestures.

Knowledge management also includes areas such as protecting the company's intellectual properties, job sharing, changing jobs within the company, and encouraging change in an organization. Effective knowledge management eliminates dictatorial management style and promotes more collaborative management style. Knowledge management follows a cycle of creating knowledge, sharing the knowledge, integrating the knowledge, evaluating the performance with metrics, and then giving feedback to create more knowledge.

The major question is: what are knowledge management technologies? This is where information technology comes in. Artificial Intelligence researchers have carried out considerable amount of research on knowledge acquisition. They have also developed expert systems. These are also knowledge management technologies. Other knowledge management technologies include collaboration tools, tools for organizing information on the web as well as tools for measuring the effectiveness of the knowledge gained such as collecting various metrics. Knowledge management technologies essentially include data management and information management technologies.

Knowledge management and the web are closely related. While knowledge management practices have existed for many years it is the web that has promoted knowledge management. Remember that knowledge management is essentially building a knowledge organization. No technology is better than the web for sharing information. You can travel around the world in seconds with the web. As a result so much knowledge can be gained by browsing the web.

Many corporations now have Intranets and this is the single most powerful knowledge management tool. Thousands of employees are connected through the web in an organization. Large corporations have sites all over the world and the employees are becoming well connected with one another. Email can be regarded to be one of the early knowledge management tools. Now there are many tools such as search engines and e-commerce tools. With the proliferation of web data management and e-commerce tools knowledge management will become an essential part of the web and e-commerce.

3.   INTEGRATING HETEROGENEOUS DATABASES

The goal of integrating heterogeneous database systems is to provide transparent access, both for users and application programs, for querying and executing transactions (see, for example, [8], and [10]). Note that in a heterogeneous environment, the local database systems may be heterogeneous. There are several technical issues that need to be resolved for the successful interoperation between these diverse database systems. Note that heterogeneity could exist with respect to different data models, schemas, query processing techniques, query languages, transaction management techniques, semantics, integrity, and security.

There are two approaches to interoperability. One is the federated database management approach where a collection of cooperating, autonomous, and possibly heterogeneous component database systems, each belonging to one or more federations, communicates with each other. The other is the client-server approach where the goal is for multiple clients to communicate with multiple servers in a transparent manner.

Federated database systems can be regarded to be a special type of heterogeneous system. As stated by Sheth and Larson [7], a federated database system is a collection of cooperating but autonomous database systems belonging to a federation. That is, the goal is for the database management systems, which belong to a federation to cooperate with one another and yet maintain some degree of autonomy. There are several challenges in developing a federated database system. First of all the schemas have to be integrated to form a federated schema. The database systems have to be autonomous and yet cooperate with each other. Security and maintaining integrity are also major challenges. Many of them are discussed in [7].

In a client-server database management system, the goal is for clients of any vendor to communicate with the servers of any vendor in a transparent manner. Various architectures for client-server communication have been examined and the three-tier approach has become quite popular. Here, the client tier is used for presentation, the server tier for database management and the middle tier for business logic.

Both the client server approach as well as the federated approach are being examined for e-commerce applications. While the client server approach is considered more suitable for business to consumer (B to C) e-commerce, the federated approach is considered to be more suitable for business to business (B to B) e-commerce.

Heterogeneous database integration is an aspect of heterogeneous information exchange. By information exchange we mean not only exchanging data, but also exchanging documents. These documents may be text documents or contain audio, video and images. One needs an organized way to exchange heterogeneous information. XML (eXtensible Markup Language) and related technologies such as SML (Synchronized Markup Language) are showing much promise. For example, XML is fast becoming a common way to represent documents. SMIL is being used for marking up multimedia documents. Such technologies are becoming critical for e-commerce and information management. XML also has applications in integrating heterogeneous databases. One specifies the schemas in XML and this way local systems can develop mappings between the XML schemas and local database schemas.

4.   APPLYING KNOWLEDGE MANAGEMENT FOR INTEGRATING HETEROGENEOUS DATABASE SYSTEMS

The advantage effective knowledge management gives us is the ability to capture the experiences as well as knowledge gained from a specific project or tasks. Integrating heterogeneous databases can be a tedious task. In many cases we may be reinventing the wheel. There could be numerous individuals who have had similar experiences, but we do not know about them. If there is a way to capture the experiences that these individuals have had in terms of integration, then this would save a corporation large amounts of resources. The developers can work on more interesting and challenging problems if they can reuse the experiences.

The experiences may be in the form of gateways and translators that have been built. These could also be in the form of schema integrators as well as repositories and mediators. Repository management techniques may also exist. Much of the effort in integrating databases is on building mediators, brokers, gateways, translators, and integrators. Knowledge management should provide a way to reuse all the experiences.

Now if the experiences are within a corporation, then we can visit the corporate Intranet and learn what has been done before. However if it is outside of a corporation, then we need methods to capture the information. In many cases the organizations are not willing to share this information. Organization A needs to give incentives to organization B if A wants to learn from B's experiences.

Furthermore, we need to develop a repository of experiences and maintain a web page that has pointers to all the efforts. This will be a challenge as who is going to maintain the web page? What if the organizations are not willing to share information? What incentives can we give? What are the benefits from sharing the experiences? Moreover, just maintaining pointers is not sufficient. We need techniques for organizing and cataloging the information. Essentially we need to maintain a digital library of integration experiences.

Such an effort will not only help the organizations with integration, it will also help organizations to carry out e-commerce activities. Many organizations are now collaboratively working together to solve problems and carry out transactions. Integrating data and information is critical for these organizations. Knowledge management will be essentially to carry out successful e-commerce between organizations.

5.   KNOWLEDGE MANAGEMENT FOR E-COMMERCE

In another paper [4] we have discussed knowledge management for collaborative commerce. We summarize some of our ideas in this section. As we stated in the previous section, knowledge management is an important technology for both B to C as well as B to B e-commerce. In B to C e-commerce, typically consumers purchase items from a business. In B to B e-commerce businesses carry out transactions between each other. In both cases, we need effective knowledge management.

First of all, we need a way for organizations to be able to advertise their capabilities and resources without compromising privacy and security. This way, consumers can learn about the capabilities of an organization and make orders and purchases. Also, in B to B transactions, organizations need to collaborate with each other and need incentives for working together. With effective knowledge management, organizations can learn from previous transasctions between them or others, things that have gone wrong, successful business practices and use the information to carry out successful e-commerce transactions.

6.   KNOWLEDGE MANAGEMENT FOR INFORMATION MANAGEMENT

Information Management is a broad area and includes a number of topics such as collaboration, multimedia information processing, training, visualization, information retrieval, data mining, among others. Knowledge management plays a role in each of these areas. We will elaborate on some.

Consider the area of data mining. The goal is to extract patterns and trends often previously unknown from large quantities of data using statistical reasoning and machine learning techniques. Usually many rules are extracted, as a result of data mining, and many of these rules may be meaningless. The goal is to find useful and interesting patterns and trends. One needs to carry out knowledge-directed and knowledge-based data mining. Prior knowledge and real-world knowledge helps a lot in extracting meaningful correlations. Knowledge management helps to organize the prior knowledge and learn from experiences. For example, if we already know of similar cases then we can with confidence state that certain rules are interesting. This area is quite immature and needs a lot of investigation.

Another area where knowledge management can help is collaboration. There is now much interest in collaborative commerce where organizations carry out e-commerce collaboratively. For example, organization A may collaborate with organizations B and C and organization B may collaborate with organization D in order to carry out a transaction say for A. One needs to have knowledge about the organizations and how they operate in order to carry out successful collaborative commerce.

We have given a brief overview of how knowledge management may contribute to information management. As mentioned earlier, knowledge management has many applications in other areas of information management including in training and visualization.

7. KNOWLEDGE MANAGEMENT AND THE WEB

While knowledge management practices have existed for a number of years, it is mainly the web that popularized knowledge management. With the web, corporations can share information within and across organizations. One can reuse the knowledge gained from experts and also use the knowledge from previous experiences. Many organizations now have knowledge management practices and are using them effectively to run the organization.

Technologies such as XML and other knowledge representation schemas can be regarded to be knowledge management support technologies. One needs to effectively capture and represent the knowledge such as documents, presentations, and briefings. XML and related technologies are an excellent way to represent the documents.

We hear a lot about the semantic web and we need knowledge management for effectively managing the semantic web. For example, the semantic web is supposed to completely manage a person's workload including fixing appointments, giving advice as well as suggesting best options [1]. One needs to effectively manage the knowledge and previous experiences in order to successfully manage the semantic web.

Essentially the web is a key tool for effective knowledge management and in turn knowledge management is essential for the successful development of the web. This is a topic that will continue to develop in the next several years.

8.   METADATA AND ONTOLOGIES

Key to effective knowledge management is knowledge representation. We discussed some issues in the previous sections. We examine here some other issues with respect to heterogeneous information exchange.

Metadata is data about the data. For the web environment, metadata not only describes the heterogeneous databases, it also has information about the resources, policies and procedures on the web. Metadata also contains information about the usage patterns. The challenge is to extract the metadata so that one can integrate and exchange information on the web effectively. The next step is to mine the metadata to extract useful patterns and trends often previously unknown.

Ontologies are key to knowledge management. Ontologies are essentially common representations so that various groups can understand what data mean. There have been ontologies for people, vehicle, animals and objects. For heterogeneous information exchange we need to develop ontologies specific to the domain. If we are dealing with biological data, we need to develop ontologies for human genes, medication as well as diseases and then use these ontologies to exchange information.

One often asks the question, what are the differences between, ontologies, and XML?

While XML deals with syntax, ontologies deal with semantics. In the specification of RDF (Resource Description Framework), ontologies play a major role. For more details we refer to the various ontologies and specifications for RDF and XML in www.w3c.org.

9.   SECURITY, INTEGRITY AND DATA QUALITY

In discussing heterogeneous information exchange, we cannot ignore security, integrity and data quality. That is, we need dependable information exchange.

Let us first examine security. We need to ensure that the information is protected at the appropriate levels. For example, consider the federated database architecture. We need consistent policy at the global level. That is, we cannot deny access to a table at the local level and then grant access to the table at the global level. We could in fact be more restrictive at the global level. That is, when we export policies to a federation, we can enforce stricter policies.

With respect to knowledge management, we need to ensure that security is considered at all levels of practices. This will involve security policies within a corporation and for sharing information across corporations. One may need to enforce strict policies for say foreign corporations. This would also involve examining the national policies as well as export and import policies. While we hear a lot about knowledge management, we believe that there is a lot of work to do on incorporating security into knowledge management practices.

Moreover, in large corporations, one builds data warehouses for storing information and knowledge so that effective decisions can be made from experiences and historical data.

Here also we need various policies for secure datawarehouses as they may be developed within an organization or across organizations. The policies differ depending on the organizations whose data is included into the datawarehouse. We have mentioned only a few issues here. A lot more needs to be done.

Other aspects are integrity and data quality. In the web environment, data could come from all kinds of sources. How do we know that the data is accurate? How do we measure the quality of the data? As data gets exchanged between organizations, the quality of the data may change also. We need to build effective tools to maintain the quality of the data. We also need tools to determine the quality of the data. One approach that is being taken is to build annotations to determine data quality [9]. Annotation management system may treat the data quality attributes as first class structures. The attributes may specify the accuracy of the sources of the data, the confidence value, etc. One then needs to develop some sort of algebra to manipulate data quality.

Security and data quality are only recently getting attention for heterogeneous database integration. We have a lot to do for exchanging information on the web. We also need to investigate security for web technologies including XML and related technologies [2]. Data quality issues for technologies such as XML also need to be developed. We also need to pay attention to privacy issues.

10. DIRECTIONS

We have provided a brief introduction to knowledge management and heterogeneous database integration and then discussed the need for applying knowledge management techniques to integrating heterogeneous database. If we can apply previous studies and experiences to our current task, then we could save large amounts of resources. We also briefly mentioned the application of knowledge management for information management, the web, and e-commerce and finally discussed security issues and data quality.

The ideas presented in this paper are just a first step. We need to determine the type of knowledge we need, how to maintain and effectively disseminate it so that organizations can take advantage of what others have done and yet maintain the security, privacy and confidentiality of their information.

REFERENCES

1. Berners Lee T., et al, The Semantic Web, Scientific American, May 2001.
2. Betino E., et al, XML Security Proceedings of the IFIP Database Security Conference, Amsterdam, August 2000.
3. Davenport T., Working Knowledge: How Organizations Manage What They Know, Harvard Business School Press, 1997.
4. Gupta A., et. al. Knowledge Management for Collaborative Commerce, Submitted for publication.
5. Harvard Business School Articles on Knowledge Management, Harvard University, 1996.
6. Morey D., Maybury M., and Thuraisingham B., (Eds), Knowledge Management MIT Press, 2001.
7. Sheth A., and Larson J., Federated Database Systems, ACM Computing Surveys, September 1990.
8. Special Issue on Heterogeneous Database Systems, ACM Computing Surveys, September 1990.
9. Thuraisingham B., and Hughes E., Data Quality: Developments and Directions, Proceedings of the IFIP Integrity and Control Conference, Brussels, November 2001.
10. Wiederhold G., Mediators in the Architecture of Future Information Systems, IEEE Computer, March 1992.

Chapter 12

The Exchange of Data in the Global Market
How to Avoid a Tower of Babel

Anna Moreno

ENEA - Italy - Email: Anna.moreno@casaccia.enea.it

Abstract: To efficiently exchange data among different users and applications, it is necessary to define and use some common standards. This paper emphasizes this problem and discusses the importance of STEP standards in the Life Cycle Assessment (LCA).

Key words: Standards, Life Cycle Assessment (LCA), STEP

1. INTRODUCTION

Nowadays the majority of product data are managed, treated and shared by computer systems. However, over the period of a few years, the development of the information society has brought different computer systems, different programs, different programming languages, different representations of the data and different structures of the data. Every day, more and more organizations around the world have to face the fact that whenever they exchange data about some products with new customers, they have to agree on a mutual format of exchange. Even for text documents the usual question is: do you use Windows, Mac OS, Linux, or yet another program? Unless an agreement is reached organizations run the risk of receiving a huge file in only few seconds without being able to read even a single word.

In the field of LCA (Life Cycle Assessment) agreement on the format of the data is becoming a must. ISO 14048 should take into account the work being done in the engineering field and try to reuse what is reusable in order to develop other data representations. As LCA is a method for assessing the environmental impact of a product through all of its life-cycle stages, it requires a massive use of materials and processes data. Nowadays, all the

H. Bestougeff et al. (eds.), Heterogeneous Information Exchange and Organizational Hubs, 169–180.

data are generated through electronic means by users who hardly ever use a standard. The main objectives should be to achieve accessibility, comparability and quality assurance of data used in LCA of products and to integrate LCA in the design process. The application of new international standards for the computerized representation of product data, such as ISO 10303, ISO 15926 and ISO 13584, will assure that LCA data will be reusable in any other computer system and will have stability and longevity. Only with the extended use of the same standards it is possible to develop the life cycle thinking and to take the environmental aspect into account in the design phase.

The use of standards for the representation of data will bring the same economic benefits to the market for LCA data as any product standardization achieves.

In addition to all of the above, it will be easier to bring under control the application of the principles reached during the Kyoto conference on the environment. In fact the use of the same standards will assure the comparability of the measures related to the life cycle impact of different products coming from different countries.

2.   DATA, INFORMATION AND KNOWLEDGE

The extended use of the Internet has convinced people that it is very easy to exchange any information across the World Wide Web. After an initial enthusiastic introduction, anybody can now imagine that it is very easy to exchange "something" through the Internet but this "something" is not always what we are looking for. One of the main problems is that there is a big difference among "words", "phrases" and "concepts" as well as "data", "information" and "knowledge". We can exchange words and data very easily through the Internet, but it is more difficult to exchange concepts and knowledge.

With natural language, we can distinguish different levels of information such as *words*, *phrases* and *concepts*. For instance the concept "the man is carnivorous" can be expressed by saying "the man can eat the lion"; this phrase is composed by words which, if put in different order, will give a different  phrase expressing a very different concept. In fact, "the lion can eat the man" expresses the concept that the lion is a predator. In short, if the same words are structured in a well-defined order, they will "represent" a concept which is very well known to anybody since the first appearance of humans on the earth. Even when writing was not yet developed, the same concept was "represented" over many centuries by pictures on the walls of caves before appearing as phrases that the evolution of languages has made more and more complex and differentiated.

Nowadays these words can be translated from one language to another, even automatically with an electronic translator, translating the words, the phrase and the concept provided that the "structure" of the phrase remains the same. An example is in the following figure.

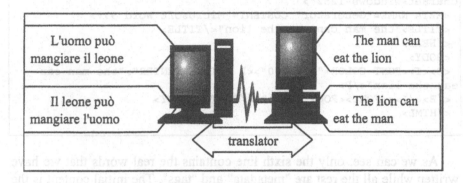

3. THE DEVELOPMENT OF THE INFORMATION SOCIETY

With the onset of the information age, there has emerged another "representation" besides the *picture* and the *human language* This representation is made by the software that is used. As for natural languages, in this case too, different software applications have been developed, and an electronic translator can sometimes translate from one "software language" to another. This means that when using the same words, phrases and concepts, the representation can be changed through the use of certain different software. Such software can misinterpret the symbols, resulting in an incomprehensible sequence of funny characters. Such is the case for a "PDF" document read with a word processor, as in this instance.

```
h >"NZ¯f -N¦vã7 ²†» Sœ 'o:? 7¹Å#¬W©   G
bú˜ŸÖhfWü=šT eÞ6- ŸA¾ê ΓÎ|É˜^ð ¤dâ[˛r[‰#‹
```

This means that the same phrase can be represented by different language programs elaborated by different software and hardware combinations. For instance, the command "save as" hides a translator that can translate the phrase in such a way that other software and hardware combinations can read the content. As an example, if the following phrase:

"the man can eat the lion"

is translated into HTML, then the result is:

```
<HTML>
<HEAD>
<META HTTP-EQUIV="Content-Type" CONTENT="text/html;
charset=windows-1252">
<META NAME="Generator" CONTENT="Microsoft Word 97">
<TITLE>"the man can eat the lion"</TITLE>
</HEAD>
<BODY>
<B><I><FONT COLOR="#ff0000"><P ALIGN="CENTER">"the man can
eat the lion"</P>
</B></I></FONT><FONT SIZE=2></FONT></BODY>
</HTML>
```

As we can see, only the sixth line contains the real words that we have written while all the rest are "metadata" and "tags". The initial content is the information necessary for the data to exist as a file, and to provide general information about the origin of the data itself. This content can be more or less complex, depending on the particular software that has generated it and how the operator wishes to keep track of information (such as author, data of the document, revision number and so on).

The tags in the body, on the other hand, are commands given by the software in order to achieve what the human eye sees without any explanation. In fact, tag <B> represents the bold font, tag <I> represents the italic style, tag <FONT COLOR="#ff0000"> represents the color black, tag <P ALIGN="CENTER"> represents the command "set the phrase in the middle of the line" and finally tag <FONT SIZE=2> represents the size of the font.

Even if all this appears rather complicated, it is in fact a simplification for all the world. HTML is the standard language used world-wide in spite of all the possible software and hardware combinations that exist. Anyone can read an HTML file as long as a browser is installed on the user's computer. The modern word processor, already provides the functionality to have the text translated into an HTML file, in such a way that any text can be transferred over the Internet without loosing its original meaning.

4. THE EXCHANGE OF TECHNICAL DATA AND LIFE CYCLE ASSESSMENT (LCA)

In the technological field, the problem of sharing and exchanging the right information is a much more complex issue. For instance, consider a very simple product such as the crown cap of a beer bottle. If this product has to be described to someone who has never seen it, it would be rather complicated to explain using simple words. If in addition the "shape and the function" of the crown cap, we also wish to describe it in order to allow somebody else to fabricate the product then the problem of exchanging the right information becomes even more complex. Such an exchange may even be impossible if we wish to describe all the processes from the raw material through to the end consumer who removes the crown cap from an actual bottle of beer.

The LCA (Life Cycle Assessment) is the description of the whole process which allows any one to know the environmental impact of the crown cap throughout its entire life cycle. With the use of a computerized system the LCA presents exactly the same situation described within the previous example.

A computer is not an "intelligent" system and is indeed rather "primitive". In fact, any information we put in a computer, whether text, calculus or images, is always stored by a sequence of bits (0 and 1). The representation of this sequence is made visible to people by the use of very well-known symbols, such as words, images, mathematical expressions all of which are related to the product that needs to be described. The more simple and intuitive the representation that is on the computer screen, the more complex the software system that represents it. For example the *word* "clown" is comprehensible to many people because it is used in many languages and is represented in a very simple way by the computer itself, (only few bits are needed to represent the word).

The *image* of a clown, on the other hand, is comprehensible to anyone who has seen a clown in his own life, but has a complex representation in the

computer. To have a good image, several hundreds of Kbits are needed. Furthermore, the word and the image of the clown represent a rather complicated concept that would be very difficult to describe to people, who use very simple language. In this case, it would be impossible to express the emotions associated with the clown whereas, for people who have already experienced a clown, it is very simple to recall those emotions by looking at the image.

5.   THE MEANING OF ENTITIES AND THEIR CONTEXT

In the technical sector, any information has to be elaborated in such a way that the computer can calculate, represent and simulate on the basis of elementary information, in a manner that is very clear and unambiguous. Therefore, it has been necessary to define the meaning of the entity to be described (terminology) and the circumstances in which that entity is valid (context) so as to ensure the possibility of elaborating data related to that entity (data elaboration). Just as with words and phrases, it is necessary to give a very well defined structure to the entity that we mean to describe as well as to the context in which this entity is valid. Otherwise the resulting information can be completely erroneous.

For instance, a screw of 5 millimeters in length and 4 millimeters in diameter is very different from a screw of 4 millimeters in length and 5 millimeters in diameter (structure of the data). If the screw is used for steel then it will be very different from the one used for wood (context). In particular, the threading will be different. The same screw will also be different depending on the aim it is used for (functionality). In fact if it is used for joining two pieces then it will have to be connected with a nut with a very defined profile (interface).

With the fast expansion of the information society into all industrial sectors, there has been a huge development of software applications as well as different computer platforms. This phenomenon has brought the development of different "electronic languages" and, as happened in the tower of Babel, it is now impossible to communicate among different computer systems unless an agreement is reached.

Everybody in his "computerized life" has to have faced the problem of trying to read documents sent by e-mail written with a certain software and being unable to read the contents. Sometimes, even if the system was the same, because of a difference in the version of the software, the computer would "refuse" to read it. One of the first more advanced fields in which the problem of too many languages has been faced was CAD

(Computer Aided Design). Very often in the supply chain there is the problem of design review, whereby sometimes it is necessary to redraw the design because the client wishes some modifications and the software used by the client and the supplier are different.

6. THE STANDARDS FOR THE EXCHANGE AND SHARING OF TECHNICAL DATA

The IGES standard was developed with the aim of transferring design data from one software application to another. That is, IGES serves as the basis for a translator between different software platforms, in the same way as the translator that can translate a phrase from English to Italian and vice versa. In order to have a suitable translation of the design, a great deal of effort was put on defining the terminology, the entities, the concepts, the data, the representation of the data, the elaboration of the data, and so on.

After the development of the IGES standard, designers have understood that in order to have a complete description of the products they need more and more information and this 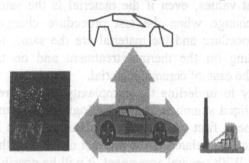 belief has brought the development of STEP (ISO 10303), the acronym originating from "standard for the exchange of product model data".

The product model of STEP can be understood in a simple way. For instance, in the diagram, the product, that is the car, exists and is unique owing to its shape, its material and the process that has been used to build it. If any of these "characteristics" are changed, the car will be different.

This product model can be used at any level of detail, even to describe the so-called "materials". For instance, if we use an aluminum foil for the body of a car, it is "only" an aluminum foil from the perspective of the car while it is quite a specific product for the manufacturer who provided the aluminum foil. In fact, the foil will have a distinct shape (thickness, width, length), a distinct "material" (a melt of different components such as aluminum, of course, but also silicon, iron, manganese, etc.) and it will be produced through a well-defined and controlled process (lamination, hardening, thermal treatment, etc.).

The same will happen for the components that the materials manufacturer uses in order to make aluminum foil. In order to obtain aluminum foil of the appropriate composition and properties, very pure components (source materials) need to be used with well-defined geometry (controlled particle-size), and the components must be fabricated in a well-defined process (milling, pouring in cold water, steering, etc.).

7.   PROPERTY DEFINITION OF MATERIALS

The same problem of the "material concept" must be faced when the property values of the so-called materials are needed for design. The "property" has a meaning only if it is specified along with the composition of the materials used, its shape and the procedure used to evaluate that property. Some properties are rather simple, such as the specific weight of a material. Others depend on so many variables that unless the environmental properties and the test conditions are well defined, the values that come from the test will be useless for property evaluation. Even the specific weight will have no meaning in the absence of gravity, as in the space.

For instance, the property "hardness" can be measured in different ways and each test produces different values, even if the material is the same. Even the measure unit will change when the test procedure changes. Furthermore, even when the procedure and the material are the same, the values may still differ depending on the thermal treatment and on the finishing of the test piece, as in the case of ceramic material.

This example was used only to underline the complexity of the "real world". This complexity has obliged scientists and technologists all around the world to come to an agreement, first of all on the product model to be used, then on the structure of the data related to the product model together with the terminology to be used. With general agreement, it will be possible, (and in some cases is already possible), to exchange and above all to share any data about anything; that is, it will be possible to share the "knowledge", and not only data or information, about any product.

8.   THE GENESIS OF STEP

ISO 10303 is one of the biggest standard undertakings within the activities of ISO. The original committee work for STEP began in 1984 and, by October 2000, ISO 10303 had 6781 pages in the ISO catalogue, and this number continues to grow.

In line with the rest of the information technology revolution, STEP is now the basis for business process change in a similar fashion to HTML being the standard used over the Internet. A good example of an extended use of STEP is "rapid acquisition of manufactured parts" (RAMP), which embodies the use of digital product data to streamline the supply chain. Instead of a physical inventory of "just-in-case" spares to support a complex engineering product such as a ship, the owner of the product is able to rely on a collection of data files, and implement a "just-in-time" order and supply philosophy.

STEP encompasses an extremely broad scope of engineering product data, throughout the product life-cycle of design, manufacture, operation, support and disposal. Materials data has always been an important part of the standard. In particular, Part 45 of STEP, "Materials", became an International Standard in May 1998, and is a STEP Integrated Generic Resource for use across the range of applications of ISO 10303. However, these Integrated Generic Resources are a specific part of the information architecture of the standard and are not suitable for general discussion of domain-specific information requirements. Thus, Part 45 contains concepts that lack specific context and have caused confusion in debates among materials researchers and engineers on the role of STEP.

The materials community gains greater benefit from participation in a different level of debate, namely around the STEP Application Protocols (AP). AP contain information requirements in the language of domain engineers and form the basis of data exchange between end-user application software. At this level, significant initiatives exist, such as the Engineering Analysis Core Model, AP 235 ("Materials information") and AP 223 ("Exchange of design and manufacturing information for cast parts").

9. ISO TC184/SC4 MISSION, STEP AND XML

The mission of ISO TC184/SC4 is to provide implementable specifications that will support the requirements for industrial automation and integration, including product model data that will enable electronic commerce among the virtual, collaborative enterprises of the 21st century. The principal deliverables of this committee, in terms of new standards are:

ISO 10303--Standard for Exchange of Product Model Data
ISO 13584--Parts Library
ISO 15531--Manufacturing Management Data
ISO 15926--Life Cycle Data for Oil & Gas Production Facilities

STEP technology is now maturing and becoming the basis for routine exchange and sharing of engineering product data. However, the Extensible Modelling Language (XML), which is an evolution of HTML, has gained rapidly increasing popularity and appears to outshine ISO 10303. A balanced approach is to recognize STEP and XML as complementary standards. In October 2000, the STEP community delivered a new draft part for the standard: Part 28, "Implementation methods: XML representation of EXPRESS schemas and data".

EXPRESS is the language used to represent the STEP information model for product. Through Part 28, new implementation routes become available. Just as HTML is now used for sending structured text through the Internet, XML can be used for sending a structured EXPRESS file. At the same time, due to the foundational architecture of STEP, what is represented through the combination of XML and EXPRESS can allow the software vendor to meet the requirements for domain engineering. By properly recognising the role of STEP, the materials community will be able to achieve greater integration of materials information into engineering processes within industry.

With XML and STEP it will be possible to exchange any technical information through the Web and, above all, it will be possible in a very simple way to collect all the data related to the environmental impact of any product. LCA will no longer be a problem, and life-oriented design could finally spread into all productive sectors.

10.   CONCLUSION

In order to avoid a Tower of Babel in the technological field, the already developed standards such as HTML, XML, STEP and so on should be used, instead of developing more and more software applications for the representation of information. Even if the standards look rather complicated to non-experts, it is always possible, with good software, to create a user friendly interface with an icon-based language that is simple and understandable to a speaker of any native language. It is therefore very important to start requesting, developing and using software that will allow for an exchange of technical information in the fastest way possible without loosing the integrity of the information we want to transfer. This can be done, as in the case of a word processor with a translator that enables through a simple "save as STEP file" the transfer of an integrated set of information to any other STEP-compliant computer.

Any attempt to simplify could lead to large errors, that may be impossible to find if the system is very complex and consists of many different computer systems produced by different companies and used by different customers. To be sure this is the case for LCA (Life Cycle Assessment) where it is necessary to keep track of the product information throughout the life cycle from cradle to grave. In some situations, the product could be rather simple and short lived as with a pair of shoes (the leather industry has one of the highest of all environmental impacts) or it could be very complex and long-lasting as with a car or ship.

It is easy to imagine the difficulty of exchanging information throughout the supply chain, in order to achieve the total data set needed to establish the environmental impact of such a product, especially if we think of the very short life that software has compared to that of the car or the ship.

The diagram below shows the flow of "information", "materials" and the "interaction with the environment" throughout the life cycle of a product.

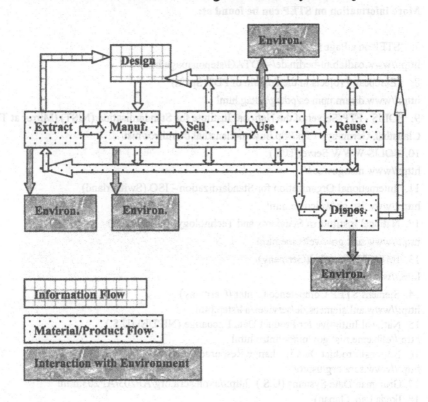

Clearly, if we wish to minimize a product's environmental impact we must take all the relevant information into account from the design. Only if this information is easily accessible throughout the supply chain can life cycle thinking become suitable and "KNOWLEDGE" (not only the information) be transferred without ambiguity.

In conclusion, only the extended use of international open standards that remain stable through time and space will avoid a new Tower of Babel, which could be a very large disaster in a globalized world where communication problems are still far from overcome.

REFERENCES

1. ProSTEP (Germany)   http://www.prostep.de
2. PDESInc(U.S.)   http://www.scra.org/
3. Ce-STEP(Italy)   http://www.polito.it/uninfo/menu.htm
4. GOSET(France)   http://www.goset.ass.fr
5. EuroSTEP(Europe)   http://www.eurostep.se
6. J-STEP(Japan)   http://www.jstep.jipdec.or.jp

More information on STEP can be found at:

7. STEP on a Page (Germany)
http://www.cadlab.tu-berlin.de/~PDTAG/steponapage.html
8. European Projects in the domain of PDT(Spain)
http://www.disam.upm.es/pdtag/pdtag.html
9. SOLIS - FTP-Server of the National Institute for Standardisation (NIST) (Mirror at TU
Clausthal, Germany)   ftp://ftp.imw.tu-clausthal.de/mirror/nist/
10. SOLIS-WWW Server(U.S.)
http://www.nist.gov/sc4/
11. International Organization for Standardization - ISO (Switzerland)
http://www.iso.ch/welcome.html
12. National Institute of Standards and Technology - NIST (U.S.)
http://www.nist.gov/welcome.html
13. IMW TU Clausthal(Germany)
http://www.igd.fhg.de/
14. Siemens STEP Competence Center (Germany)
http://www.anl.siemens.de/services/a4/step.htm
15. National Initiative for Product Data Exchange (NIPDE) (U.S.)
http://elib.cme.nist.gov/nipde/Intro.html
16. National Product Data Exchange Resource Center (USPRO) (U.S.)
http://www.scra.org/uspro/
17. Grumman Data Systems (U.S.)   http://axon.scra.org/AP203/AP203.html
18. Ikeda Lab. (Japan)
http://www.hike.te.chiba-u.ac.jp/ikeda/documentation/STEP.html

Chapter 13

Knowledge Discovery in Heterogeneous Environments

Magdi N. Kamel[1], Marion G. Ceruti[2]
[1]Naval Postgraduate School, [2]Space and Naval Warfare Systems Center, San Diego
Email: mnkamel@nps.navy.mil

Abstract: This chapter addresses the topic of knowledge discovery in heterogeneous environments. It begins with an overview of the knowledge-discovery process. Because of the importance of using clean, consistent data in the knowledge-discovery process, the chapter focuses on the problems of data integration and cleansing by presenting a framework of semantic conflicts identification and an algorithm for their resolution. The chapter then describes the various data-mining tasks that can be performed on the cleansed data, such as association rules, sequential patterns, classification and clustering. It also discusses data-mining models and algorithms, such as those related to neural networks, rule induction, decision trees, K-nearest neighbors, and genetic algorithms. The chapter concludes with a summary.

Key words: Knowledge discovery, semantic conflicts identification, semantic conflicts resolution, data mining, data mining tasks, data mining algorithms

1.   INTRODUCTION

The explosive growth of government, business, and scientific databases has overwhelmed the traditional, manual approaches to data analysis and created a need for a new generation of techniques and tools for intelligent and automated knowledge discovery in data. The field of knowledge discovery is an emerging and rapidly evolving field that draws from other established disciplines such as databases, applied statistics, visualization, artificial intelligence and pattern recognition that specifically focus on fulfilling this need. The goal of knowledge discovery is to develop techniques for identifying novel and potentially useful patterns in large data

181

H. Bestougeff et al. (eds.), Heterogeneous Information Exchange and Organizational Hubs, 181–204.
© 2002 U.S. Government.

sets. These identified patterns typically are used to accomplish the following goals [9]:

- to make predictions about new data,
- to explain existing data
- to summarize existing data from large databases to facilitate decision making, and
- to visualize complex data sets.

Knowledge discovery is as an interactive and iterative process that consists of a number of activities for discovering useful knowledge. The core activity in this process is data mining, which features the application of a wide variety of models and algorithms to discover useful patterns in the data. Whereas most research in knowledge discovery has concentrated on data mining, other activities are as important for the successful application of knowledge discovery. These include data selection, data preparation, data cleaning, and data integration. Additional activities are required to ensure that useful knowledge is derived from the data after data-mining algorithms are applied. One such activity is the proper interpretation of the results of data mining.

Whereas most efforts have been on knowledge discovery in structured databases, there is an increasing interest in the analysis of very large document collections and the extraction of useful knowledge from text. More than 80% of stored information is contained in textual format, which cannot be handled by the existing knowledge discovery and data mining tools. With the popularity of World Wide Web, the vastness of the on-line accessible information has opened up a host of new opportunities. At the same time, it accelerates the need for new tools and technologies for textual-content management and information mining.

2.   THE KNOWLEDGE-DISCOVERY PROCESS

In its simplest form, the process of knowledge discovery is an iteration over three distinct phases: data preparation, data mining, and presentation. The first phase, data preparation, can be further broken down into two steps: 1) data integration and cleansing and 2) data selection and preparation. Data integration is the process of merging data from multiple heterogeneous sources or databases. Data cleansing is a collection of processes that aim at improving the quality of the data. These processes may include the removal of duplicate data, handling missing values, identifying and resolving semantic ambiguities, cleaning dirty sets, etc. Because integration and cleansing issues are common with those found while building a data warehouse, having a data warehouse in place greatly facilitates the knowledge-discovery process. However, data mining does not require a data warehouse to be built, rather select data can be downloaded from operational databases, integrated, cleansed and input to a data-mining processor.

Data selection and preparation involve identifying the data required for mining and eliminating bias in the data. Identifying the data relevant to a given mining operation is a difficult task that requires intimate familiarity with the application-domain data and the mining operation being performed on those data. Identifying the bias in the data is an equally important step, since bias in data can lead to the discovery of erroneous knowledge. Therefore, bias in data should be detected and removed prior to performing any data-mining operations.

Data mining actually occurs in the second phase of the knowledge-discovery process. Integrated and cleansed data generated in the first phase are accessed by the data-mining processor directly or through a middleware.

The third phase of the knowledge-discovery process is the presentation of facts discovered during the data-mining process. The presentation can be done by the data-mining processor or by a separate presentation front-end tool.

In the remainder of this chapter we address data integration and cleansing issues and the data mining process itself.

3. DATA INTEGRATION AND CLEANSING IN HETEROGENEOUS ENVIRONMENTS

As discussed in the previous section, a crucial step for knowledge discovery is the integration and cleansing of data from heterogeneous sources. Integrating data in this environment involves resolving the heterogeneity on three main levels, namely, the platform, data model (sometimes termed "syntactic") and semantic levels. (See, for example [4], [5], [6].) Platform integration addresses the coarsest level of heterogeneity, such as database management system (DBMS) vendors, DBMS transaction processing algorithms, and DBMS query processing [4].

Data integration involves removing inconsistencies that arise from different schemata or data models, different DBMS query languages and versions, different integrity constraints, etc. [4]. Detecting and resolving errors on this level is more complicated than that of the platform level because it involves merging business-process models and policies that may conflict, assuming that they are all known. For example, a data administrator in organization A may require that employees must enter their names, social-security numbers, full addresses, phone numbers, and vehicle license-plate number as "not-null" attributes. In contrast, a data administrator from organization B may require as mandatory only the name, social-security number, phone number, and address but allow the home phone-number and vehicle-license-number attributes to be null. When the organizations merge, the employee databases also would need to merge. Consequently, in the absence of any additional policy guidance, the database administrator must choose whether to relax the not-null constraint for the attributes in the employee database of organization A, or to require the employees of organization B to provide their home phone numbers and vehicle license numbers.

In next two sections we address the issue of identifying and resolving semantic conflicts of data collected from multiple heterogeneous sources.

4.   SEMANTIC CONFLICTS IN HETEROGENEOUS ENVIRONMENTS

The most challenging level at which to integrate data is the semantic level. (See, for example [4], [5], [6].) To be sure that a data set contains all semantically consistent data is a task that is NP complete, due to the combinatorial explosion. That is, as the number, N, of data elements approaches infinity, the number of two-way comparisons rises faster than a polynomial in N. Given that this is the case, one must look toward heuristics to simplify that task into the realm of tractability. (See, for example, [8]).

Semantic heterogeneity is an adverse condition characterized by disagreement about the meaning, interpretation, or intended use of the same or related data [13]. Semantic heterogeneity can be classified broadly into two categories, schema and data.

Schema conflicts include homonyms and synonyms, as well as differences in data types, length, units of measure, and levels of object abstraction. Schema conflicts such, as homonyms and synonyms, can be determined at schema-definition time. Other schema conflicts, including differences in data domains and units of measure, also can be determined at schema-definition time, provided this information is specified as part of the attribute name [6]. In other cases, it can be obtained from data dictionaries.

Data conflicts are best discovered and can be verified only at run time using queries against various database components. Data-fill heterogeneity includes different units of measure, different levels of precision, different data values for the same measurement, and different levels of granularity. The heterogeneity classification process can include three distinct, but related levels of semantic heterogeneity [6]. This classification contributes to a logical progression to simplify and facilitate the development of the algorithm described in Section 5.

Levels of abstraction or granularity pertain to objects and also to the information describing them. For example, levels of object abstraction in semantic heterogeneity pertain to physical or notional entities, such as a fleet of ships (coarse), and individual ships (fine). Categories of semantic heterogeneity can be arranged conveniently according to information granularity. For example, conflicts in the data category arise from differences in data values returned by similar queries against different databases with attributes representing the same objects. Kamel has described a detailed classification of semantic conflicts with examples from Naval Administrative Databases [10].

4.1   Level-One Granularity – Relations

Relations are database-structural components at the most coarse-grained level of information. This level is limited to names and definitions of relations, both in comparison to the names and definitions of other relations as well as in comparison to those of attributes. The resolution of semantic inconsistencies at level one does not require access to the data fill. Relation-attribute homonyms occur when a relation and an attribute have the same name. To avoid ambiguity, all relations and attributes should have unique names, but this is not always the case when merging data sets that originated from different organizations into the same data warehouse.

4.2   Level-Two Granularity – Attributes

The attribute level of granularity includes data-element names, definitions, meanings, data types and lengths. For example, a synonym occurs when the same entity is named differently in different databases, e.g. "vessel" in database A and "ship" in database B. Analysis at level two can resolve semantic conflicts to produce unique attribute names, definitions, data types and lengths for entities in a global, integrated schema. Attributes with different representations in the local schemata that have the same representation in the global schema after analysis at level two can be called "equivalent attributes" [6].

Data-type conflicts occur when equivalent attributes have different data types (e. g., character vs. numeric), particularly when integrating data managed in different Database Management Systems (DBMSs). For example, one DBMS may use an integer type, whereas another may use a numeric type for the same purpose. Similarly, length conflicts occur when equivalent attributes have different lengths. Type conflicts are quite common when dealing with databases designed for different implementations, whereas length and range conflicts are more likely to occur as a result of semantic choices [10]. The risk of synonyms increases if two users adopt vocabularies at different abstraction levels [2].

A homonym occurs when different objects or concepts (e.g. entities and attributes) are assigned the same name in different component databases. The risk of homonyms generally is higher when the vocabulary of terms is small, whereas the risk of synonyms is higher when the vocabulary of terms is rich [2]. In a data warehouse that contains integrated databases, all instances of semantic heterogeneity at level one and most at level two can be discovered by analyzing the results of appropriate queries on the metadata, assuming the metadata are consistent with and correctly represent the database design. Homonym analysis at level two frequently can be performed without consulting the data fill. Detecting synonyms is more difficult because the wording of data definitions can vary whereas the meanings remain identical [6].

4.3   Level-Three Granularity – Data Fill

Level three has the finest granularity and is needed because many semantic conflicts cannot be resolved at the schema level due to incomplete specification of the metadata. Detection of semantic heterogeneity at level three requires access to the data fill to obtain a more precise specification of the domains of attributes that appear to be equivalent at level two in order to determine whether these attributes represent the same or different objects. Semantic conflicts in different domains at this level arise from different units of measure, different levels of precision, and different ranges of allowable values [6].

Conflict resolution at level three requires an understanding of domains, which are the sets of all allowed data-element values for attributes. The resolution of semantic inconsistencies at the data-fill level has been hampered by the complexity of domain issues. Frequently, the schema is not sufficiently explicit to specify the domains. Resolution of semantic inconsistencies at this level can be very difficult. Precise domain definitions are required for the complete resolution of semantic heterogeneity. Strong typing is one way to address this problem, but this can be time consuming and expensive [6].

Given this constraint, the most comprehensive solution at the data-fill level that is theoretically possible can be achieved only by considering data updates and data implementation, which are outside the scope of this chapter. Therefore, we offer a partial solution that depends on assumptions necessitated by the lack of strong typing. One such assumption is that a "select-distinct" query will represent the domain sufficiently for semantic-conflict resolution to occur [6].

5. SEMANTIC-CONFLICT-RESOLUTION ALGORITHMS

Alternatives are available to simplify the semantic-integration task. For example, one can focus on data that are used most often and also resolve conflicts in data that are of known critical operational importance [8]. Other pragmatic approaches include resolving conflicts that are easy to identify with a minimum of expended resources, or focusing on data in specific categories that have been known to exhibit semantic conflicts in data sets previously observed [8].

When the search domain has been restricted sufficiently, some algorithms become tractable to use on small- to moderate-sized data sets. For example, [6] contains a detailed algorithm that is designed to resolve some conflicts on the three levels described in Sections 3 and 4. This algorithm addresses the semantic level by systematically searching for the following kinds of semantic heterogeneity: synonyms, homonyms, conflicts in data lengths, types, and units.

5.1 Sample Data Set Description

The algorithm is explained below in terms of an example from the Global Command and Control System - Maritime, (GCCS-M), which is the result of a comprehensive systems-integration effort that supports the U. S. Navy, the Marine Corps and the Coast Guard. A significant contribution to GCCS-M and its predecessors comes from the Naval Warfare Tactical Database (NWTDB), which is the standard, authoritative data source for all Naval tactical warfare systems [4], [7]. Due to the diverse data sets of NWTDB, the database integration necessary to form NWTDB served as a model for the GCCS-M database integration which includes not only data from NWTDB but other databases required to support a wide variety of maritime Command, Control, Communications, Computers and Intelligence (C^4I) applications with diverse DBMSs. These database-integration efforts provided metadata for case studies in integrating data dictionaries and identifying semantic conflicts [4], [5], [6].

Table 1 presents sample metadata of some NWTDB components. Because the GCCS-M federated database (FDB) resulted from an integration of several different data sources, the GCCS-M data categories are represented explicitly in the NWTDB and also in Table 1. Component databases designated under "DB" represent NWTDB data sources: "GR" – GCCS-M FDB readiness data from GCCS-M ashore; "GT" – GCCS-M FDB track data from GCCS-M ashore; "M" – Modernized Integrated Database (MIDB) from GCCS-M afloat [6].

Table 1 shows an example of a Synonym-Homonym Group (SHG) which is a set of two or more attributes related by synonymy or homonymy or both [4], [5]. SHGs also can be called "semantically heterogeneous groups." The use of SHGs enables a clear focus on the common ground and the diversity among related component databases. The SHG in Table 1 includes both synonyms and homonyms. Other researchers also have used clustering techniques similar to SHGs to identify trends in data. (See, for example, [12]).

Attribute name	Relation name	Data Type	Data Length	DB*	Attribute Definition
HULL	ESS_MESSAGE_D_E	CHAR	6	GR	Hull number.
HULL	TRKID	CHAR	24	GT	Hull number of ship, submarine, squadron number for fixed-wing aircraft.
HULL_NUMBER	IDBUQL	CHAR	15	M	Hull number of a vessel.

DB* = Database; GT = GCCS-M Track Database; GR = GCCS-M Readiness Database; M = Modernized Integrated Database

Table 1. Examples of Synonym-Homonym Group Derived from C⁴I Data Sets in the Naval Warfare Tactical Database [6]

5.2 Algorithm Features

In this section, we summarize an algorithm for identifying and resolving semantic heterogeneity using heuristics. (For a detailed description of the algorithm, see [6].) The objective of the algorithm is to construct a consistent, global, integrated schema for databases A and B that can facilitate data mining and knowledge discovery. Each phase of this algorithm is based on one of the levels of information granularity described above in Section 4. Connection points are also specified for navigation between levels so that transitions between levels can proceed in a logical manner when resolving conflicts. For example, when the inconsistencies are resolved at the relations level, attention then is directed toward the attributes level [6].

This algorithm can be generalized to apply to the schemata of any number of component databases in a data warehouse and is useful in identifying most, if not all, of the SHGs present in the aggregate of the component databases. This approach enables data from operational systems to be cleaned periodically and ported into an integrated data warehouse [8].

The algorithm was designed to identify and resolve a hierarchy of semantic conflicts, some of which can be resolved by data-dictionary comparison and some of which will require an analysis of the data fill and/or specific domain knowledge at schema-definition time. The algorithm features a systematic procedure designed to ensure that the analyst will not omit inadvertently the comparisons between relations, attributes, and data fill of the component databases [8].

The methodology was designed to resolve semantic inconsistencies at each level before progressing to the next lower level. One proceeds to the next level only when finished at the higher one or when information is needed from a lower level to complete the analysis at the higher one. The algorithm is intended to be applied recursively to the metadata until each instance of semantic heterogeneity is resolved. Thus, the algorithm can be applied to the entire metadata in case all SHGs are not identified, although SHG formation prior to algorithm usage facilitates efficiency by ignoring attributes without semantic inconsistencies. The methodology is designed to eliminate from further consideration metadata irrelevant to semantically related groups, such as SHGs [8].

5.3 Example of Algorithm Application

The following application of some of the heuristics in the algorithm illustrates a relatively simple example of the identification and resolution of semantic heterogeneity in the ship-identifier SHG in Table 1.

The algorithm can be applied to all metadata at the relations level to generate the SHGs by conducting pairwise comparisons between all relation names and attribute names in the three databases. (Some minor details of the procedure have been omitted for brevity in this example.)

The following heuristics were extracted from the algorithm. Each heuristic is followed by an observation concerning the result of its application [8].

• Compare the names of the relations in databases GR, GT and M. All relation names are unique.

- Compare names of relations to names of attributes. All three relation names differ from all three attribute names.

- Compare relation descriptions. Whereas examples of relation descriptions are not included in this paper, an analysis of the relation descriptions indicates that the relations were designed for unique purposes. Thus application of this heuristic reveals no semantic inconsistencies at the relations level.

- Continue analysis at the attribute level.

- Compare attribute names in database GR to those in databases GT and M, etc. HULL occurs in two of the three databases.

- Compare attribute definitions. HULL has different definitions in databases GR and GT; thus, they are homonyms.

- Compare meanings of attribute definitions. HULL in database GR has a definition equivalent to HULL_NUMBER in database M.

- Compare data-element types and lengths. The application of this heuristic reveals same data type, but different lengths. Thus, HULL in database GR and HULL_NUMBER are class-two synonyms.

- Continue analysis at the data-fill level.

- Compare domains of data fill for HULL-related attributes in all three databases. The domains for HULL and HULL_NUMBER are the same in databases GR and M, respectively. This domain is a subset of the domain for HULL in database GT.

- Return to the attribute level.

The semantic conflicts are identified using the information obtained at the data-fill level. Therefore, the algorithm returns to the attribute level to resolve the inconsistencies.

- Rename HULL in database schema GR and HULL_NUMBER in database schema M. The new attribute name is "HULL_VESSEL."

- Change the attribute definition in database GR to "*Hull number of a vessel.*"

- Increase the length of the "HULL_VESSEL" attribute in database schema GR from 6 to 15 characters.

Semantic heterogeneity is identified and resolved at the attribute level.

Table 2 shows the results of the algorithm's application in which the semantic heterogeneity in the ship-identifier SHG from Table 1 has been resolved. Table 2 displays the modified metadata in **bold italics**.

Attribute name	Relation name	Data Type	Data Length	DB*	Attribute Definition
HULL_VESSEL	ESS_MESSAGE_D_E	CHAR	15	GR	*Hull number of a vessel.*
HULL	TRKID	CHAR	24	GT	*Hull number of ship or submarine, squadron number for fixed-wing aircraft.*
HULL_VESSEL	IDBUQL	CHAR	15	M	Hull number of a vessel.

DB* = Database; GT = GCCS-M Track Database; GR = GCCS-M Readiness Database;
M = Modernized Integrated Database.

Table 2. Processed Metadata from Table 1 with Semantic Conflicts Resolved [6]

5.4 Limitations of the Methodology

The methodology includes decisions about resolving semantic heterogeneity that are somewhat arbitrary because of the arbitrary nature in which many attribute and relation names and definitions are selected in autonomous, legacy databases. Moreover, the manner in which attributes and data fill are separated in the autonomous databases also is arbitrary.

The methodology depends on the assumption that an analyst can judge whether data entities are the same or different. Sometimes the context is ambiguous, particularly with class-two synonyms if they cannot be resolved at the data-fill level. Analysis at this level is the most difficult because knowledge of data updates and implementations may be required for the resolution of some data-type heterogeneity. For example, if an attribute requires a numerical data type, a format error could result from an update to the attribute if the allowed data-type requirement has been relaxed to the more general character data type.

This methodology covers several properties of relations, attributes and their data fill. Heterogeneity with respect to nullness; differences in levels of security; data updates; and some kinds of data granularity, except at the relations level, were ignored.

The methodology can report character-numerical domain mismatches, but it cannot resolve them without the input of a data analyst or the use of knowledge-based techniques. Similarly, heterogeneity due to different levels of precision can be discovered but not resolved at the data-fill level.

An implicit assumption during the implementation of this algorithm is that no updates or modifications of any aspect of the component databases will be allowed because these changes could interfere with conflict discovery and resolution.

Whereas this section is intended to describe a framework for the systematic resolution of semantic inconsistencies, more work is needed in this area, especially to address conflicts arising from data updates and intended use. Because of the variety and complexity of semantic problems, this methodology is appropriate for detecting and resolving some, but not all semantic inconsistencies.

Finally, the algorithm's performance is expected to degrade in the limit of large data warehouses. This is the reason for restricting the search-domains prior to the application of the algorithm. (See, for example [8].)

Certain costs and tradeoffs are associated with selecting the degree of restriction in the search domain. The more restricted the domain, the more efficient the integration task. However, many data sets will be excluded from consideration. A broader domain will lead to a more comprehensive integration result but the task will be much more complex, resource intensive, and time consuming.

As with any effort, practical consideration must be given to the resources available to perform the data integration and the resolution of semantic heterogeneity. Cost and schedule must be considered, especially when dealing with very large data sets that easily could occupy several database administrators for many months with integration-verification tasks. As in so many other areas, a tradeoff exists between cost, schedule and completeness of a data-integration task. For this reason, it is important to build into the schedule sufficient time for data quality control and integration of heterogeneous data sources.

Artificial intelligence techniques, such as the use of ontologies as aids to semantic integration also have proven useful. (See, for example [3]).

6. DATA MINING TASKS

Data are ready for mining when they have been selected, cleansed, and integrated. A data-mining task needs to be selected before data mining can occur. A data-mining task refers to the type of problem to be solved. In this chapter we discuss the four prominent types of problems to be solved by data mining: association, sequential patterns, classification, and clustering.

6.1 Association Rules

Association rules associate a particular conclusion (e.g., the purchase of Brand X) with a set of conditions (e.g., the purchase of several other brands). An association rule is presented in the form:

CONCLUSION ⇐ CONDITION 1 & CONDITION 2 & ...& CONDITION N

For example:

Beer ⇐ Cigarettes & Frozen Foods

This rule indicates that people who buy cigarettes and frozen meals are likely to buy beer too. Each rule is assigned two measures to indicate the strength of the association for each rule. These measures are called **coverage** (or **support**) and **accuracy** (or **confidence**). **Coverage** is the proportion of records in the data set that have the set of CONDITIONS occurring together. **Accuracy** is the proportion of those records that have the CONDITIONS and CONCLUSIONS. These measures are often represented in the following format:

CONCLUSION ⇐ CONDITIONS (Number of records: Coverage, Accuracy)

For example:

Beer ⇐ Cigarettes & Frozen Foods (2341: 10%. 0.8)

which indicates that 10% of the customers (out of 2341 individuals in the data set) bought cigarettes and frozen foods. Of these 10% (234 individuals), 80% also bought beer.

The aim of the algorithm that discovers associations is to find all association rules with coverage >= minimum coverage and accuracy >= minimum accuracy, where minimum coverage and minimum accuracy are specified by the user.

Discovery of associations is the process of finding answers to questions such as: When people buy brand X do they tend to buy brand Y? If people have high cholesterol do they tend to have high blood pressure?

Discovering associations in data sets is very useful in applications such as brand positioning, advertising, direct marketing, medical diagnosis, and in military battlefield planning.

6.2   Sequential Patterns

In a sequential pattern task, sets of related records collected over time are analyzed to detect frequently occurring chronological patterns. For example sequential patterns can be used to identify the set of purchases that frequently precede the purchase of a microwave oven. Another example could be the discovery of a pattern that 70% of the time when Stock X increased its value by at most 10% over a 5-day trading period and Stock Y increased its value between 10% and 20% during the same period, the value of Stock Z also increased in a subsequent week. Since records occurring at different times need to be related, this approach requires that individual records be tagged with the identity of the entity that they represent.

6.3   Classification

Given a set of records, each comprised of a number of predicting attributes and a goal attribute that classify each record depending on its value, the goal of a classification task is to discover the relationship between the predicting attributes and the goal attribute. The discovered relationship is used to classify new records of unknown classification by predicting the value of the goal attribute. The class description generated by a classification task may be expressed explicitly by a set of rules describing each class or implicitly using a mathematical function which derives the class to which a record belongs to when this record is given as input to this function.

The algorithms and techniques used for class description are commonly called "predictive modeling," since the inputs are used to predict the value of an output. Many classification models have been developed. They include linear regression models, decision-tree models, rule induction, and neural network models. Rule-induction classifiers are examples of explicit classifiers whereas neural-network classifiers are examples of implicit classifiers.

A well-suited application for the classification task is that of credit analysis. A bank or credit card company usually has records about its customers that include characteristics of these customers such as income, age, number of children, number of credit cards, etc. For those customers for which their credit history is known, their records also include an attribute that describes their credit risk (e.g., Good, Medium, or Poor). A predictive model can examine these records and produce an explicit or implicit description of these classes. For example, an implicit model would produce a rule that specifies a "Good" credit risk for those customers who earn more than $40,000, are between the ages of 40 and 50 and have no children.

Classification is used extensively in applications such as credit risk analysis, portfolio selection, health-risk analysis, image and speech recognition, etc. Classification is particularly important for image-identification application, such as those used in military intelligence activities.

6.4 Clustering

Unlike the classification task, the clustering task input records do not contain a goal attribute. No classes are known at the time the clustering model is applied. The goal of the clustering task is to produce a reasonable classification of the set of input records according to some criteria defined by the clustering model. In some respects, the clustering model 'invents' classes by grouping records with similar attribute values into the same class. Similar to classification models, clustering models may produce explicit or implicit descriptions of the resulting segmentation.

Example applications that can use clustering tasks are market segmentation, discovering affinity groups, and defect analysis.

It is important to note that different data-mining tasks can be used in a cooperative fashion. For example, an association task could be used to identify a group of products that are likely to be purchased together or a sequential pattern function can identify a group of customers that are likely to purchase a specific product after purchasing other products. A classification function can then be used to produce a generalized description of products or customers in this class. Similarly a clustering task can be used to classify a set of records according to some criteria. After clustering, classification methods can be applied to discover rules to predict membership in a given class.

7. DATA MINING MODELS AND ALGORITHMS

Whereas data-mining tasks refer to the type of problems to be solved, data-mining models and algorithms are the methods used to solve a particular data-mining task. Several combinations of data-mining tasks and data-mining algorithms are possible. This means that a data-mining task can be accomplished using several data-mining algorithms, and a data-mining algorithm could be used to complete several data-mining tasks.

7.1   Neural Networks

The neural-network approach is based on constructing computers with architectures and processing capabilities that attempt to mimic the architecture and processing of the human brain [11]. A neural network is a large network of simple processing elements (PEs) which process information dynamically in response to external inputs. The processing elements are simplified representation of brain neurons. The basic structure of a neural network consists of three layers: input, intermediate (called the *hidden layer)*, and output. Figure 1 depicts a simple three-layer network.

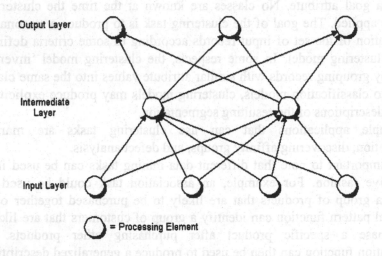

Figure 1. A three-Layer Neural Network Architecture. The Layers of the Network are the Input, Intermediate (Hidden), and Output Layers.

Each processing element corresponds to a predictor variable. It receives inputs, processes the inputs, and generates a single output. Each input corresponds to a decision factor.

For example, for a loan approval application, the predictor variables may be the income level, assets, or age. The output of the network is the solution to the problem. In the loan approval application a solution may be simply a "yes" or "no." A neural network, however, uses numerical values only to represent inputs and outputs.

Each input x_i is assigned a *weight* w_i that describes the relative strength of the input. Weights serve to increase or decrease the effects of the corresponding x_i input value. A summation function multiplies each input value x_i by its weight w_i and sums them together for a weighted sum y. As Figure 2 illustrates, for j processing elements, the formula for n input is:

$$y_j = \sum_j w_{ij} x_i$$

Based on the value of the summation function, a processing element may or may not produce an output. For example, if the sum is larger than a *threshold value* T, the processing element produces an output y. This value may then be input to other nodes for a final response from the network. If the total input is less than T, no output is produced. In more sophisticated models, the output will depend on a more complex activation function.

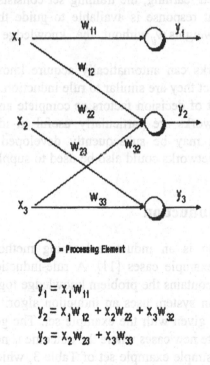

$$y_1 = x_1 w_{11}$$
$$y_2 = x_1 w_{12} + x_2 w_{22} + x_3 w_{32}$$
$$y_3 = x_2 w_{23} + x_3 w_{33}$$

Figure 2. Summation Function for a Number of Neurons.

The knowledge in a neural network is distributed in the form of internode connections and weighted links. These weights must be learned in some way. The learning process can occur in one of two ways: *supervised* and *unsupervised learning*.

In supervised learning, the neural network is repeatedly presented with a set of inputs and a desired output response. The weights are then adjusted until the difference between the actual and desired response is zero. In one variation of this approach, the difference between the actual output and the desired output is used to calculate new adjusted weights.

In another variation, the system simply acknowledges for each input set whether or not the output is correct. The network adjusts weights in an attempt to achieve correct results. One of the simpler supervised learning algorithms uses the following formula to adjust the weights w_i :

$$w_i(new)=w_i(old)+\alpha*d*\frac{x_i}{|x_i|^2}$$

where α is a parameter that determines the rate of learning, and d is the difference between actual and desired outputs.

In unsupervised learning, the training set consists of input stimuli only. No desired output response is available to guide the system. The system must find the weights w_{ij} without the knowledge of a desired output response.

Neural networks can automatically acquire knowledge from historical data. In that respect they are similar to rule induction. They do not, however, need an initial set of decision factors or complete and unambiguous sets of data. Neural networks are particularly useful in identifying patterns and relationships that may be subsequently developed into rules for expert systems. Neural networks could also be used to supplement rules derived by other techniques.

7.2 Rule Induction

Rule induction is an inductive learning method in which rules are generated from example cases [11]. A rule-induction system is given an example set that contains the problem knowledge together with its outcome. The rule-induction system uses an induction algorithm to create rules that match the results given with the example set. The generated rules can then be used to evaluate new cases where the outcome is not known.

Consider the simple example set of Table 3, which is used in approving or disapproving loans for applicants. Application for a loan includes information about the applicant's income, assets, and age. These are the decision factors used to approve or disapprove a loan. The data in this table show several example cases, each with its final decision. From this simple example case, a rule-induction system may infer the following rules:

1. If income is high, approve the loan

2. If income is low, assets are high, approve the loan
3. If income is medium, assets are medium, and age is middle or higher, approve the loan

Name	Annual Income	Assets	Age	Loan Decision
Applicant A	High	None	Young	Yes
Applicant B	Medium	Medium	Middle	Yes
Applicant C	Low	High	Young	Yes
Applicant D	Low	None	Young	No

Table 3. Example Data Set from a Loan Application Database Used for Rule Induction

The heart of any induction systems is the induction algorithm that is used to induce rules from examples. Induction algorithms vary from traditional statistical methods to neural computing models.

Rule induction offers many advantages. Unlike decision trees, rule induction does not force splits at each decision level. Therefore, one can look ahead and perhaps find different, and sometimes better, patterns for classification.

Induction systems, however, suffer from several disadvantages. Unlike decision trees, the rules generated may not cover all possible situations. Also unlike trees, the rules generated may be conflicting, in which case a conflict resolution strategy is needed to choose which rule to follow. Further, they can generate rules that are difficult to understand. They may require a very large set of examples to generate useful rules. In some cases, the examples must be sanitized to remove exception cases. Additionally, the computing power required to perform the induction grows exponentially with the number of decision factors.

7.3 Decision Trees

Decision trees are a graphical representation of a problem domain search space. A decision tree is composed of nodes and branches. Initial and intermediate nodes represent decision attributes, and leaf nodes represent conclusions. A path from the root node to a leaf node leads to a class or value. Figure 3 shows a decision tree for investment decisions based on age, amount of investment, and investment style.

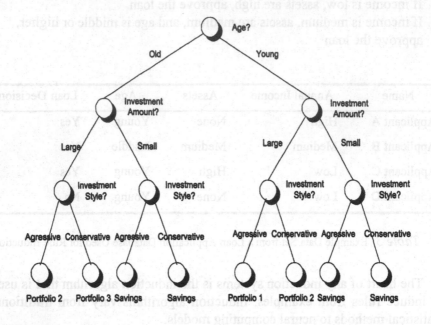

Figure 3. Example of a Decision Tree for the Investment Decisions.

Decision trees are commonly used as predictive models. Decision trees used to predict categorical variables are called *classification trees*, and those used to predict continuous variables are called *regression trees*. Different types of algorithms may be used for building decision trees including Chi-squared Automatic Interaction Detection (CHAID), Classification and Regression Trees (CART), Quest, and C5.0 [1].

A main advantage of decision trees is that they can explain their classification process and the order in which input data are requested, and since they make few passes through the data, they are very efficient. They also handle categorical data very well. Decision trees are however susceptible to growth without bound and thus risk overfitting the data. They need to be controlled through *stopping rules* that limit their growth, for example by specifying a maximum depth or by establishing a lower limit on the number of records in a node. They are not allowed to split the tree below this limit. Another approach to limit a tree's growth is to prune the tree after allowing it to grow to a full size, using either heuristics or through user intervention.

Another disadvantage of decision trees is their inability to look ahead when choosing a split, and therefore may not consider different and sometimes better patterns for classification. Furthermore, most algorithms used in decision trees consider only one predictor variable at a time. This approach limits the number of possible splitting rules to test and makes relationships between predictor variables hard to detect.

7.4 K-Nearest Neighbor

K-nearest neighbor is a classification algorithm that classifies a new object by examining k of the most similar objects or neighbors. It counts the number of objects of each class, and assigns the new object to the same class to which most of its neighbors belong.

The application of the algorithm is as follows. First, the distance between the objects is calculated. Next, a set of already classified objects is selected as the basis for classifying new objects. The size of the neighborhood in which to do the comparisons is then selected, and the weight given to the different neighbors is decided upon (e.g., nearer neighbors are given more weight than farther neighbors). Figure 4 indicates a new object N would be assigned to the class X because the number of X's within the neighborhood outnumber the number of Y's [1].

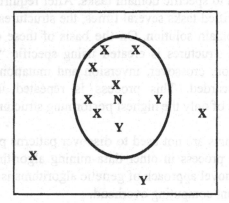

Figure 4. K-Nearest Neighbor. N is a New Object.

The challenge in applying the K-nearest neighbor algorithm is to find a suitable metric for measuring the distance between attributes in the data and then calculate it. Categorical variables present a particular challenge. For example, what is the categorical distance between a hostile submarine and a friendly merchant ship?

K-nearest neighbor is a computationally demanding algorithm as the computational time is proportional to the factorial of the total number of objects. Unlike a neural network or decision tree, the algorithm requires a new calculation to be made for each new object to be classified.

However, K-nearest neighbor models are very easy to understand when there are few predictor variables. They can also accommodate non-standard data types, such as text, as long as an appropriate metric is identified.

7.5   Genetic Algorithms

Genetic algorithms refer to a variety of problem-solving techniques that are based on models of natural adaptation and evolution [11]. They are designed the way populations adapt to and evolve in their environments. Members that adapt well are selected for mating and reproduction. The descendants of these members inherit genetic traits from both their parents. Members of this second generation that also adapt well are selected for mating and reproduction and the evolutionary cycle continues. After several generations, members of the resultant population will have adapted optimally or at least very well to the environment.

Genetic algorithms start with a fixed population of data structures that are candidate solutions to specific domain tasks. After requiring these structures to execute the specified tasks several times, the structures are rated for their effectiveness as domain solution. On the basis of these evaluations, a new generation of data structures is created using specific "genetic operators" such as reproduction, crossover, inversion and mutation. Poor performing structures are discarded. This process is repeated until the resultant population consists of only the highest performing structures.

Genetic algorithms are not used to discover patterns per se, but rather to guide the learning process in other data-mining algorithms such as neural nets. Whereas the novel approach of genetic algorithms is an interesting one, it requires significant computing overhead.

7.6   Other Models and Algorithms

Other models and algorithms have been suggested to mine data. Some represent new approaches, whereas others are simply variations of algorithms that have been published in computer science or statistics journals. These models and algorithms include Multivariate Adaptive Regression Splines (MARS), logistic regression, discriminant analysis, Bayesian networks, and Generalized Additive Models (GAM).

8. CONCLUSION

Knowledge discovery offers great promise in helping organizations to uncover hidden patterns in their data, to explain existing data and make predictions about new data. Although the selection of appropriate data-mining algorithms and models is a vital step in the success of the knowledge-discovery process, it is equally important to collect, cleanse, and integrate the data properly prior to the application of data-mining algorithms.

ACKNOWLEDGEMENTS

The authors thank the Office of Naval Research, the Space and Naval Warfare Systems Center, San Diego Science and Technology Initiative, and the Center for Reconnaissance Research, Naval Postgraduate School for financial support of this work. This chapter is the work of U.S. Government employees and no copyright subsists therein. It is approved for public release with an unlimited distribution.

REFERENCES

1. Introduction to Data Mining and Knowledge Discovery, Two Crows Corporation, 2000.
2. Batini C., Certi S., and Navathe S. B., Conceptual Database Design: An Entity-Relationship Approach, Benjamin/Cummings Publishing Co., 1992.
3. Ceruti M. G., Application of Knowledge-Base Technology for Problem Solving in Information-Systems Integration, Proceedings of the 14th DOD Database Colloquium '97, pp. 215-234, Sep. 1997.
4. Ceruti M. G., and Kamel M. N., Semantic Heterogeneity in Database and Data Dictionary Integration for Command and Control Systems, Proceedings of the DOD Database Colloquium '94, pp. 65–89, Aug. 1994.
5. Ceruti M. G., and Kamel M. N., Heuristics-Based Algorithm for Identifying and Resolving Semantic Heterogeneity in Command and Control Federated Database Systems, Proceedings of IEEE Knowledge and Data Engineering Exchange Workshop, KDEX'98. pp. 17–26, Nov. 1998.
6. Ceruti M. G., and Kamel M. N., Preprocessing and Integration of Data from Multiple Sources for Knowledge Discovery, in a special issue of International Journal on Artificial Intelligence Tools, (IJAIT), vol. 8, no. 2, pp. 152–177, June 1999.
7. Ceruti M. G., Rotter S. D., Timmerman K., and Ross J., Operations Support System (OSS) Integrated Database (IDB) Design and Development: Software Reuse Lessons Learned, Proceedings of the Ninth Annual AFCEA Database Colloquium '92, Aug. 1992.

8. Ceruti M. G., Thuraisingham B. M., and Kamel M. N., Restricting Search Domains to Refine Data Analysis in Semantic-Conflict Identification, Proceedings of the Seventeenth AFCEA Federal Database Colloquium and Exposition '00, pp. 211–218, Sep. 2000.

9. Fayyad U., Piatetsky-Shapiro G., Smyth P., and Uthurusamy R.., Advances in Knowledge Discovery and Data Mining, MIT Press, 1996.

10. Kamel M. N., Identifying and Resolving Semantic Conflicts in Distributed Heterogeneous Databases, Proceedings of the Tenth Annual DOD Database Colloquium '93, AFCEA, San Diego, CA, Aug. 1993.

11. Kamel M. N., Knowledge Acquisition, in Wiley Encyclopedia of Electrical and Electronics Engineering, J. G. Webster, Ed. John Wiley & Sons, vol. 11, pp. 107–122, 1999.

12. Mehrotra M., and Wild C., Multi-viewpoint Clustering Analysis, Proceedings of the 1993 Goddard Conference on Space Applications in Artificial Intelligence, pp. 217–231, May 1993.

13. Sheth A. P., and Larson J. A., Federated Database Systems for Managing Distributed, Heterogeneous and Autonomous Databases, ACM Computing Surveys, vol. 22, no. 3, pp. 183–236, 1990.

Chapter 14

Heterogeneous Information Exchanges in the Construction Industry
Tthe SYDOX/MATCOMP/Xi Prototype

Anne-Françoise Cutting-Decelle[1], Jacques-Emile Dubois[2]
[1]Université d'Evry, 91025 EVRY, France [2]Université Paris-VII, ITODYS, 75005 PARIS, France. Email: afcd@univ-savoie.fr

Abstract: Construction activities have always been basic contributions to our societies. Their wide scope and diversity largely contribute to their heterogeneity, and it must be noticed that even a systemic analysis is not sufficient to handle their complexity with success. The objective of this paper is to present the general System SYDOX, designed to deal with complex data and information, and aimed at facilitating and enhancing communication between construction experts, designers, manufacturers and end-users.

Key words: Construction industry, heterogeneous information exchange, ontology, complex data management, SYDOX

1. INTRODUCTION

Construction activities (CONST) have been and are still basic contributions to our societies. Their wide scope and diversity are such that even a systemic analysis is not sufficient to handle their complexity with success.

A general SYstem SYDOX, designed to deal with Complex Data and Information (DOX) is designed to facilitate and enhance communication between CONST experts, designers, manufacturers and end users. We combine two strategies to generate an optimised representation of the MATCOMP information and its attributes, both for storage (archiving) and intelligent access. The first strategy is a bottom up creation of MATCOMP data and information representation, carried out to produce a practical CONST ontology and thesaurus recognised by all experts in the field. To

H. Bestougeff et al. (eds.), Heterogeneous Information Exchange and Organizational Hubs, 205–222.

downsize our work we have limited the project through the choice of a few CONST components, notably the "window component". In the second strategy, we use a top-down holistic mechanism, using specific scenarios through which we identify the part played by some CONST data at different levels and time locations of the CONST cycle. Since we plan to exchange and use *"external data and information"* we must stress the importance of standardizing materials and product data in our evaluation. Special attention is paid to standardization work undertaken in the domain of the *Industrial Data* (ISO TC 184/SC4 International Committee), leading to the development of the STEP standard (ISO 10303 - Industrial automation systems and integration - Product data representation and exchange) [12], notably the ISO part 10303-45 [13], in the domain of "materials" and P-LIB (ISO 13584 - Parts Library) for the development of libraries of components [11].

In the modern construction context, the volume of inter-relations increases among heterogeneous people and fields Thus, the initial objective of improving communications between this heterogeneous set of people (composed of architects, engineers, clients, quantity surveyors and companies of industrial CONST components) has proved to be a powerful approach to the future of the sector.

2.　INFORMATION NEEDS IN THE CONSTRUCTION SECTOR:
INITIALISATION PHASE

Information systems become increasingly important in industrial companies for acquiring, structuring, and exchanging complex technical data that they have to handle during the production process. The intrinsic complexity of the information becomes yet more complex with the relational structuring of the data. This structure is necessary in order to select among the set of possible solutions the most competitive ones in answer to given specifications. This information system is mainly aimed at SMEs, since they are often exposed to situations for which they have neither the necessary skills nor the tools enabling a permanent follow-up of the normative texts, nor a continuous updating of the technical information needed by the projects they work on.

Fundamentally, this point is common to numerous industrial sectors. The methodology developed in this project must be applicable to different industrial sectors, with possible consequences for the level of complexity of the information system (IS). A selection must be made between the complexity of the degrees of freedom in the choosing of candidate solutions, and the technological level of the sector (i.e. high level technology with low degree of freedom, or low level technology with high degree of freedom).

The construction industry is characterised by:

- *Increasing complexity* with an acceleration of the relations among the partners, alongside a dramatic reduction of the lead-time between the call for tender and the operation of the building;
- *Increasing diversity* of the information and data handled, mainly due to the development of new representation structures (use of standard messages such as EDIFACT messages [3], use of product data *-de facto or de jure-* standards: STEP, P-LIB and IFCs [10]) ;
- *The development of new software tools* capable of dealing with the increasing volume and diversity of information, although, most of the time, without any interoperability between them ;
- *Great heterogeneity of the information handled*, since a normal construction project requires several documents simultaneously. These include drawings, calculation, technical notes, bills of materials and other kinds of technical analysis, as well as documents (legal or not) with information related to the different building components.

The evaluation of the degree of elaboration of an information system starts with the possibility to identify and to interface, when possible, existing document repositories or product databases, regardless of their structuring and location [16].

This project started with an analysis of data circulated during the production process of a building. This analysis has led to:

- *Identification of the information needs* in the building sector, from the results of a previous sociological study, whose aim was to analyse the ways in which professionals in the sector accessed the information;
- *Identification of the professional stakes* of information related to products, materials and components;
- *Usual practices in research of information* related to products and materials : generally combining different information sources resulting from a permanent follow-up, or searching a practical information related to specific points. Needs for specific information necessary to take decisions have also been mentioned;
- *Legal aspects of the information*: these are mandatory requirements, such as codes of practice or other legal documents.

In the second stage, we tried to locate data related to materials and components within the overall building project. We also explored several ways of classifying information and meta-data.

The inventory of the *sources of information* was developed through the research into possible "categorization" by means of a table, comprising:

- *Columns* representing possible "approaches" to the construction, in terms of life-cycle stages and features of the construction. This leads to the following headings: *constitutive elements, general features, achievement, regulation, environment, certification, safety, logistics*;
- *Lines* representing "themes" proposed for the information sources, based on a functional approach of the building. These lines were then developed further to increase the adequacy between the theme of a source and the headings of the columns.

A questionnaire was sent to the different Technical Research Centres that were partners in the project. The responses received mainly deal with materials such as timber and timber-related products, concrete and derived products (focusing on regulations, classifications, nomenclatures) and steel profiles. An in-depth analysis of the responses highlighted several common characteristics:

- The *magnitude and diversity* of information sources; these *information sources were not commonly computerised* (at least at the beginning of the project), the main part of the information is essentially obtained from paper documents (this was the most surprising feature we discovered through this project);
- The *situation described above is evolving* with the growth of computerised catalogues, CD-ROM, use of the Internet/WWW capabilities -- however there is little research of compatibility among them;
- The *heterogeneity of the information sources:* the information lacked consistency and the descriptive parameters and variables did not deal with similar characteristics [4].

3.   THE SYDOX/MATCOMP/XI PROJECT: ANALYSIS PHASE

The analysis was done through three axes:
- *A database approach* structuring a collection of basic information needed by the system ;
- *A query approach* to help formalize interrogations on the databases;
- *A communication approach* to define the whole set of communication procedures needed by the important heterogeneity of the storage/retrieval facilities, the communication protocols and the geographical location of computers.

3.1   Objectives of the Project

SYDOX ("*Système de données complexes*" - complex data management system) defines an information system built on an integrated data based approach. Its use in the domain of construction products and materials (SYDOX/MATCOMP) must provide the user with key-information, including innovative materials and/or use. The project can be viewed at several levels :
- SYDOX : software system providing access to complex documents;
- MATCOMP : applied to the domain of materials and components;
- Xi : application to a specific sector, in this case theconstruction sector.

The aim of the project is to develop an "*information access* point" as an Internet WWW server enabling:

- A *dissemination of basic knowledge* essential for industrial companies which have to organize and process their internal data and data use from clients, sub-contractors, professional associations;
- An *update and dissemination of information* related to the status of new standards and rules (decisions or discussions capable of generating subsequent modifications);
- The *development of relationships between "providers" and "users"* of technologies and tools for complex technical data structuring and processing;
- *Training* by means of interactive examples of the fabrication of products using entity-relationship or object oriented modeling: industrial subsets or components.

In order to develop an interactive information system as quickly as possible while demonstrating the feasibility of the basic concepts of the methodology, we proposed to limit the application field of the prototype to materials and industrial subsets used in the construction sector, focusing on upstream production processes only. We believe that companies in this sector (mainly SMEs) have the most urgent need for data structuring systems.

The objective of the project is to develop both learning (base of information) and know-how (base of methods) allowing companies to structure data related to materials/components according to their needs, in France and in Europe at large. In this project, we analyze the methodology, leading to the elaboration of the information and communication system. This work resulted in the elaboration of a software tool prototype aimed at providing simple information, tailored to the needs of the user and to the kind of question he may ask. This software can also be used as a training tool for the purpose of these new *Information technologies*.

3.2   Structure of the Project and Partnership

The project was organized into four tasks to meet its objectives :

- *Data identification and structuring: state of the art* - review to make an inventory of the existing data bases and information sources. This work relies on the Technical Centres' knowledge of the construction domain ;
- *Identification of methods and tools necessary for data representation and structuring*: to identify, when they exist, the corresponding software tools;
- *Formal specifications of the information system*: the main result of the project, providing a generic way for structuring the information. The end-users of the information system are defined in scenarios that are considered as sets of typical requests corresponding to the type of information generally expected ;
- *Software prototype of the information system*: to build on an interactive software system, running in a client/server mode, with several input levels and several types of users. The prototype enables a short term validation of concepts defined in the project.

The partners of the project are: *CODATA France* doing the scientific co-ordination (The SYDOX software is a development of SYCOGMA SA); the *University of Savoie/ESIGEC/LGCH* ("*Laboratoire Génie Civil et Habitat*"); *Technical Research Centres*: CSTB ("*Centre Scientifique et Technique du Bâtiment*"), CTBA ("*Centre Technique du Bois et de l'Ameublement*"), CTICM ("*Centre Technique Industriel de la Construction Métallique*").

4.   THE SYDOX/MATCOMP/XI INFORMATION SYSTEM: DEVELOPMENT PHASE

In this section, we present the information system developed within the framework of the project, the methodology used for data structuring, and the description of the general structure of the IS and the user interface.

4.1   Methodology Used for Data Structuring

The methodology used to structure the data from the analysis of the responses in the questionnaire is close to the structuring proposed by the *American Concrete Institute Committee 126* "*Database Formats for Concrete Materials Properties*", described in its report [14]. This format defines a framework for cross-referencing cement properties, data and other information. The format seemed generic enough, was powerful, simple and well suited to computerised databases and WWW interfacing, thus suitable to be customised to our needs [5]:

The basic principles for data structuring are such that information related to products and materials is represented using similarly complete sets of data, all of them together constituting the material and product database. This information is represented using the following concepts, separated into abstract data type (ADT) and concrete fact (CF):

- *Object* (ADT): item selected on a "column" - the highest level of the hierarchy;
- *Constituent* (CF): first level detailed information about the object;
- *Meta-segment* (ADT): set of information of the same nature related to a constituent;
- *Segment* (CF): subdivision of the meta-segment into data table, definitions, figures;
- *Meta-element* (ADT): collection of information of the same kind;
- *Element* (CF): item of information.

The SYDOX methodology can deal with a special gateway concept used to connect heterogeneous data sets [6]. In fact, mapping of the description of concrete elements (composition) with related properties (description, regulation, safety measures, standards, etc.) is achieved through a standard ordered hierarchical graph, whose nodes are either primitive or reference properties (environment, etc.) and formal properties (certification, etc.).

For each concept, the number of related sub-concepts has to be kept low enough to keep visible the menu selections (headings) on the screen.

4.2 Structure of the SYDOX/MATCOMP/Xi Information System and Software Prototype

The general structure of the information system prototype corresponds to the schema represented in Figure 1. The following features are considered:
- A *database*: containing the information about products and materials. The organization of the information has been described above ;
- A *data dictionary*: providing, when needed, a correspondence between the concepts handled by the scenarios and the data of the database;
- A *user interface*: a way to access the system, according to the type of user. Users might include those who want to obtain general information on products, architects wishing to find a precise detail about properties of a product, technical engineers wishing to obtain specific information (e.g. thermal behavior) for use in construction or refurbishing.

This user interface includes:

> - *information menus*: headings, as possible choices, resulting from the analysis of the responses in the questionnaire;
> - *some scenarios*: pre-defined "navigation routes" within the information system, that users will have to follow. These "routes" are pre-defined today. The addition of dynamic features to the current software system would decrease their rigidity. The examples mentioned in the prototype were chosen from scenarios in several stages of the life-cycle of the construction; they are a part of a special computer aided interface [8].

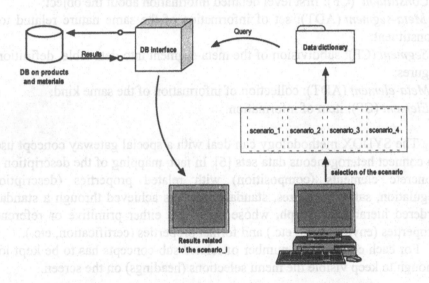

Figure 1. Structure of the SYDOX/MATCOMP/XI Information System

A communication interface has been developed for the Internet. Its corresponding information system is an interactive, hypertext software, accessible through HTML browsers such as Netscape Navigator™ or MS-Internet Explorer™.

To date, most of the developments have focused on applications to specific products, such as a window and floors. This is the case for the following reasons.

Firstly, since the aim of the project is to validate a methodology, it seems better to restrict it to one product and to fully develop all the information related to this product.

Secondly, the validity of the answers provided by the system heavily relies on the amount of information put in the database. Since this information did not previously exist under this format, we also had to build on the contents of the database.

Finally, the end product provides a computer aided interface to help designers or specific users (interested in the environment, comparisons, aesthetics, emerging concepts) - coupled with the technical database oriented to a search of construction industrial components and information to use them.

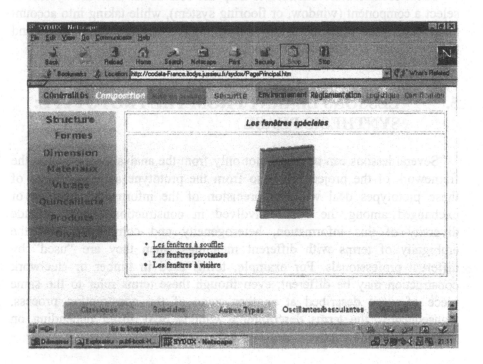

Figure 2. Information Menu for a Scenario or for a Direct Request

Figure 2 shows an example of a screen corresponding to the selection of the following headings (example of a window) :

- upper menu ("object"): *"composition"*: (constitutive elements);
- left menu ("constituent"): *"formes"*: shape;
- lower menu ("meta-segment"): *"spéciales"*: specific;
- right window ("segment", "meta-element" or "element" depending on the structuring of the information): properties, usage, characteristics.

The IS also offers the possibility that once *Composition/Produit* (constitutive elements/product) is selected, then *"fournisseur"* headings (supplier) will obtain a list of products classified according to given properties.

Several scenarios were developed within the framework of the project, dealing mainly with *windows* and *floorings*. For *windows*, scenarios were developed for an architect (new construction and refurbishing); and for a thermal engineer (thermal evaluation of a window). For *floorings*, scenarios were developed for an architect, a contractor and a client.

These scenarios are intended to help the user of the software system to select a component (window, or flooring system), while taking into account restrictions or considerations imposed on the product due to the nature and the specifications of the construction.

5. LESSONS LEARNT FROM THE PROTOTYPE: SYNTHESIS PHASE

Several lessons can be learnt, not only from the analysis done within the framework of the project, but also from the prototype achieved. Most of these prototypes deal with the precision of the information handled or exchanged among the actors involved in construction. These include diversity of this information, heterogeneity and complexity, and the ambiguity of terms with different meanings when they are "used" by different professionals. For example, terms used in timber or steelwork construction may be different, even though these terms refer to the same piece of work described at another stage of the construction process. Consequently, the terms describing a window may differ depending on whether timber or aluminum is used for the framework.

5.1 Ways of Using the Information System

Since the IS may be operated in several ways, the information contained in the answers it generates must be adapted to the type of questions asked. The two main types of interrogations of the IS are direct requests and scenarios:

- *Direct question* (or request for further information) *about a specific technical or regulatory text or else a given product, through a key-word based access.* Most of the time, the answer provided is simple (schema, and/or text), provided that the question is non-ambiguous and well-posed. In such a case, an answer is available from the database, no transformation is needed;

- Direct request for a list of specific information: list of windows of some kind, list of rules applicable to construction on seismic zones, etc.;

- Scenarios: in this approach, the end-user of the IS is identified by specific categories of professionals in the construction sector. In the feasibility study leading to the prototype, the categories selected were an architect (new construction, or refurbishment) and a thermal engineer. Through use of the scenario, the end-user gets only the kind of information suited to the profile he has declared. For example, if a window is to be used for refurbishment and the user has described himself as a thermal engineer, the thermal characteristics of the window will be obtained, rather than rules related to the categories of materials.

5.2   Problems Encountered

Several problems were encountered during this project. Most of them can be split broadly into two categories:
–   problems related to the non-availability of the information required by the end-user,
–   problems related to the rigidity of the scenarios (proposal of only pre-defined "tracks").

One peculiar category of problems was related to the simultaneous management of the different ontologies defined behind the objects or components that were proposed in the menus.

More precisely, the two categories of problems we met have different origins:

- Non-availability of the information required: an example is provided by the case of an end-user, who is not necessarily an expert in thermal behavior, but who is aware of the regulations in this domain. This end-user asks for the value of the GV coefficient (overall thermal loss applicable to housing buildings) of the building within which he lives, on the basis of the thermal conductibility coefficients related to the windows, floors, walls, etc. The evaluation of the GV coefficient is not trivial at all, since it takes into account the inner volume of the building, the total heating loss due to ventilating, and the overall loss coefficient related to the different partition walls. To date, the information system is not able to provide the user with this kind of complex information on the sole basis of data contained in the database;

- Structure and content of the scenarios: as they have been proposed for the prototype, the scenarios are rigid; this means that the user is obliged to follow the pre-defined path proposed by answering a series of very precise questions in order to receive a possible solution to his problem. To date, the scenarios do not handle questions closer to the reality of the problems met by

professionals (or close to the initial design phase of the project). It seems such scenarios are incapable of dealing with the incompleteness and inconsistency of *"human"* reasoning (the *"human"* user of the information system is not always capable of providing the system with precise, complete or perfectly right data). Sometimes also, this information is not yet known, according to the stage of the project to which they refer. Besides, the scenario cannot evolve, e.g. suggest other proposals on the basis of the previous answers (no reasoning embedded).

To date, the existing concept of "scenario", as dealt with in the project does not enable the development of scenarios involving more than one kind of actor simultaneously, such as possible exchanges between the architect of a building and the structural engineer during the detailed design phase, and/or with the thermal technician in charge of the HVAC facilities. All of them will not consider, for example a wall (or a partition-wall) in the same way, nor with the same functionality (separation of spaces, aesthetics, loading -- whence the thickness, or the acoustical behavior of the concrete wall, given its thickness). For these three actors, the wall will not at all appear as the same *"object"*, even though, there is only one physical element once the building is completed.

In other words, the current structure of the scenarios does not enable real interactions among different actors at the same time. The decision making process can only be handled step by step in a continuous consultation.

- Heterogeneity of the information handled: another kind of problem encountered in this project is related to the apparent heterogeneity of the information handled by the information system. This heterogeneity (in content and structure) appears on two levels, which can be described as follows:

▪ *structuring of the information mentioned in the menus*: for example, on the upper menu, eight possibilities are proposed to the user. Each possibility has a specific structure of the data or items of information contained. According to the *"object"* selected in this menu, the *kind* of information retrieved may be of various types, including, plain text (e.g. rules), figures, text and figures, hypertext, etc. The information needed is then generally accessed through the left menu, whose content varies according to the *object* of the upper menu (see Figure 2).

All this means that the information system must be able to simultaneously handle eight different ontologies related to the topics the *objects* refer to. The problem we faced was finding a way of managing the coordination among these ontologies. One ontology was related to codes of practice and regulations applicable to construction in France, another to some *"rules of thumb"* whose knowledge is necessary to install e.g. a window, others to safety rules, commonalties and general features, certification and logistics. Of course, the concepts provided by these ontologies differ and are expressed neither in similar ways nor with similar terminology.

This way of managing several ontologies simultaneously is not a trivial issue, but it has been made more difficult (in this project) by the fact that the granularity of the information expressed in the ontologies is not the same.

For example, some *"rules of thumb"* to be followed in installing a window for refurbishing are sometimes far more detailed than the mere list of the components (as provided by the manufacturer of the window) that the user of the IS will have to buy.

The terms used to describe them may also be different, since a piece may have a completely different name according to the role it will play once placed on the wall or on the roof. However, during the initial phases of a project, the future location of the pieces is not yet defined.

- *means of accessing the information system*: this problem can be seen as a second level of information heterogeneity. It can be defined as follows: when the end-user enters the information system, access is achieved through a first ontology, belonging to the list mentioned in the upper menu. The problem is which access? In other words, must we consider the possibility of managing all the possible accesses, or do we favor a specific kind of access, used, for example, by most users of the IS? Again, this problem is not trivial, particularly given the difference in granularity between the ontologies. In our opinion, we must favor a specific access, through the ontology whose granularity is the smallest, since this option seems to be easier to propose and then define correspondences to other ontologies with less precision.

In terms of *navigation among the ontologies*, it is important to define relevant criteria. At the lowest level, the criteria is defined through the use of the smallest possible items of information, that is through pre-defined key-words, or sentences. Another approach is to use correspondence rules defined on trees homothetic with respect to granularity proportions.

We must, however, pay attention to the fact that some terms have legal meanings whereas some of their homonyms may denote the same concept but they are not really homonymous from a legal point of view.

The last part of this study suggests both a new approach to scenario development and a way to use IS, on the basis of ontology engineering.

6. KNOWLEDGE MANAGEMENT WITHIN SCENARIOS THROUGH ONTOLOGY ENGINEERING:
NEW SEMANTIC APPROACH OF THE CONSTRUCTION INDUSTRY

One of the problems we faced in this project lies in the research of correspondences between concepts ([1], [2]) handled by various professionals of the construction sector. These concepts differ both in their meaning (semantics), and in the "*granularity*" of the item of knowledge to which they refer. They may also vary according to when they occur during the different phases of the construction project life cycle. For example, some temporary parts needed only during the on-site construction, are added, later on, to other structural elements of the building where they become permanent. This is frequently the case in steelwork construction.

This aspect has not been the subject of an in-depth development in this study, since, at the beginning of the project, we faced other (and unexpected) problems, notably the low level of computerized information related to the products and components used in construction. Furthermore, the aim of the project was mainly to demonstrate the *feasibility* of an approach in terms of information related to products and components in construction.

The approach we propose here focuses on the problem of developing correspondences between items of knowledge, of whatever kind, contained within the *information exchanges* in the construction industry.

These correspondences are expressed by means of ontologies. Here, the role of the scenarios is two-fold. On the one hand, they facilitate the *engineering* of the ontologies, thus providing a bottom-up approach to the problem (from the reality to its conceptualization). On the other hand, once defined and integrated into the system, they provide the user of the IS with a *user-friendly* interface, *de facto* perfectly suited to his needs.

Of course, the process of engineering an ontology does not stop at the mere development of a set of informal questions related to the topic of the scenario. In fact, this process ends with the translation of this informal knowledge into formal specifications able to be implemented into the *physical* information system.

For any given ontology, the goal is to agree upon a shared terminology and set of constraints on the objects in the ontology [9]. We must agree on the purpose and ultimate use of our ontologies. We must also provide a mechanism guiding the design of ontologies, as well as providing a framework for evaluating their adequacy. Such a framework allows for a more precise evaluation of different proposals for an ontology, by demonstrating the competency of each proposal with respect to the set of questions that arise from the applications. These justify the existence and properties of the objects with the ontology and also contribute to validating the approaches proposed by the scenarios through cross-referencing of the dual approach: from the applications to the system and vice versa. A more general guideline would be to work within given ontologies but with a program to enrich the ontology by implementing new information in real time and/or to change the ontology graph interactively.

6.1 Ontology Engineering
Ontology Dynamic Reshaping

The process of engineering an ontology starts with *scenarios* describing the applications that the system is to support [9].

Motivating Scenarios: The development of ontologies is motivated by scenarios that arise in the applications. In particular, such scenarios may be presented by construction partners as problems they encounter in their relationships with the other partners. The motivating scenarios often have the form of story problems or examples which are not adequately addressed by existing ontologies. A motivating scenario also provides a set of intuitively possible solutions to the scenario problems. These solutions provide a first idea of the informal intended semantics for the objects and relations that will later be included in the ontology.

To develop a specific CONS/Ontology, three steps are considered:

– definition of a set of informal competency questions ascribed by the system to represent the information/application correspondences;
– production of an initial terminology comprising objects, attributes and their relations;
– conclusion of a definitive refined ontology based on precise and unambiguous terms adopted through interactive processes.

To proceed from the first step to the third, one uses an informal competency questioning leading to a bottom up extraction of knowledge relations.

Informal Competency Questions: Given the motivating scenario, a set of queries arises which connects demands to an underlying ontology. We can consider these queries as requirements in the form of questions that an ontology must be able to answer. These are the informal competency questions, since they are not yet expressed in the formal language of the ontology.

Ideally, the competency questions should be defined in a stratified manner, with higher level questions requiring the solution of lower level questions. The ontology would not be considered well designed if all competency questions took the form of simple lookup queries; there should also be questions that use the solutions to simple queries.

These competency questions do not generate ontological commitments; they are instead useful to evaluate the ontological commitments that have already been made. They evaluate the expressiveness of the ontology required to represent the competency questions and to characterize their solutions.

6.2   From Informal Queries to Formal Specifications

Once informal competency questions have been posed for the proposed creation or extension of a working ontology, the terminology of the ontology must be specified using first-order logic.

An ontology is a formal description [9] [17] of objects, properties of objects and relations among objects. This provides the language that will be used to express the definitions and constraints in the axioms. This language must provide the necessary terminology to restate the informal competency questions.

The first step in specifying the terminology of the ontology is to identify the objects in the domain of discourse. These are represented by constants and variables in the language. Attributes of objects are then defined by unary predicates, and relations among objects, which are defined using n-ary predicates.

The axioms in the ontology specify the definitions of terms in the former and constraints on their interpretation; they are defined as first order sentences using the predicates of the ontology. It is important to understand the significance of using axioms to define the terms and constraints for objects in the ontology. Simply proposing a set of objects alone, or proposing a set of ground terms in first-order logic, does not constitute an ontology. Axioms must be provided to define the semantics, or meanings, of these terms.

It is also important to realize that this is not the implementation of the ontology; it is its specification. The implementation of the ontology has to be translatable into formal representations such as KIF [7], [15] or Z [18].

The process of defining axioms is perhaps the most difficult aspect of producing ontologies. However, this process can be guided by the formal competency questions. As with the informal competency questions, the axioms in the ontology must be necessary and sufficient to express the competency questions and to characterize their solutions. Axioms are essential to handle both questions and their solutions.

Further, any solution to a competency question must be entailed by or consistent with the axioms in the ontology alone. If the proposed axioms are insufficient to represent the formal competency questions and to characterize the solutions to the questions, then additional objects or axioms must be added to the ontology until they are sufficient. This development of axioms for the ontology with respect to the competency questions is therefore an iterative process.

It is important to note that although there may be many different ways to axiomatize an ontology, the formal competency questions alone do not generate these axioms. Once the competency questions have been formally stated, we must define the conditions under which the solutions to the questions are complete. This forms the basis for completeness theorems for elaborating the ontology.

7. CONCLUSION

We have built our ontologies with a bottom up method around structured vocabularies and scenarios, specific to the construction world. At the level of a prototype it appears that the requirements for satisfying topologies, even in limited applications, are very great. Substructures in the construction world are sometimes difficult to assess and, although our SYDOX/CONST strategies are efficient, difficulties occur. Future scenarios should be more numerous, more flexible and accept some fuzzy description. They should also be useful for interactive discussions involving several experts. Although the SYDOX/CONST has satisfactory abilities for answering and dialogue, its generalization implies not only testing new scenarios, but also finding new mechanisms to produce, almost on line, appropriate creation or extension of the ontologies concerned. Future work must also concentrate on navigation problems through ontology graph structures.

Construction is a broadly scattered sector, with regard to both skill and geographical location; it needs a powerful communication medium endowed with language flexibility and translational ability. As it is also a human endeavor dealing with homes and man-made environments, its complexity and diversity will require significant efforts if the numerous data and viewpoints are to be considered in their globality.

ACKNOWLEDGMENTS

The authors wish to thank Karim FRAOUA for his contribution to the SYDOX/CONS project.

REFERENCES

1. Bestougeff H., Salzano G., Construction et Génération d'Ontologies pour Fédérer des Bases de Données Relationnelles, ISIS - UMLV, Rapport n° 99- 19 – Université de Marne la Vallée, 1999.
2. Bestougeff H., Salzano G., Recherche de Correspondances en Vue de la Fédération de Bases de Données Relationnelles, ISIS - UMLV, Rapport n° 98- 15 – Université de Marne la Vallée, 1999.
3. BSR Rules, Guidelines and Methodology, ISO CD 16668, 1999.
4. Cutting-Decelle A.F., SYDOX/MATCOMP/Xi : Rapport Final en Collaboration avec les Partenaires du Projet SYDOX, Ministère de l'Industrie DGSI / SERICS, Juin 1999.
5. Dubois A.M., Fies B., Lanvin J.D., Bonfils P., Chabrolin B., Dubois J.E., Messabih A., Cutting-Decelle A.F., Mommessin M., Hamchaoui M., SYDOX/MATCOMP/Xi, Identification et Structuration des Données, Rap.1.1, 1998.
6. Dubois J.E., Fraoua K., Mapping a Description of Objects and their Related Properties with an Ordered Hierarchical Graph, CODATA International Conference, New Delhi, November 1998.
7. Genesereth M., Fikes R., Knowledge Interchange Format (Version 3.0) - Reference Manual, Computer Science Dept., Stanford University, Stanford, CA, 1992.
8. Genthon S., Resident E., Aide à la Conception de Bâtiments: Produits et Composants Utilisables, Identification de Scenarios de Conception et Traduction en Termes d'Information sur les Gammes de Produits et Composants, TFE, ESIGEC, April 1998.
9. Gruninger M., Fox M.S., The Logic of Enterprise Modeling, in : Modeling and Methodologies for Enterprise Integration, Bernus P., and Nemes L., (Eds), Chapman & Hall, 1995.
10. http://www.iai.com
11. Industrial Automation Systems and Integration - Parts Library, ISO IS 13584-1, Part 1: Overview and Fundamental Principles
12. Industrial Automation Systems and Integration - Product Data Representation and Exchange, ISO IS 10303-1, Part 1: Overview and Fundamental Principles, 1994.
13. Industrial Automation Systems and Integration - Product Data Representation and Exchange, ISO IS 10303-45, Part 45: Overview and Fundamental Principles, 2000.
14. Kaetzel L.J., Galler M.Z., Proposed Format for Data on Cements in a Material Properties Database, NISTIR 6034, June 1997.
15. Knowledge Interchange Format, Part 1 : KIF-Core, ISO/JTC1/SC32/WG2, WD, 1999.
16. Mommessin M., Cutting-Decelle A.F., Dubois A.M., Dubois J.E., SYDOX/MATCOMP/XI : An Information System Adapted to the Needs of Construction Actors, Vancouver, Juin 1999.
17. Uschold M., Building Ontologies : Towards a Unified Methodology, AIAI, TR 197, 1996.
18. Z notation, Final CD 13568-2, ISO JTC1/SC22/WG19, 1999.

Chapter 15

Databases and Design
Discovering New Ideas in Old Facts

Shuichi Iwata
RACE, The University of Tokyo.
4-6-1 Komaba, Meguro-ku, Tokyo, Japan
Email: iwata@race.u-tokyo.ac.jp

Abstract: Discovering new ideas in old facts often implies extracting the knowledge
associated with facts and with organized previous experience. The history of
scientific and technological progress highlights different mechanisms such as
copying and assembling which, over time can be done ever faster and, in
greater detail and complexity. Transferring information from databases to the
management of design processes and plans is a way of identifying the
knowledge features and their potential abilities. Discoveries often result from
knowledge and data previously used in similar or related examples. The search
for improvement with a copying mechanism using information technology
potential can generate original views of a projected application, provided the
associated learning method is open and not application bound. The essential
mechanisms of evolving progress are considered with respect material design
examples, underlining the need to cope with growing complexity and
emerging knowledge.

Key words: Knowledge discovery, discovery process process, copying mechanism,
materials design, structure map, STEP/CALS

1.   INTRODUCTION

"Bene latuit, bene vixit" is an old Latin saying which suggests the role of
data in society. From data we create systems, that in turn make materials,
(chips and other components), which then become products, which change
the world. Good data can be copied and transferred easily from one to
another due to their own universal feature and their added value, until finally
the data become useful to many people. This is generally a condition for the

H. Bestougeff et al. (eds.), Heterogeneous Information Exchange and Organizational Hubs, 223–240.
© 2002 *Kluwer Academic Publishers.*

world to change rightly, but there are many exceptions and new possibilities are also emerging.

The cutting edge of science and technology is to train people to present things that are novel and different, comprehensive and universal. Through evolutionary refinement, this approach ultimately generates a set of complex networks of original data and models. Many attribute such novelties to intuitions of genius, yet this is rarely the case. In fact, these novelties are usually the product of copying, imitating and modifying former models, in a process of trial and error; thus, small modifications can lead sometimes to successful results and sometimes to mistakes. Learning starts with copying, and original discoveries come later. In this paper I will focus on the changes that occur in the preparatory phase preceding discovery, changes that become a big and new wave of "Bene latuit, bene vixit" in our current Information Technology (IT) era. I leave the history of discovered results to another occasion.

2.   CHANGES EVOKED THROUGH COPYING

Copying has historically evoked various phase changes and the spiritual effects of which were critically reviewed by W. Benjamin [2]. Original paintings that were, at one time, privately owned by limited persons, have since been transferred to museums for open viewing. Icons of Jews, Buddha, Kannon and so on have rendered certain grounds sacred for each. The mass production of bibles was made possible by Johannes Gutenberg, a trained goldsmith, who invented moveable characters. This mass production paradigm contributed at first to mission work and later to effective propagation of information. Jikjisimgyong of Koryo is another historical example of moveable type printing for Buddhist texts in Asia.

Through the ages, copying has continued to make marvelous advances on image and sound technology, from lithographs and etching to phonographs, photographs and films, to recent digital technology. Media of information have evolved from clay plates, to papyrus and sheepskin, to paper and now to silicon chips and CD-ROM disks.

Memex, written by Vannevar Bush early in the 1930s, is a device in which an individual copies all his/her books, records, and communications; today we have the predicted ability to navigate the enormous data through a handy hardware connected to computers by network.

Even the sense of touch is copied into VR (Virtual Reality) machines and their peripheral extensions.

Tasting and smelling have been also dealt with although indirectly in cosmetic and food industries. Even the "sixth sense" has been of interest this century in such contexts as brain science, artificial intelligence, tacit knowledge and the arts.

Using information technology, we can now copy data and logic easily. Knowledge, if explicitly described, can be shared by everyone. By taking advantage of the above potentialities, people obtain new options for going to church without making a pilgrimage, to museums, theaters, or watching TV rather than visiting actual spots, and enjoying virtual adventures in amusement parks or with a liquid crystal display device.

What may happen to Science and Technology in this kind of artifactual environment? The topic of my paper is to describe different approaches to materials, energy systems and other related issues from the viewpoint of copying.

3. MAKING A COPY OF MATERIALS WORLD IN A COMPUTER NETWORK FOR MATERIALS DESIGN

Making a copy of materials world aims at establishing an information environment in which to design materials with a higher degree of freedom, so as to meet various requirements. The first straw man we made is shown in Fig.1-a.

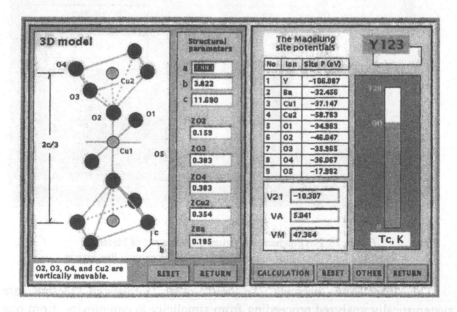

Figure 1a. Environment for Virtual Experiments of Materials Design Windows forVirtual Atomistic Manipulations.

It is a copy of essential features of high Tc superconducting materials; namely, structural units for atomistic manipulations by MOUSE models. It helps to calculate essential parameters correlating structural units manipulated and properties of interests.

To build this window, much data was compiled to derive a correlation between the Mardelung site potential and the critical temperature Tc. Data extraction of high quality was also a key in getting an insight on complex materials at that time.

Materials experts expect each material to provide a set of functions in a system where the material is used. In their minds they have vivid copies of the materials world through repetition of making materials. Figure1-b is a window to trace processing procedures where the available data is evaluated, classified, and browsed.

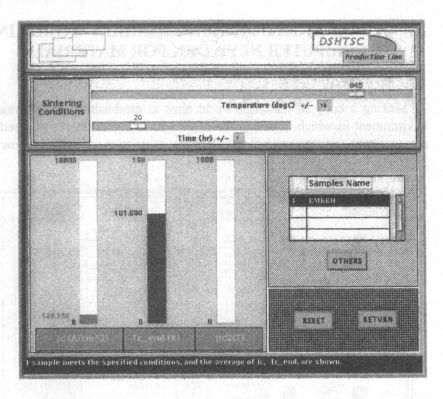

Figure 1b. Environment for Virtual Experiments of Materials
Windows for Virtual Production Line to Trace Processing Procedures.

The correlation between Tc and other influenced factors are systematically analyzed proceeding from simplicity to complexity, from one dimension to three dimensions and from macro-level to micro-level. Suitable models for further understanding of materials are also developed based on the available information and the new data produced.

Traces of experts thinking can be abstracted as a network. Static snapshots of these networks were linked and implemented as a production system over the last three decades. However, such approaches have not helped materials design, except in well articulated cases for optimization. To get rid of the ad hoc features of production systems, systematization of models has been attempted independently in the last two decades due to marvelous computer developments.

Basic relations between structures and properties for materials design (namely, electronic, atomistic, mesoscopic and macroscopic aspects of materials) have been in a process of integration by different groups, namely, multi-scale modeling, multi-principle modeling, seamless integration of models and virtual experiments/laboratories.

However, in reality, it is nearly impossible to cover the whole domain of materials with these approaches, so that we need meta approaches in order to find a suitable solution for each problem. Among the many factors that determine properties of materials, structure plays a key role on a physical basis, not only due to its visibility but also to its continuity.

Geometric manipulations of structures, more precisely on sets organized in structural hierarchies, such as move, add, subtract, replace, deform, twist, rearrange will also stimulate thought.

The example in Figure 1-a,b is a copy showing how people will think, getting an insight by a "do it yourself" approach.

The next step concerns attitudes consisting of "thinking together" and "thinking differently". As a consequence of large efforts to get better explanation on materials, materials information becomes huge and complex with many layers of descriptions, depending on structures and compilation levels from raw data to design data. Therefore, we have different possibilities to take on challenges to explore materials as shown in Figure 2.

In particular, much data on structure of crystalline compounds are now organized into a number of crystallographic databases, providing a unique opportunity to investigate the structural primitives from a global perspective.

What is important now is what we can do with a wealth of large databases, for instance, data mining for knowledge discovery. To display, access, and extract general principles from this enormous volume of information, a graphical approach such as a structure map is essential. It is the intrinsic role of a structure map to bridge processing methods and properties. It can also be thought of as a convenient road map for navigation of materials design around databases and models.

Therefore, based on the above case studies, identification of basic tools and implementation of their parts have been tried, not only to prepare for freedom of enjoying calculation, but also to form an "embryo" of a set of tools with interoperability and adaptability to other huge resources.

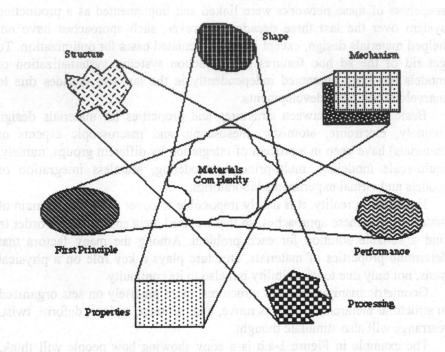

Figure 2. Strategic Challenges to Extract Values from Materials.

As an extension of this approach two dimensional figures applying principles on such complex systems as genes, proteins, nuclear fuels and materials, nuclear reactors, environmental data, factual databases, bibliographic databases, patent databases and landscapes are under compilation for creating sets of maps guiding discoveries of design solutions and/or acquiring insights into complex phenomena. Structure maps, creep mechanism maps, fish bone charts, decision trees and so on, are exemples of such features, and a focal point of this research is to establish practical procedures for creating such maps through data mining and knowledge discovery. Such maps are positioned in a set of decision making nodes and branches, guiding users to better solutions along each context. In addition intuitive maps are now emerging by taking advantage of databases and inverse problem solving.

Surveys of factors governing crystal structures have been carried out through databases, first principles and molecular dynamics calculation.

Figure 3 presents an example of structural primitives extraction for materials design, where a set of theoretical structure maps have been obtained using a tight binding approach based on a new classification approach of crystal structures – atomic environment types (AET). The structural trends for all AB compounds produced in calculated maps agree with corresponding semi-empirical structure maps. A detailed investigation on the structural properties of typical AB intermetallic compounds has been carried out by the first principle approach (LMTO), which provides a microscopic explanation for the structural regularities, and shows the key factors governing the structure of materials.

These factors include, within the framework of LDA, the competition of band energy to the remaining terms. In the semi-empirical TBA model, the electronic factor (the difference of atomic energy level and valence electron number) and size factor (bond length) are key factors corresponding to the empirical concepts, electronegativity and atomic size. Through this calculation a new factor to describe the relative strength of attractive and repulsive interaction has been introduced.

This work, an interplay between data and models, sets up a method for obtaining a description of materials complexity beyond the implication of experimental data. This kind of besieging and versatile method makes the procedure of materials design flexible and promising for candidate solutions. It is usually unsuitable for a data service to directly give users a set of discrete data retrieved from databases. Providing users with a comprehensive picture of interesting materials is welcomed as it enables a user to imagine/think "something on demand".

The discovery of high Tc superconducting materials still implies the superiority of experiments to the full set of information resources, in spite of big developments of mining and knowledge discovery tools. However, rules on materials properties are categorized by structural primitives and model primitives, after obtaining a certain amount of data based on statistical causalities among complex data. Available physical frames are to be referred for the next step.

Taking advantage of digitized information, comparative studies on materials are just entering our scope, since different systems, players and scenarios are ready as digital information. Redesigning established exemplars through optimization of controllable parameters for a given need has been the most effective way of improving materials properties so as to reduce the ambiguities there. Nearly all industrial materials have been developed gradually in this way, due to the very complexity of engineering applications.

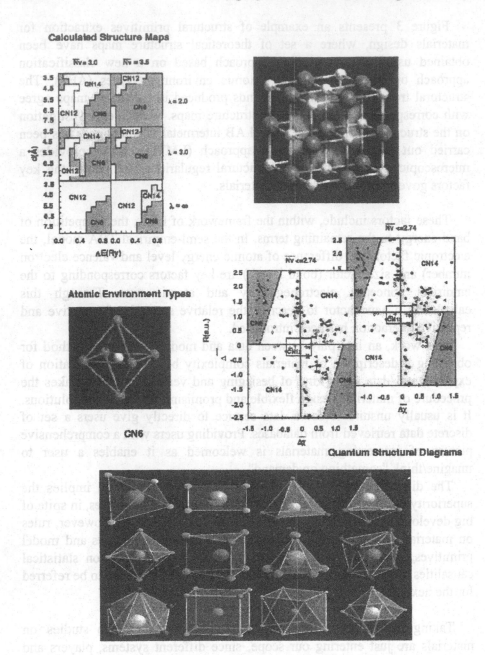

Figure 3. Fusion of Databases and Models with a List of AET (Atomic Environment Types),[4, 5].

Innovations in materials design are to be focused on replacing components and/or schema of design exemplars, and their possibilities are discussed in the following three steps.

Get Intentions: How to cause a new idea to emerge and to discover multi-variate patterns through the mining of data; browsing of continuous, heterogeneous information via filtering/focusing/erasing/selecting/ rearranging/reasoning to extract useful information, with fluctuating/ changing viewpoints.

The browsing of different information available through networks can give new ideas as it is becoming really effective and more and more used recently.

Get View: How to define, reduce dimension of, and get a design window to reach a solution.

Setting up a Strawman for Further Improvements: How to set up/select an initial specification on the trial model and to carry out further improvements in the way of redesigning material, shape and process.

Overall surveys of materials comes next by changing compositions and process parameters in promising domains.

Figure 4 shows a set of copies on basic thinking operations of materials engineers.

These can be linked along structural hierarchies and grouped under four types: cutting/selecting, articulating, combining and tailoring. It appears to cover everything but is insufficient to develop design skills. Critical thinking swinging between structural primitives and needs are required to reach a solution as shown in Figure 5, where bi-directional approaches, (namely, analytical and synthetic) are mixed up to reach a target solution as a prototype.

Different kinds of thinking are required to arrive at innovative solutions, which will be accelerated by the quality and quantity of digitized information, if well organized. A mixture of hindsight and foresight sometimes stimulates a breakthrough as was the case for high Tc super conducting materials and superalloys. In the latter case, changes at meta level structures, for example, from polycrystal to directionally solidified materials and finally to single crystal, from nickel base to iridium base alloys, played a very important role for "switching gears". However in the former case, similar explanations from NaCl type to A15 type and to perovskite seem like "hindsight". In both cases, explanations on their solution spaces were given by adding new terms on electronic aspects to develop design windows from one dimensional to multi-dimensional ones.

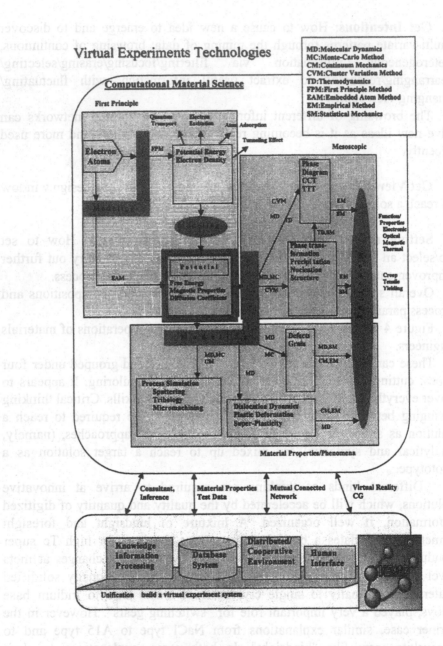

Figure 4. A Schema (after M.Nihei) for Link Models for Virtual Experiments.

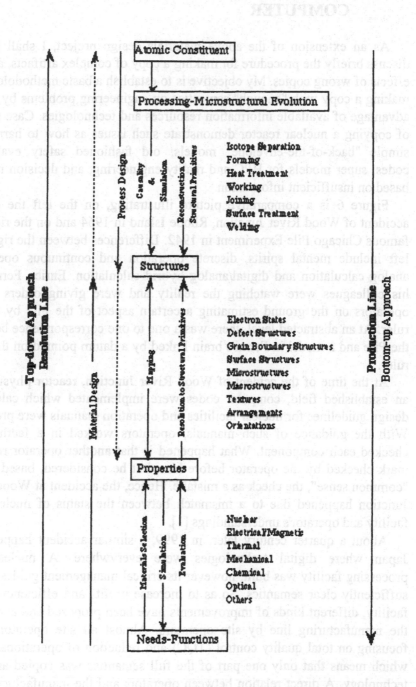

Figure 5. Back (=Analysis) and Forth (=Synthesis) in Design.

4.   MAKING A COPY OF ARTIFACTS IN A COMPUTER

As an extension of the above materials design project, I shall like to discuss briefly the procedure for making a copy of complex artifacts, and the effects of wrong copies. My objective is to establish a basic methodology for making a copy with "enough" semantics on engineering problems by taking advantage of available information resources and technologies. Case studies of copying a nuclear reactor demonstrate such issues as how to harmonize simple "back-of-the-envelope" models, old fashioned safety evaluation codes, super models for HPC and reality engineering, and decision making based on insufficient information.

Figure 6 is a comparative picture illustrating, on the left the critical accident of Wood River Junction, Rhode Island in 1964 and on the right the famous Chicago Pile Experiment in 1942. Differences between the right and left include mental spirits, discrete operation and continuous operation, analog calculation and digital/analog hybrid calculation. Enrico Fermi and his colleagues were watching the reality and were giving orders to the operators on the ground estimating a certain aspect of the Pile by a slide ruler. At an abstracted level, there was a one to one correspondence between the Pile and a model in Fermi's brain linked by a datum pointed on the slide ruler.

At the time of the ccident of Wood River Junction, reactor physics was an established field, computer codes were implemented which calculated design guidelines for nuclear facilities and operation manuals were prepared. With the guidance of such manuals, operators worked in a facility and checked each component. What happened is that another operator read the mark checked by the operator before him, but he considered, based on his "common sense", the check as a mistake. Hence, the accident at Wood River Junction happened due to a mismatch between the status of nuclear fuel facility and operator's understandings [1].

About a quarter century later, in 1999, a similar accident happened in Japan where digital technologies were everywhere. A nuclear fuel processing facility was built, however its critical management guides lacked sufficiently clear semantics. So as to increase profits and efficiency of the facility, different kinds of improvements have been proposed and applied to the manufacturing line by site operators. Almost all site operators were focusing on total quality control (TQC) and reduction of operational steps, which means that only one part of the full semantics was copied as a key technology. A direct relation between operators and the manufacturing line was disturbed by simplified inaccurate manuals, selective reactions of operators whose training was biased towards TQC.

•What kinds of differences?

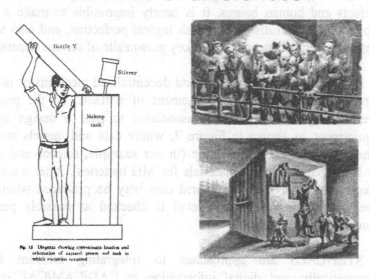

Figure 6. Difficulty to Pass Suitable Information Rightly

Domain differentiation or specialization around established disciplines have sometimes not succeeded due to the very features of human nature or the current high technology society. We must be very careful how we make copies with respect to quantity, quality, timing, contents, and information path by extracting suitable parts from enormous amounts of information, (e.g. tons of documents and millions of articles for nuclear facilities at least).

5. DISCUSSION

The Basics for designing materials are equivalent to that for solving other issues of engineering in the following ways:
1. Knowledge through interactions with objects,
2. Articulation of complex phenomena by resolution into parts with manageable hierarchies, and modeling of evolving procedures of such parts.

Materials have been developed by information and/or expectations of occurrences, learning by practice with graceful interface and repeating interactions, and finally by acquiring insights into complexity - intelligence.

A focal point for managing these aspects is to understand the essential feature of *homo faber* through observation of history as a relation between artifacts and human beings. It is nearly impossible to make a full set of copies in different disciplines with logical perfection, and also to carry out messages from a data source to a key person/site of serious necessities.

Hybridization of centralized and decentralized mechanisms is required to improve the quality and management of artifacts. At the product level, relevant engineering data are associated to pass a design specification requirement, as shown in Figure 7, where data and models are integrated coherently within one discipline (in our example, science and engineering for hydrogen absorption materials for MH batteries). After a series of such integration and evaluation, hybrid cars may be produced where an upper level schema at the product level is checked as possibly perfect along structures and semantics.

STEP/CALS are approaches to integrating relevant information systematically, and digital information in CAD/CAM/CAE continues to generate new issues. Consequently, there appear more efficient mass production, homogenization of products, globalization of manufacturing systems, higher level competitions from function to design and something special, mega competitions and uncontrollable wastes. As for engineering information, this kind of approach is 100% digital with respect to geometric information, while others are not.

Decisions are made prior to, during and after the design phase. A product comes in the market as the symbol of a company's capabilities after overcoming all the hurdles of criticism and the business criteria for release. Here the product is a copy of all the ideas and competence of workers who contributed to the production in the company and it is not a copy that can be reproduced mechanically. Histories to reach the product are to be compiled into a set of knowledge so as to obtain a similar product, but the dynamics of decision makings will lead to different solutions.

Recycling has been taken into account in recent years, but as a whole there is still no turning back. The new product will now have to prove its worth in the market place combination with other products.

Only sales figures tell the company whether its assumptions were right or wrong, and not the value of the product for the society.

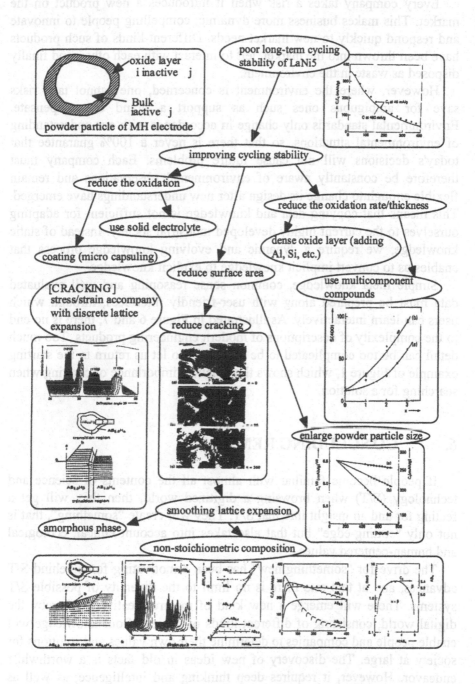

Figure 7. A Scenario to Develop Materials for MH Batteries.

Every company takes a risk when it introduces a new product on the market. This makes business more dynamic, compelling people to innovate and respond quickly to new market needs. Different kinds of such products have been thrown into the market, left to interact with each other, and finally disposed as waste in the environment.

However, where the environment is concerned, one cannot take risks save for ambiguous ones such as support a brand or compensate. Environmental standards only change in accordance with our understanding of environmental situations, so that there is never a 100% guarantee that today's decisions will not cause future problems. Each company must therefore be constantly aware of environmental observations and remain flexible enough to change its design after new understandings have emerged. This means that copying data and knowledge is not sufficient for adapting ourselves to the current highly developed industrial society. Instead of static knowledge, we require a dynamic and evolving knowledge process that enables us to convert implicit knowledge to explicit knowledge.

Simple meta knowledge, common sense reasoning and well evaluated data must be prepared along with user-friendly interfaces, through which users can learn interactively. As illustrated in Figure 6 and 7, there is no end to the complexity of descriptions of modern engineering products. Too much detail can be too complicated to be practical. So let us return to the starting example of Figure 1, which shows the practical importance of copying when searching for a solution.

6.   CONCLUDING REMARKS

If people become familiar with almost all the contents of science and technology (S/T) when browsing a digitized world, then they will get a feeling for and an insight into that S/T. They will create "something", that is not only "cutting-edge" but that also takes into account ethical, ecological and human-centered values.

The drive for "something new" has been a motivating force behind S/T advances, and at this rate there is no limit to the diversity of possible S/T systems. There will emerge a new kind of mature creativity, whereby the digital world, consisting of different kinds of copies of our knowledge will enable people and companies to determine their own values and solutions for society at large. The discovery of new ideas in old facts is a worthwhile endeavor. However, it requires deep thinking and intelligence, as well as elaborate developments of information systems. IT presents new possibilities for copying, in which we do not simply transfer information but rather learn from old facts so as to create something truly excellent.

As a conclusion, it is perhaps time to advise everyone to become an Edison. With the help of fruitful information environments, not only DB/KB/Network but also interfaces enabling interactive manipulation of such information, it is possible to get insights through interactive learning and find hints for solutions to complex problems.

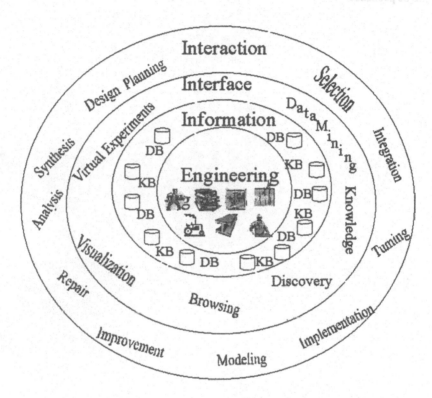

Figure 8. Hierarchy of Interactive Learning

REFERENCES

1. Auxier J.A., Nuclear Accidents at Wood River Junction, Nucl. Safety No.3 pp.298-301, 1965.
2. Benjamin Walter. Abhandlungen, Gesammelte Schriften, Band I-2, Surkamp, 1974.
3. Chen Hailong, Research and Development of A Data System for Materials Design, Doctoral Thesis, The Univ. of Tokyo, 1993.

4. Chen Y., Iwata S., Liu J., Villars P., and Rodgers J., Structural Stability of Atomic Environment Types in AB Intermetallic Compounds, Modeling Simul. Mater." Sci. Eng.4 pp.1-14, 1996.

5. Villars P., Brandenburg K., Berndt M., LeClair S., Jackson A., Pao Y.-H., Igelnik B., Oxley M., Bakshi B., Chen P., and Iwata S., Binary, Ternary and Quaternary Compound Former/Nonformer Prediction via Mendeleev Number, J.Alloys and Compounds 1, 2000 to be published.

INDEX

A

abstract data type (ADT), 47, 48 ,49, 211
accuracy, 167, 193
active data warehouse system, 105
active rules, 95, 105, 106, 107, 108, 109,
  111, 112, 114, 121
agent, 34, 36, 37, 38, 39, 40, 102
association rules, 181, 193
autonomy, 17, 18, 21, 25, 26, 30, 73, 162

B

BLOOM, 18, 22, 32, 134, 136, 140
broker agent, 39, 40
brokers, 163

C

canonical data model (CDM), 1, 18, 33,
  34, 36, 38, 47, 133, 134, 138, 139, 140
classification, 4, 48, 67, 113, 181, 184,
  185, 193, 194, 195, 199, 200, 201, 229
clustering, 181, 188, 193, 195
complex data management, 205, 209
components, 2, 4, 33, 35, 36, 43, 44, 45,
  88, 89, 93, 114, 136, 146, 175, 184,
  185, 187, 206, 207, 209, 213, 215,
  217, 218, 223, 231
conceptual model, 2, 4, 12, 33, 41, 43,
  45,53
construction industry, 207, 218
cooperative information systems, 59, 61
copying, 223, 224, 225, 234, 238
coverage, 150, 193

cube, 92, 105, 107, 108, 109, 111, 113,
  114, 116, 118, 119, 121, 135, 137
common warehouse metamodel, (CWM),
  87, 88, 92, 102, 103

D

data mart, 93, 105, 123, 133, 138, 141
data mining, 108, 164, 165, 181, 182,
  183, 188, 193, 227, 228
data models, 45, 60, 61, 62, 63, 65, 66,
  69, 71, 73, 74, 77, 89, 126, 132, 137,
  162, 183
data quality, 102, 159, 160, 166, 167,
  168, 192
data warehouse, 4,16, 85, 87, 105, 106,
  109, 110, 113, 114, 117, 118, 121,
  136, 167, 183, 185, 186, 189, 192
data warehouse architecture, 87, 106, 118,
  121
database integration, 1, 9, 73, 85, 159,
  162, 187
database management, 77, 89, 162, 183
decision support, 87, 89, 106, 110
decision trees, 181, 199, 200, 228
design process, 170, 223
discovery process, 181, 183, 203, 223

E

e-commerce, 159, 160, 161, 162, 163,
  164, 165, 168
entity-relationship, 45, 75, 77, 209